PRODUCING REPRODUCTIVE RIGHTS

With events and movements such as #MeToo, the Gender Equality UN Sustainable Development Goal, the Irish and Chilean abortion policy changes, and the worldwide Women's March movement, women's rights are at the top of the global public agenda. Yet, countries around the world continue to debate if and how women should have access to reproductive rights, and specifically abortion. This book provides the most comprehensive comparative review of this topic to date. How are reproductive rights produced? This book analyzes three spheres of influence on abortion policymaking: civil society, national government, and international bodies. It engages scholars as well as undergraduate and graduate students in social sciences, law, gender studies, and development and sustainability studies. With insights into the influence of intergovernmental bodies, international health organizations, state-level political representatives, and religious civil society players, this book will be of interest to policymakers, organizations, and individuals concerned with influencing reproductive policy.

Udi Sommer is Senior Lecturer at the Political Science Department at Tel Aviv University. He has also taught political science at Columbia and SUNY at Stony Brook. He is Chair of The Israel Young Academy and Head of the Center for the Study of the United States at Tel Aviv University. Sommer is the author of over 20 articles in peer-reviewed journals and 2 books: *Supreme Court Agenda Setting* (2014) and *Legal Path Dependence and the Long Arm of the Religious State* (2016). He is the recipient of grants and fellowships from the European Union, Fulbright, and the NSF and was a finalist in the LSA 2nd Half-Century Project.

Aliza Forman-Rabinovici is a PhD candidate at Tel Aviv University. Her research focuses on the intersection between gender and public policy, and the role and impact of female leadership in politics. Forman-Rabinovici has had articles published in top peer-reviewed journals and serves as the academic advisor to the Israeli Ministry of Science and Technology's Council for the Advancement of Women as well as a policy researcher and advisor for major political parties and figures in Israel.

Producing Reproductive Rights

DETERMINING ABORTION POLICY WORLDWIDE

UDI SOMMER

Tel-Aviv University

ALIZA FORMAN-RABINOVICI

Tel-Aviv University

CAMBRIDGE
UNIVERSITY PRESS

University Printing House, Cambridge CB2 8BS, United Kingdom

One Liberty Plaza, 20th Floor, New York, NY 10006, USA

477 Williamstown Road, Port Melbourne, VIC 3207, Australia

314–321, 3rd Floor, Plot 3, Splendor Forum, Jasola District Centre,
New Delhi – 110025, India

79 Anson Road, #06–04/06, Singapore 079906

Cambridge University Press is part of the University of Cambridge.

It furthers the University's mission by disseminating knowledge in the pursuit of
education, learning, and research at the highest international levels of excellence.

www.cambridge.org
Information on this title: www.cambridge.org/9781108493161
DOI: 10.1017/9781108694407

© Udi Sommer and Aliza Forman-Rabinovici 2019

First published 2019

Printed and bound in Great Britain by Clays Ltd, Elcograf S.p.A.

A catalog record for this publication is available from the British Library.

Library of Congress Cataloging-in-Publication Data
NAMES: Sommer, Udi, author. | Forman-Rabinovici, Aliza.
TITLE: Producing reproductive rights : determining abortion policy worldwide /
Udi Sommer, Aliza Forman-Rabinovici.
DESCRIPTION: New York : Cambridge University Press, 2019. | Includes bibliographical
references and index.
IDENTIFIERS: LCCN 2019016919 | ISBN 9781108493161 (hardback)
SUBJECTS: LCSH: Human reproduction – Law and legislation. | Reproductive rights. |
Abortion – Law and legislation. | BISAC: POLITICAL SCIENCE / Political Freedom &
Security / Human Rights.
CLASSIFICATION: LCC K2000 .S66 2019 | DDC 342.08/4–dc23
LC record available at https://lccn.loc.gov/2019016919

ISBN 978-1-108-49316-1 Hardback

Udi dedicates this book to his beloved wife, Michal.

Contents

Figures

Tables

Preface

Women's reproductive needs have existed since the dawn of history. Indeed, abortion appears in artwork in Angkor Wat and in the text of Assyrian Law. Likewise, references to abortion procedures are found in the "Egyptian Ebers Papyrus (1550 BC), the Latin works of Pliny the Elder (23 to 79 AD) and Dioscofides (De materia medica, c. 58 to 64 AD), and the Greek writings of Soranus (Gynecology, c. 100 AD)" (Potts and Campbell, 2002). Today, societies across the globe continue to debate questions of reproductive policy and rights, in some cases even if and how they should exist. In the modern state system, these debates manifest as political and policy questions, as the state is given the responsibility to decide what is, and what is not, a woman's right.

As medicine and technology advanced, the question of if and how women should have access to abortion became more pressing in the nineteenth and twentieth centuries. With such changes, abortion became a more relevant option and the dangers of unregulated abortion procedures starker. It is in this context that states began to feel the need to formulate policy on this issue. Rather than provide a comprehensive historical review of abortions, our goal in this book is to focus on policymaking in this area, particularly in recent decades. We are less interested in the evolution of medical technology and more concerned with the involvement of state governments in policymaking in this context and the panoply of influences on those governments.

Since abortion entered the modern political agenda, the policy and political landscapes have been ever shifting. In the United Kingdom, the Infant Life (Preservation) Act of 1929, an Act of Parliament, amended the Offences against the Person Act 1861 and allowed abortion to save the life of the mother. The Soviet Union became the first European government to legalize abortion in the Decree on Abortion in 1920, with far-reaching policy consequences. It recriminalized the procedure later on (Avdeev, Blum, & Troitskaya, 1995).

The Decree set "to permit such operations to be made freely and without any charge in Soviet hospitals, where conditions are assured of minimizing the harm of the operation" (Semashko, 1924, p. 24).

Cases such as these, from the early and mid-twentieth century, while important in their own right, are at best precursors for the swirl of political activity surrounding abortion issues in the historical period we focus on in this book. Today we live in a conspicuously different era. New players, technologies, and global networks redefine how we talk about abortion and who determines the boundaries of the discussion. It is in such an era – with currents that go deeper than national governments and well beyond the territory of any particular state – that we find such a political climate. This climate leads to the solidification of webs of organizations, political norms, and policy practices that span multiple spheres including the international system, the state sphere, and civil society.

Such a climate has produced momentous political battles over the question of abortion. These battles continue to play out and today they find additional stages in social networks and new media. Likewise, it is in such an era that global phenomena such as International Safe Abortion Day, recognized in dozens of countries around the world, transpire. It is in this context that we embark on a course to re-examine how abortion rights are shaped in the late twentieth and early twenty-first centuries.

We develop an analytical framework that accounts for this new era by focusing on international, national, and civil society effects on abortion policy. Such a framework is powerful in its ability to shed new light on abortion policy in a comparative perspective. While the structure of this book dictates that these spheres are mostly analyzed separately, we dedicate the concluding sections to recognizing their interconnectedness and interdependence. In the book's final sections, accordingly, we put those three spheres back together as we focus on agents, institutions, and norms that travel among them to influence the production of reproductive rights.

New York, NY
Tel Aviv, Israel
Fukuoka, Japan

Acknowledgments

As always when it comes to writing a book, I am indebted to many who supported me. I would like to take this opportunity to thank those individuals and organizations by name. First, it has been a pleasure working with my student and coauthor, Aliza Forman-Rabinovici. It is always a delight to see how a student grows into a young scholar. Aliza's creativity and fresh perspective made working on this book a real pleasure. Furthermore, I am indebted to my dedicated research assistants, students, and members of my research team, Ms. Anne Bauer and Ms. Moran Shechnick. Their work on data collection on Chile, Bahrain, Rwanda, and New Zealand was vital.

Funding support has been invaluable in making this project possible. I would like to thank the Israel Institute in Washington, DC, and the Institute of Israel and Jewish Studies at Columbia University of New York. Thanks also to IIJS directors, past and present, including Michael Stanislowski, Jeremy Dauber, and Elisheva Carlebach as well as wonderful Assistant Director, Dana Kresel. Furthermore, an internal grant at Tel Aviv University supported some of the research assistance necessary for this project, in particular through the International Masters Program in Conflict Resolution and Mediation. At Columbia University, I was lucky to work with fantastic colleagues at the Department of Political Science where I was also able to interact with some of the leading figures in the field, including esteemed guest speakers such as Rose McDermott, Frances McCall Rosenbluth, and Amaney Jamal. At the Columbia Law School, the advice of Olatunde Johnson was invaluable. At the School of International and Public Affairs, I was lucky to have the ideal work environment to work on this book and the kind support of Dean Merit Janow. At Cambridge University Press, working with Mr. John Berger has been a true pleasure. John's helpful comments and suggestions for how to develop the project proved remarkably useful for my work. The reviews of the manuscript by anonymous readers were astute, constructive, and helpful. This book will hopefully live up to their expectations, but it was surely improved thanks to their efforts. Also at Cambridge, Danielle Menz's help was invaluable. I am also grateful to colleagues from the College of Law in the University of Bahrain, for their help in understanding legal provisions and political circumstances related to abortion policy in their country.

Earlier versions of some of the analyses in this book appeared in various conference papers, such as at the International Studies Association, as well as in articles published in *World Development, Public Administration*, and the *Journal of Public Policy*. I am grateful to the editors and the reviewers at the journals for their priceless help and insightful comments.

Our dear friends, Zurn, Delano, Batya, Dennis, Jane, Irene, Greg, Miriam, Charlene, Bob, Lilach, Mati, Doron, Leah, Michal(s), Idan, Lara, Yoav, Guy, Dana, Ron, Hila, Kelly, Daniel, Ayala, and close family all gave me the supportive community I so vitally needed when working on this book. I am grateful to my three kids, Talia, Ori, and Inbal for being there. Their distractions were fantastic excuses to take time off, which proved to be an invaluable passageway to creativity and new ideas. And to my beloved wife, Michali, to whom this book is dedicated.

1

Introduction: Producing Reproductive Rights

The global push for women's rights has entered a new era, embodied in the #metoo campaign, worldwide mass marches for women's rights, and a popular push for reproductive rights such as in the case of the Irish abortion referendum, among many other examples. In 2018 alone, this new wave has seen legislation initiatives in Argentina, judicial challenges in Brazil, and the Kavanagh U.S. Supreme Court confirmation battle in the United States, to name a few cases. The topics of gender equality, women's physical autonomy, and abortion rights dominate headlines as much now as ever.

Around the globe, countries continue to debate gender equality in general, and in particular if and how women should have access to abortion. In the Paraguayan capital of Asunción, Casa Rosa Maria is a shelter for young mothers. Some are young teenagers. Many of these girls have been denied abortion under the country's restrictive reproductive policies. In Uzbekistan, with a Muslim majority of 90%, abortion is available on demand. At times, it's even used as a form of contraceptive. Until 2018, every year thousands of Irish women engaged in "abortion travel," hopping the channel to undergo in England a simple procedure that until recently was almost entirely illegal in their home country. These are the stories that do not always make the news. When they do, they are often treated as isolated incidents, relevant in their individual countries but disconnected from greater worldwide trends. However, policy is not made in a political void. This book poses the following question: how can we explain the dramatic differences in how countries legislate women's reproductive rights and autonomy?

We focus on three spheres of influence. The first is the level of civil society, which is analyzed in Part I of this book. The influence of civil society on policy in general is well established in the literature. Through a range of actions – such as lobbying, campaigning, and mobilizing – factors within the sphere of civil society affect policy. We isolate a single factor within civil society, religion, as a tool to analyze the sphere's overall powers. Faith civil society is of particular importance in the context of abortion policy. What is more, for the type of comparative exercise this book offers, religion is advantageous methodologically. While civil society may consist of different types of groups and institutions in different parts of the world, focusing on religion facilitates the type of broad comparative framework we attempt here.

The second sphere is that of the nation-state. We delve into the influence of the state sphere on abortion policy in Part II of this book, examining systematic trends as well as offering some analysis of case studies. For many, this would be the first thing that comes to mind when considering questions of policymaking in general and abortion policy in particular. Our analysis of the national sphere focuses on dimensions of representation, as we examine questions related to the links between descriptive and substantive representation and their implications for abortion policy. As abortion is inherently a part of women's rights, examining female representation is critical.

Completing the analyses of faith civil society and state-level influences on abortion policy, in Part III we look at the international sphere. There are debates in the literature regarding mechanisms to explain how policy travels around the world and across borders. Some theories suggest that international institutions are the catalysts for this process. The policy they make or advocate trickles down to the states in various ways and through an array of institutions. Others suggest that diffusion among countries, in particular, neighboring countries, accounts for policy dissemination. Those debates inform our discussion of international influences on abortion policy, where we focus on one type of key player – intergovernmental organizations.

The importance of reproductive health – and specifically abortion rights – cannot be overstated. According to the World Health Organization, of the 56 million induced abortions annually, nearly half are unsafe abortions, mostly taking place in the developing world. By some estimates, one in every seven maternal deaths can be attributed to an unsafe abortion, and the annual costs of medical treatments following these procedures exceed half a billion dollars worldwide (Ganatra et al., 2017; Say et al., 2014; Vlassoff et al., 2008). Abortion rights are often used as a measure for how a country views gender equality and women's physical autonomy more broadly.

Accordingly, this book contributes directly to the United Nations' (U.N.'s) Sustainable Development Goals (SDGs) and, in particular, to SDG5, Gender Equality. Set by the U.N. General Assembly, these 17 goals are a part of U.N. Resolution 70/1: *Transforming Our World: The 2030 Agenda for Sustainable Development*. Encompassing a broad range of interrelated objectives, the SDGs cover issues of social and economic development running the gamut from gender equality, water, health, education, and global warming to poverty, hunger, sanitation, energy, the environment, social justice, and urbanization. Of key importance to us is Goal 5: Gender Equality. The aim of SDG5 is to achieve gender equality and empower all women and girls.

The current literature on this topic provides limited information on how laws on abortion are generated worldwide. This book sets out to fill key theoretical and empirical gaps, as we explore different levels of influence on reproductive rights around the world. Combining large-scale comparative quantitative analyses with a series of case studies, the book allows us insight into some of the causal mechanisms underlying this critical aspect of the politics of gender.

This book significantly advances our knowledge of the determinants of reproductive policy. In theoretical development and in empirical scope, the project reaches beyond the Western case studies that have dominated abortion policy studies to date. We study reproductive rights using a theoretical framework that identifies the three spheres of influence discussed above: the international arena, state government, and civil society. In each sphere, we focus on agents and institutions that influence reproductive policy. We identify them and compare their degrees of influence. As such, this project takes a novel approach. Not only do we develop innovative theoretical frameworks to explain the evolution of women's rights, but we also use quantitative analysis to compare dozens of states and to observe policy development over time.

Who are the actors and players determining the norms of women's rights around the world? Do policies regarding women's rights correspond with norm change within civil society, sovereign state bodies, the international community, or some combination thereof? To examine this set of questions, we plan to look at actors in all three spheres, studying their actions both within these arenas, but also comparing influence among the three spheres. To get our discussion started, let us examine some of the key theories we use in the book. Along with these theories, we offer some examples of social media activity, which prove how timely and salient those topics are in various political settings and in different parts of the world.

THE CIVIL SOCIETY SPHERE

Walzer defines civil society as "the space of uncoerced human association and also the set of relational networks—formed for the sake of family, faith, interest, and ideology—that fill this space" (1990, p. 1). Kimmerling describes it as "all [of] the social activities that are performed outside of the state's direct instructions, and beyond family or primordial frameworks" (Gidron, Bar, & Katz, 2004, p. 142). Edwards and Foley (1998) present two main theories of the role of civil society. Civil society can be seen as a sphere independent of the state, whose role is to push back against the state and to act as a counterbalance. The second theory of civil society sees it as a sphere unrelated to the state, where citizens can unify and come together.

In this book, we think of civil society as a "social sphere" that involves political activity but excludes official state institutions. Players in civil society include actors that function outside the confines of the state and above the level of the family unit (Salamon, Anheier, List, Toepler, & Sokolowski, 1999). For our analysis, we choose to use religion as an example of a civil society player that can have great influence over state policy. Faith civil society suits our purposes well since religion is a ubiquitous aspect of almost any culture or social group. Likewise, despite certain disagreements regarding who is included in civil society, there is a general consensus in the literature regarding the fact that religion is in this sphere. Additionally, religion is of particular interest when we examine women's welfare policy, as organized religion is often assumed to have a negative impact on the status of women and gender equality policy. Yet, this common understanding has yet to be fully tested in a comparative context. Lastly, while certain organs of civil society may not exist in all types of regimes, religion is pervasive around the world. This makes it a perfect choice for the comparative exercise we are interested in for this book, which is intended to reach beyond the democratic sphere, empirically as well as theoretically.

Naturally, by focusing on religion, we do not attempt to address multiple aspects of civil society, but rather isolate one of its features. This feature serves as an example to demonstrate the effects and powers of the sphere. We see religion as critically important and believe this trade-off is worthwhile. We leave investigations into additional important elements of civil society for future research.

In different countries, including the United States, faith civil society has made concerted efforts in the area of reproductive rights. A recent example on social media comes from a Providence, Rhode Island, bishop. Bishop Thomas Tobin called on Twitter in April 2018 for a "#metoo movement for unborn children." His was one among many tweets voicing the pro-life sentiment in a country where the question of abortion is still being constantly debated. Despite being settled constitutionally by the U.S. Supreme Court in *Roe v. Wade* over four decades ago and a long progeny of cases since, is still a major fault line in the political landscape. The influence of faith civil society is discussed in depth in Part I of the book, quantitatively in Chapter 2 and using the case studies of Chile and Bahrain in Chapter 3. The theories developed in Part I and the findings presented also inform much of the discussion in the chapters in Parts II and III.

THE NATIONAL GOVERNMENT SPHERE

Of the different spheres we examine in this book, the state is the most obvious and direct source of policy influence. Many countries have recently seen the ground shifting in their abortion policy. A campaign in Argentina has brought the issue of abortion to the nation's legislature, with the Argentinian Senate failing in 2018 to pass a bill legalizing abortion. The fact that the bill even made it to the floor, though, and the fierce debate in parliament, suggested winds of change at the state level. In its neighbor to the north, Brazil, the possibility of changes in abortion policy is also rising via the courts.

According to the Brazilian Health Ministry[1], more than a quarter of a million women annually are hospitalized due to abortion-related medical complications, and approximately 1 million abortions are performed every year. Clandestine and unsafe abortions have cost the medical system over $130 million over the past decade and, in 2016 alone, 203 women died as a result of failed abortions. While women who can afford the trip may have an abortion overseas, a strong movement at the civil society level has pushed toward decriminalization in recent years, even in the face of a conservative government. As late as August 2018, the Brazilian Supreme Court considered whether constitutional protections made Brazil's restrictive abortion law void. Dr. Maria de Fátima Marinho, a representative of the health ministry and an activist in international bodies dealing with reproductive health such as the Pan American Health Organization, testified before the court as to the public health challenges unsafe abortions created. Dr. Maria de Fátima Marinho addressed issues ranging from improper facilities to maternal mortality rates. These two countries, Brazil and Argentina, represent 40% of Latin American women. Changes in the Brazilian judiciary or the Argentinian legislature could be momentous for women across the region.

Probably the most prominent recent example of influence from the state sphere on abortion policymaking is what occurred in Ireland. The Eighth Amendment of the Constitution of Ireland, approved by referendum in 1983, recognized the equal right to life of the mother and the unborn: "The State acknowledges the right to life of the unborn and, with due regard to the equal right to life of the mother, guarantees in its laws to respect, and, as far as

---

[1] www.brazilgovnews.gov.br/presidency/ministers/ministry-of-health

practicable, by its laws to defend and vindicate that right." With close to 67% of the referendum votes cast in support of a Yes decision, the Amendment restricted both legislation and judicial interpretation of the Constitution (abortion had been criminalized in the country since 1861), allowing abortion only in circumstances where the life of a pregnant woman was at risk. This legal reality lasted several decades but changed dramatically in 2018.

Thirty-five years after the Eighth Amendment was ratified by popular fiat, on May 25, 2018, a new referendum was conducted. After years of political debate, 66.4% of voters who participated in the referendum voted Yes to the Thirty-Sixth Amendment of the Constitution of Ireland. Taking effect after the president signed it into law on September 18, 2018, this amendment permitted legislation for abortion by the Parliament of Ireland (Oireachtas). A day later, Justin Trudeau, the Canadian Prime Minister tweeted: "What a moment for democracy and women's rights. Tonight, I spoke with Taoiseach @campaignforLeo and his team and congratulated them on the Yes side's referendum victory legalizing abortion in Ireland." The political change in Ireland and the international attention it garnered reflected not only one country's change, but the global discussion it represents.

Trudeau was not alone on social media when it came to the Irish abortion referendum. Both No and Yes supporters took to the networks to influence reproductive rights in the country. Presenting themselves as "Ireland's most active pro-life organization," @YouthDefence, a far-right organization, used hash tags like #youthdefence, #savelives, and #savethe8th when waging the No campaign. On the other side of the issue was @Together4yes, a national civil society campaign supporting the repeal of the Eighth Amendment. These are but two examples of a plethora of such movements and organizations on both sides of the campaign aiming to change (or preserve) abortion policy by the national government in the Oireachtas Éireann.

Patterns of activity on social media by both local and foreign politicians and political organizations are but another expression of how different state and non-state actors influence policy. We delve into the theoretical complexity of this topic as we focus on the concept of representation – specifically, female political representation – as a significant influence over reproductive health policy. The importance of female leadership in determining state abortion policy is based on the connection between descriptive and substantive representation. This is the idea that women are best positioned to comprehend, and thus represent, the needs of women. The more women are present in the legislature, the more likely it is that women's issues are addressed. We take this theoretical discussion a step further, as we are interested in the link between descriptive and substantive representation beyond the democratic state. We want to understand abortion policy worldwide. Do women exercise the same powers of representation around the world? The answer to this question is probably no. Yet, can they carry some influence on abortion policy beyond the sphere of developed democracies? This question is particularly interesting for us in this book, and we believe the answer here is yes.

The state government sphere and the dimensions of representation at the heart of its influence on abortion policy are examined in Part II. We focus on quantitative analyses in Chapter 4, and then briefly examine two case studies in Chapter 5: New Zealand and Rwanda. These examinations are neither comprehensive nor exhaustive. Rather, without writing an entire book about those countries, the case studies in Chapter 5 illustrate and bring to life the patterns identified in Chapter 4. They also help shed light on some of the theoretical complexities the large-N quantitative results do not address.

THE INTERNATIONAL SPHERE

A quick survey of social media reveals the many actors in the international sphere who are trying to influence state abortion policy. There is a universe of international institutions advocating abortion policy. They are going beyond traditional websites, taking to various social media platforms to promote international discussions. The International Planned Parenthood Federation (@ippf) prominently states on their website, Facebook, and Twitter that the organization is "committed to delivering sexual and reproductive healthcare services around the world." Focused on the world's disadvantaged, Marie Stopes International (@MarieStopes) uses its various platforms to promote its goal to deliver "reproductive healthcare to millions of the world's poorest and most vulnerable women." Promoting #AbortionIsNormal, one of the oldest currently active global feminist groups, @IntlWomen The International Women's Health Coalition (IWHC), states on its page that it aims to secure "sexual & reproductive rights & health for women & girls around the world." Indeed, new media has become a sphere for international players to attempt to influence abortion policy worldwide with hashtags and campaigns such as #GenderEquality, #SheDecides, #LetsTalkAbortion, #SafeAbortionDay, and #IDecide.

Of the range of bodies operating in the international sphere, in this book we focus on intergovernmental organizations. The quintessential intergovernmental institution is the United Nations. U.N. Women is a U.N. agency that, according to its Twitter page, is "the UN entity for #genderequality & women's empowerment." Thus, an implicit goal of U.N. Women is to change international norms in the area of reproductive rights. While this book is not about social media, this handful of examples out of an ocean of social media buzz on the topic illustrate how invested the international sphere is in influencing norms of abortion policy around the world.

Global norms are the shared normative frameworks that exist among a large enough number of states and other international actors. Norms can be applied to states, intergovernmental organizations, and a variety of non-state actors (Khagram, Riker, & Sikkink, 2002). In general, norms are guides for conduct. They dictate behavior and imply what ought to be and what one ought to do (Hage, 2005; Martinsson, 2011). They are essentially the expression of a group expectation of behavioral standards (Hage, 2005; Katzenstein, 1996; Shannon, 2000). Change in abortion policy reflects a social norm concerning women's autonomy, secular definitions of gender equality, and the common view on the question about the beginning of life.

There are competing theories of why and how norms and policies diffuse. Some believe that states comply with international norms only when it is consistent with their material and security interests (Martinsson, 2011; Hyde, 2017). Others claim that states will actually accept burdensome norms imposed by the international sphere to send credible signals to other states and international entities, and to increase the share of and access to internationally allocated benefits and resources.

The key debate in the literature is between policy diffusion and the World Society framework. Both theories are based on an assumption of interdependence (Gilardi, 2012). Yet, they differ on where this sense of interdependence is communicated and how pressure is applied to and by different actors. Policy diffusion theory describes a process in which pressure for policy innovation comes from outside the polity, spreading from one state government to another (Braun & Gilardi, 2006; Shipan & Volden, 2008). The mechanisms driving policy diffusion include changing conditions in one country altering the benefits of a certain policy in another, regional influences and trends, and more information becoming available because of an experiment in a neighboring state (Simmons & Elkins, 2004; Shipan & Volden, 2008).

Within the World Society framework, policy proliferation is driven by intergovernmental organizations (True & Mintrom, 2001). Many features and norms of the nation-state are derived from global culture. The nation-state's desire to conform to World Society encourages diffusion. Within this theory, bodies such as the United Nations and the African Union (AU) serve as the "organizational frame" for World Society. Procedures defined in these international bodies can strongly influence practice at the nation-state level, even when a nation may resist the influence initially or even later on in the process (Meyer, Boli, Thomas, & Ramirez, 1997; Stone & Ladi, 2015).

In Part III, we argue that, for multiple reasons, the World Society framework – rather than the policy diffusion one – is appropriate to explore abortion policy in the context of the international sphere. Part III analyzes influences from the international sphere on abortion policy. Empirically, we present evidence for the systematic effects of intergovernmental organizations (IGOs). We argue that the stated goals – such as those stated on social media platforms – are also translated into actual policy change. Yet, the way IGOs try to influence abortion policy, how their internal debates are handled, and the final agreements they produce are of critical importance to their eventual influence. We further delve into the causal mechanisms underlying IGO influence on the production of abortion rights around the world using case studies. This sphere is addressed quantitatively in Chapters 6 and then using case studies in Chapter 7. Finally, it is further integrated into the more general debate in Chapter 8.

Data

Data for this project are taken from a variety of sources including the Global Abortion Policies Database, U.N. Population Division, the World Values Survey, the World Health Organization, the Inter-Parliamentary Union, the Quota Project, the Human Development Index, and the Polity Project.

We created a new index for state abortion policy. The U.N. Department of Social and Economic Affairs has published a global review of abortion policy periodically since 1992. All reviews published between 1992 and 2013 were examined. Seven criteria under which state law may allow access to abortion services are specified:

1. Saving a woman's life
2. Preserving a woman's physical health
3. Preserving a woman's mental health
4. In case of rape or incest
5. In case of fetal impairment
6. For social or economic reasons
7. On request

In the original index we created, the Comparative Abortion Index (*CAI*), each country-year was given a score based on the number of legal criteria accepted as grounds for abortion. In Chapter 2 we extensively detail the index and the measurement strategy involved. Countries are given a score between 0 and 7, based on the number of criteria accepted. An additional weighted index was

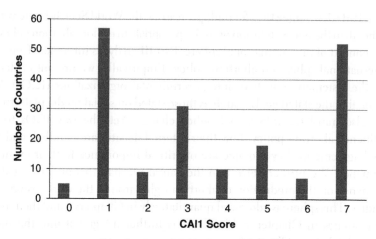

FIGURE 1.1: Distribution of CAI1 Scores Globally (1992–2013)

created that gives scores based on the frequency of all the criteria. In the following chapter, we go into the details of the index.[2]

While similar indexes have been used (Pillai and Wang, 1999; Hildebrandt, 2015), our data set is unique in its breadth and inclusion of numerous considerations. Figure 1.1 shows the global distribution from the conservative end at 0 (leftmost column) to the liberal 7 (the column on the right). The first thing that is clear is the substantial variance in how countries approach abortion rights around the world. The distribution is largely bimodal. A total of 57% of states had a score of either 1 (restrictive abortion policy) or 7 (most permissive reproductive policy). After 1 and 7, 3 was the most common score, on average accounting for 16% of states. Figure 1.1 illustrates the considerable variance in how abortion policy is distributed around the world. While many countries are permissive in their abortion policy, even more are not. The three spheres of influence we analyze – civil society, state government, and the international system – provide invaluable insight into how such policy develops and why.

CHAPTER SYNOPSES

The book is divided into three sections, each two chapters long. Each section takes up a different sphere, examining it theoretically and empirically. The first chapter in each part provides large-scale quantitative

---

[2] The full collection of indexes is included in the 2019 addition of the Quality of Government Institute Database, and can be accessed at https://people.socsci.tau.ac.il/mu/udis/the-comparative-abortion-index-project/.

analyses that aim to demonstrate how players within the given sphere systematically influence abortion policy. The second chapter in each part brings qualitative case studies into the discussion. The qualitative components illustrate the findings from the quantitative analyses and shed additional light on the causal mechanisms underlying the production of reproductive rights.

Part I – Civil Society Sphere
Chapter 2

We start our investigation of abortion policymaking with the civil society sphere. Within civil society, we take religion as a defining feature that has long been assumed to have a fractious relationship with women's rights and gender equality. This discussion contributes to our understanding of how a given aspect of civil society ultimately influences policy concerning women's rights. The effects of religion in the area of gender equality have been considered substantial in academic work as well as in popular and political discourse. A common understanding is that religion depresses women's rights in general and reproductive and abortion rights in particular.

The literature on reproductive rights, however, is disproportionately focused on Western cases, and is limited in its definition of religion as a variable. What happens, though, when we switch to a more inclusive framework? To what extent do a variety of religious variables correlate with policy on reproductive rights outside of the Western context? We examine the relevance of the religion-abortion link in a broad comparative framework looking at religious sect, religiosity, religious diversity, and the relationship between religion and the state. Norris and Inglehart contend that sexual liberalization is "the most basic cultural fault line" (2002, pp. 235–236). As the traditional caregivers, women are seen as the moral guardians and teachers of culture and norms. Religious institutions, therefore, often push to maintain traditional family structures and gender roles. Law regarding the role of women, particularly as mothers, can be especially sensitive to religious influence.

We find that reproductive rights correlate only with some religious denominations, while others have no significance. Additionally, while religiosity correlates with reproductive policy, variables such as religious freedom, separation of religion and state, and religious diversity show no correlative effects. This strongly suggests that the connection between religion, as it is manifested in faith civil society, and women's reproductive rights is far more nuanced than previously thought.

Chapter 3

This chapter looks at Chile and Bahrain as two countries that demonstrate the effects, interactions, and dependencies of faith civil society and abortion policy. With no official state religion, and a massive Catholic constituency but a fairly secular population, Chile had a total ban on abortion until August 2017. The ban was so extreme that in 2015 a pregnant, 11-year-old rape survivor was denied the procedure. In early 2015, President Michelle Bachelet submitted a bill to Congress to decriminalize abortion. Decriminalization was to apply when the mother's life was at risk, in the case of rape,[3] or in cases of non-viability. The opposition's request to declare the law unconstitutional was rejected by the high court of the land in August 2017, paving the way for abortion legislation in Congress. On September 14, 2017, President Bachelet, the first woman president of the country, signed the law. Public provision and medical coverage became available early the following year.

With an 85% Muslim population and Islam as the official state religion, Bahrain on the other hand has a much more permissive abortion policy, particularly salient in comparison to other countries in the same region. While suffrage was extended to Bahraini women only in 2002, they have had access to legal abortion on request since 1976. Some organizations in the country, such as the Bahrain Reproductive Health Association (affiliated with the above-mentioned @IPPF), have supported abortion in the country since the 1970s.

The analyses in this chapter use case study methodology in an attempt to deepen our understanding of the effects of faith in the civil society sphere on the production of reproductive rights. The value of case studies is not limited to the illustration of the systematic quantitative findings in the previous chapter. Rather, this methodology allows us to explore causal mechanisms in the relations between the civil society sphere and abortion policymaking.

Part II – State Government Sphere
Chapter 4

Within the sphere of the nation-state, we focus on dimensions of representation in the national government. That women can offer substantive representation in a democratic environment is well established. However, can women

---

[3]   In cases of rape, a woman can access abortion services if she is still in the first trimester. A minor can access abortion services up to 18 weeks gestation.

representatives do so under compromised forms of democracy? Extant literature suggests that representation has little meaning in nondemocracies. Yet, as less than half of the nearly 3.8 billion women in the world live in democracies, analyzing the connection between women's descriptive and substantive representation outside of the context of democracy is crucial. We hypothesize that even in nondemocracies and developing democracies, women exercise substantive representation in the sense that their presence in government will positively influence the likelihood of permissive abortion policy. We develop three theoretical frameworks to explore why there might appear to be a connection between descriptive and substantive representation: pandering to international norms, a generally favorable stance toward gender equality, and a lenience toward policy areas where women most commonly exercise influence.

In this chapter, we explore the state government level and the effects of degree of democracy, representative institutions, and gender quotas on policy outcomes. By focusing on different aspects of representation, we offer a conversation that engages several bodies of literature including regime typology, descriptive and substantive representation, the importance of female political participation, and questions pertaining to the legitimacy and efficacy of gender quotas. Disparate types of quotas – which are also examined in conjunction with the effects of international norms in Chapter 6 – interact with women's rights in different ways. Those interactions are contingent on features of the general political environment, such as the number of women legislators and the overall democratic nature of the system. The discussion of quotas in this chapter is mostly theoretical. We add empirical inquiries into this question in the following chapters.

The findings in Chapter 4 indicate substantive representation in non, developing, and established democracies. In other words, the link between descriptive and substantive representation does survive beyond the realm of democracies. The case of Michelle Bachelet is not an exception. Female leadership correlates with the production of reproductive rights even when democratic institutions, norms, and standards are not fully in place. We discuss the findings within the broader scope of dimensions of representation and the influences on abortion policy from the national sphere.

Chapter 5

Building on the findings in the previous chapter, Chapter 5 uses the case studies of Rwanda and New Zealand to more deeply explore the conduct of the nation-state in generating abortion policy. Rather than intending to provide a comprehensive analysis of these two cases, the case study methodology in this chapter serves to focus on particular aspects pertinent to the influences on abortion policy from the sphere of the nation-state. By the nature of things, other students of abortion policy in those countries may point to additional important aspects. Granted, while we omit certain aspects, we believe that the variables and dynamics we highlight and analyze are invaluable to advance our understanding of the influence of state-level politics on abortion policy.

Rwanda is still far from a democracy, yet proponents of gender equality may applaud the progress the state has made. Institutionalization of gender issues is well developed in the country, with a gender-based budgeting system, Ministry of Gender and Family Promotion, and a designated Gender Monitoring Office. The Gender Monitoring Office, for instance, was established to "ensure compliance and effective implementation of the various national, regional and international commitments, (...) with a mandate to monitor the respect of Gender Equality principles, promote gender accountability at all levels and fight against Gender Based Violence and related injustices" (www.gmo.gov.rw/ @GenderMonitorRw).

The country ranks in the top five countries for gender equality according to the World Economic Forum's 2017 "Global Gender Gap Report." Since reconstruction following the 1994 civil war and genocide, the government has been going to great lengths to entrench the value in state institutions. In projects of national development, in education, and in the health care system, the commitment to gender equality has been growing stronger for several decades. Indeed, the Rwandan Parliament has the highest rate of female legislators in the world. Rwanda's female majority in the legislature is a result of both the political history of this country and the implementation of gender quotas. In 2012, correlating with its increased rate of female representation, Rwanda liberalized its restrictive abortion policy.

New Zealand, on the other hand, has had universal suffrage since 1893. The country has had significantly more female representatives in parliament than the global average for decades. Even with this longstanding history of female representation in a developed democracy, however, New Zealand has a relatively restrictive abortion law. Indeed, the country's reproductive legal code has only undergone a minor change since 1977.

These case studies bring up issues concerning the efficacy of female leadership and the importance of how those leaders are situated politically, whether in the ruling authoritarian party, outside of it, or in a democratic regime. As far as electoral quotas and their efficacy are concerned, societal acceptance of gender equality seems to be of defining significance in the extent to which women elected can exercise substantive representation. Societal norms seem to trump the effects of institutions such as quotas.

Part III – The International Sphere
Chapter 6

The Convention on the Elimination of all Forms of Discrimination Against Women (CEDAW), the SDGs, and the International Conference on Population and Development (ICPD) Programme of Action (PoA) are but a few salient examples of how the international sphere attempts to influence abortion policymaking. Within the international sphere, we review a range of actors and then focus on intergovernmental organizations to see how they impact reproductive policy. Our theory distinguishes regional from international intergovernmental bodies and goes into detail about the rationale for this distinction. The first significant finding here is a heretofore-overlooked relationship between international entities and reproductive health, which to date has been largely neglected in comparative abortion policy literature. Our theory distinguishes regional from universal intergovernmental bodies. The theoretical framework goes into detail about the reasons why we draw such a distinction. The protocols that we tested are essentially an expression of the norms that are being processed in IGO forums as global norms. When a certain value or principle is shared among enough states, it becomes a global norm. These norms can then be codified in treaties and protocols. Thus, they are translated into standard practice even for states that have yet to adopt the norm. Additionally, we compare the influence of international organizations with domestic government measures, such as quotas, meant to increase women's substantive representation. Chapter 6, thus, also incorporates discussions from Chapters 4 and 5.

Chapter 7

To further elucidate the effects of the international sphere, this chapter examines specific international treaties and protocols to see how IGOs attempt to influence reproductive policy. We take the ICPD PoA and the Maputo Protocol (interchangeably referred to as the African Union Protocol or the Protocol to the African Charter on Human and Peoples' Rights on the Rights of Women in Africa). These two documents, while both addressing women's reproductive health and rights, are dramatically different. Comparisons between their writing and ratification processes, their texts, and their impact – which can be found in detailed illustrations of the findings in Chapter 6 – shed new light on the underlying causal mechanisms.

The ICPD PoA communicated that abortion was an acceptable form of family planning and practice in women's health. Its mentioning of abortion and endorsement of safe abortion procedures took steps to normalize this medical procedure. Simultaneously, its indecisive, and at times discouraging, language undermined this message. Writers of the U.N. ICPD PoA avoided controversy, used restrained language, and generated a document that ultimately did not take a firm stance on abortion. In comparison, the AU writers did not shy away from taking a strong stance, benefitted from the work of NGOs leading up to the event, and eventually produced the first document of its kind proclaiming abortion as a woman's right (under certain circumstances).

In the AU charter, the language was significantly more decisive, without the wavering or hesitation found in the ICPD PoA. This kind of verbiage sends a considerably stronger message about norms of abortion. Our findings imply that organizations in the international arena are powerful. Such organizations may also produce transnational epistemic communities that further support and sustain an international agreement drafted, ratified, and then implemented by the members of this group. In the context of reproductive rights, such groups of experts with common normative and analytic frameworks may be essential for translating common understandings at the level of the IGO into policymaking at the level of the nation-state.

Chapter 8

This chapter summarizes and further ties together findings, cases, and theories from the previous chapters. By bringing conclusions pertaining to all three spheres of influence – faith civil society, dimensions of representation at the national level, and intergovernmental effects – into one chapter, we are able to paint a simultaneously broad and high-resolution picture. We look at how actors in different arenas interact with, and complement, each other. We compare their influence and discuss the ramifications of actors at one level on actors at the other levels. Finally, what questions remain open for future exploration? We discuss venues for further research and encourage readers to draw their own conclusions about what still needs to be discovered to more fully understand the determinants of women's welfare policy and reproductive rights around the world.

PART I

CIVIL SOCIETY SPHERE

2

The Civil Society Sphere: Religion and Reproductive Health

Civil society and the range of groups, associations, and organizations that operate within it can be a powerful source of influence over government and public policy. Civil society constitutes the realm that falls outside the boundaries of the regime but beyond the private domain of the family. It is here that cultural groups, social groups, and religions function (Cohen & Arato, 1994; Hann & Dunn, 1996; Taylor, 1990; Fukuyama, 2001). In both democracies and nondemocracies, civil society encompasses players that try to influence state structure and policy. For a range of reasons and motivations, state institutions will be aware of and responsive to the preferences expressed by organs of civil society. In democracies, representatives will follow civil society activity as a means of gauging the desires of constituents and gathering voter support. Likewise, they are likely to be responsive to lobbying efforts by civil society.

In non-democracies, states will monitor civil society preferences. At least one key motivation would be the fact that this sphere is a potential source for opposition and regime insecurity. Pandering to certain civil society preferences can ensure regime stability. What is more, the regime may find that providing civil society sufficient freedom to operate serves its own interests. Indeed, as we will fully elaborate in Chapters 6 and 7, civil society may serve the goals of the regime in spheres of lesser concern domestically, but of major importance in terms of its international relations and standing in the world.

As we mentioned in the introduction in Chapter 1, there are multiple definitions of "civil society." Walzer (1990), for example, defines it as "the space of uncoerced human association and also the set of relational networks – formed for the sake of family, faith, interest, and ideology – that fill this space" (p. 1). Kimmerling describes it as "all [of] the social activities that are performed outside of the state's direct instructions, and beyond family or primordial frameworks" (Gidron, Bar, & Katz, 2004, p. 142). In Chapter 1, we also mentioned the two theories of civil society presented by Edwards and Foley

(1998). Civil society can be seen as a sphere independent of the state, whose role is to push back against the state and to act as a counterbalance. The second theory of civil society sees it as a sphere unrelated to the state, where citizens can unify and come together. Within the latter theoretical framework, civil society does not work against the state; rather, it complements and strengthens it. The function of civil society may be contingent on the system of government in place. In democratic regimes, civil society may serve a complementary function, while in non-democratic states, it is often the location of resistance and opposition (Edwards & Foley, 1998; Cohen & Arato, 1994). Those various theoretical approaches to civil society have the shared feature of seeing it as a "social sphere" that involves political activity but excludes official state institutions. There is general consensus in the literature that this sphere includes actors that function outside the confines of the state and above the level of the family unit (Salamon, Anheier, List, Toepler, & Sokolowski, 1999). This definition includes social associations and cultural organizations. There is a debate among scholars, however, as to whether and how to include market players and non-profit, or third-sector, players (Schwartz & Pharr, 2003; Foley & Edwards, 1996).

Civil society can be a source of influence over public policy. While in an election people may express their opinions and preferences through voting, both during and between elections they express their desires through social, cultural, and political organizations within the sphere of civil society. Politicians need to be aware of the preferences of players in civil society and to pander to them to gain support both during and between election cycles. Even in non-democracies, the state must be aware and considerate of the nature of civil society, as this sphere serves as a location of potential resistance and opposition. Indeed, compromising in order to appease civil society forces may be important to ensure regime stability and durability.

We consider civil society players as sources of influence over public policy in all types of states. For our analysis of civil society, we use religion as an example of a player that can have great influence over state policy. Religion suits our purposes well for a number of reasons. First, it is a ubiquitous aspect of any culture or social group. One can hardly think of a society where religious aspects are totally absent. Even in political and social experiments in the past, where this was attempted, religion resurfaced in various ways and forms. Second, despite certain disagreements regarding who is included in civil society (as mentioned earlier), there is a general consensus regarding the fact that religion is in this sphere.

Additionally, faith civil society is a particularly interesting element in an examination of women's welfare policy for several reasons. First, issues of family policy, fertility, and reproductive rights are at the heart of perceptions of various organized religions. Second, organized religion is often assumed to have a negative impact on the status of women and gender equality policy, but this common understanding has not been extensively tested in a comparative context. This leads us to the last reason why organized religion and its role within civil society is a good choice for the focus of our research. While certain types of organs of civil society may be typical only of democracies, religion is ubiquitous around the world. Thus, this variable is useful for the type of comparative work we undertake here. To study the effects of civil society on the production of reproductive rights around the world, religion is an invaluable predictor. While other elements of civil society may be hard to compare across such a wide range of political systems, religion is quite amenable to such an analytic exercise. Naturally, by focusing on religion we do not address many other elements of civil society. The aim here is to demonstrate how civil society can influence policy. To that end, we choose to isolate religion as a representative variable. With the benefit of deeply understanding the effect of faith civil society on abortion policy, we forego the analysis of other elements of civil society. Since we see religion as critically important, we believe this trade-off is worthwhile and leaves additional important investigations of other features of civil society for future research.

Religion and Reproductive Rights

Religion, women's rights, and reproductive policy have frequently been the topic of discussion in recent academic work as well as in public discourse (Echavarri & Husillos, 2016; Ross, 2008; Joshi & Sivaram, 2014). Those topics did not just attract attention as unrelated issues, but have been addressed extensively in relation to each other (King, 2012; Norwood, 2016; Wang & Sun, 2016; Wald &Wilcox, 2006, inter alia). For a variety of scholars and observers, the ties between religion and gender equality generally and reproductive policy specifically are inherent. As the degree of religiosity and the clout of religion increase, common wisdom would have it, so does patriarchal treatment of women. However, when checked on empirical validity and theoretical soundness, we find that such links are not as clear.

Insofar as it is a feature of the human experience, religion will inevitably find its way into and permeate politics. Religion can influence public policy as well as civil rights and liberties in many ways, whether directly through state action, or indirectly through the influence of faith civil society. The state may interact with and be influenced by religion through formal institutions such as a state religion, laws based on religious doctrine, or state sponsorship of religion. Even for a state that strives to separate itself from religion, religious influence will pervade through politician and voter ideology, religious lobbying, and so forth. Despite its potential for influence, religion is often overlooked in the social sciences and not appreciated for the complex variable that it is (Fox, 2001, 2018).

The relationship between religion and women's rights in general, and reproductive rights in particular, is especially relevant for our discussion. Organized religion is often perceived as being associated with patriarchal structures and gendered role enforcement (Bakht, 2007), and feminism has long regarded religion as a patriarchal institution (Sultana, 2011). For the maintenance of patriarchal religious ideologies, women, in their role as child bearers and educators, are necessary for the transmission and reproduction of religious symbols. Women, therefore, must be both maintained and seen in this role as part of religious adherence. The image of motherhood as the apex of the female experience is often deeply embedded in religion and protected by its teachings, principles, and institutions. Of course, this reflects a sweeping view of how religion defines and imposes upon female identity. It does not fully help us understand how religion might affect public policy. Furthermore, some areas of public policy are more amenable and sensitive to religious doctrine than others. This chapter and the next one delve into those questions theoretically and empirically.

Various theories see the link between religion and reproductive policy as particularly strong. Even those who argue that only certain types of women's welfare policy may be influenced by religion see abortion policy as highly susceptible to such influence (Htun & Weldon, 2010). Yet, we know little about how religion and abortion policy interact, especially outside of the Western context. Thus, while there is reason to think that organized religion, as a key civil society player, would influence abortion policy, there is still much to discover about the religion-abortion policy link (Forman-Rabinovici & Sommer, 2018a, 2018b). Let us discuss some of the literature about abortion and how it considers the potential, and real, influences of religion.

Abortion and Religion – Limitations in the Current Literature

By and large, abortion literature falls into one of two broad categories: U.S.-focused scholarship or comparative analyses. U.S.-based research has addressed the effects of Catholic, Protestant, and Jewish voters, as well as religiosity on various aspects of reproductive health and abortion policy. Yet, its findings are limited to a single country, the United States, and are based on a public opinion perspective (Combs & Welch, 1982; Jelen &

Wilcox, 2003; Berkman & O'Connor, 1993; Cook, Jelen, & Wilcox, 1993; inter alia). In the comparative literature, the connection between abortion and religion has also been discussed from an opinion perspective, rather than a policy perspective. It has also largely limited itself to European and Western contexts, leaving out many features of the religion-state interaction.

A focus on public opinion makes sense when the cases under investigation are democracies. In such government systems, there is a set of institutions designed to translate public opinion into public policy. By design, representatives must be attentive to the ebb and flow of public wants and needs. Public preferences on questions of reproductive policy are expected to influence reproductive health provisions. When delving into the comparative dimensions of this question, however, the institutional logic of democracies is no longer universally relevant. Instead, we deal with a range of governmental systems, many of which lack the institutions designed to guarantee representation. The will of the people is not necessarily reflected, nor is it expected to be reflected, in government decision making. Inherently, officials may have additional and often different motivations, incentives and influences in the decision making process. Indeed, in some systems, not only is public opinion not expected to influence public policy, it is not even measured in a valid manner.

The shortcomings of existing literature on the religion-abortion connection are not just limited to the focus on public opinion. Where religion has been examined in the study of reproductive policy (both in the United States and internationally), only limited dimensions of religion were included. For instance, most studies to date have focused on different denominations of Christianity. The second- and third-largest world religions, Islam and Hinduism, which represent a combined 2.6 billion people (upward of 38% of the world population), are largely absent from scholarship on this topic. Still, Norris and Inglehart (2002) describe gender equality and sexual liberalization as "the most basic cultural fault line between the West and Islam" (pp. 235–236). Considering the significantly different ways various religions approach gender equality, it is critical to look beyond Western Christian states and the Judeo-Christian traditions.

Furthermore, the approach to religion in the literature has ignored a range of features in the relationship between religion and policy. For instance, no large comparative quantitative study has been conducted, to our knowledge, to observe the effects of religious variables such as religiosity, religious diversity, or the formal laws of the religion-state relationship. Moreover, the above-mentioned fact that much of the previous research has focused on public attitudes toward abortion, rather than the actual reproductive policy in place, means that extant literature has put process over outcome.

A New Approach

We propose improvements on those various aspects. First, we look at religion as a complex and multifaceted entity, exploring both different denominations and different variables of the religion-policy relationship. Second, we think of women's welfare policy as multidimensional, looking at religion's effects on both doctrinal reproduction policy and non-doctrinal political rights policies. This gives us insight into how to think about abortion policy in the greater context of women's rights policy. It is only such an examination of the multifaceted interplay between religion and women's welfare policy that allows us to re-evaluate common perceptions concerning the effects of religion on women's rights. The results suggest that when both religion and women's welfare are treated as nuanced and multifaceted variables, the connection between them is more complex than previously thought.

The discussion in this chapter is dedicated to exploring these questions through large-N quantitative analyses, using ordinal regression models and multiple indexes to test for robustness. We generate original indexes, based on reports of the United Nations, that reflect the various grounds on which a state will allow an abortion. Along with abortion policy, we also look at women's political rights, so as to distinguish between doctrinal and non-doctrinal policies. Doctrinal policy is theorized to be more sensitive to religious doctrinal influence (Htun & Weldon, 2010). Both types of policies are included so as to capture the nuances of the relationship between women's welfare policy and religion. We examine both abortion and political rights indexes in correlation with characteristics of the religion-state relationship. This includes various religious denominations, degree of freedom of religion, religiosity, and more.

This chapter aims to present both a theoretical discussion and an empirical examination of how religion interacts with reproductive rights. We will first present a general discussion of the relationship between religion and the state, religion and gender equality policy, and religion and reproductive rights. Next, in addition to the brief discussion in the introduction to this chapter, we look more in depth into what the literature has had to say so far about religion and abortion rights. In order to set up our theoretical framework, we will explore various features of the state-religion relationship and theorize how these features might determine the relationship. This will be followed by statistical analyses, including a range of regression models empirically testing those connections. The chapter concludes with a discussion of the findings and some conclusions leading up to the case studies in the following chapter. The case studies of the effects of faith civil society on abortion in Chile and Bahrain in Chapter 3 allow us to illustrate the findings from the current chapter. Moreover, thanks to the case study methodology employed, the actions and strategies of the Catholic Church in Chile and Islam in Bahrain also demonstrate causal pathways we outline here.

Religion and the State

A feature of the human experience, religion permeates politics at various levels and in different ways. Religion can influence public policy and civil rights and liberties directly through state action or indirectly through the influence of civil society. As Robert Benne (2010) writes, "the vast and complicated interplay of religion and public life … simply cannot be shut down" (p. 14). Overlap between religious communities, institutions and traditions, and state governance is inevitable. In fact, governments may be as involved in religion today as at any other point in history. All countries have some manner of support and restriction of religion (Fox, 2018).

Given that we are discussing religion as an institution, let us define it for the sake of the discussion. We use Fox's (2018) definition:

> Religion seeks to understand the origins and nature of reality using a set of answers that include the supernatural. Religion is also a social phenomenon and institution which influences the behavior of human beings both as individuals and in groups. These influences on behavior manifest though the influences of religious identity, religious institutions, religious legitimacy, religious beliefs, and the codification of these beliefs into authoritative dogma, among other avenues of influence." (p. 6)

For a number of reasons, this definition fits the study of religion in the social sciences and specifically in political science. First, it recognizes religion as both a phenomenon and a social institution that influences human behavior. Second, it differentiates religion from other ideologies by defining it as an ideology or belief system that includes a supernatural element or entity. This is useful for our purposes, as we need to isolate religion as a social phenomenon separate from ideology and political doctrine. Further, we want to analyze religion as both functioning as an institution and as influencing human and state behavior.

The interaction between religion and the state can take many formal and informal forms. As Fox (2018) suggests, the interface of religion and the state includes features such as (1) secularization, (2) religious identity, (3) religious worldview or doctrines, (4) religious legitimacy, (5) religious institutions and political mobilization, (6) religious fundamentalism, (7) religion and conflict, (8) government policy toward religion, (9) political secularism, (10) religious freedom, and (11) religion in international relations. At the level of formal state relations, a country might have an official religion. In more extreme cases, a state might limit other religions, impose a certain religion, or make law on the basis of religious doctrine. Even in liberal democratic states there can be an official religion, a state sponsorship of religion, or religion-based political parties. Informally, religious doctrine and religious leaders may influence citizen views on a wide range of political issues.

Even in a system with separation of religion and state, the informal opportunities for religion to enter politics are abundant. As much as any state might try to relegate it to the private sphere, it is near impossible to avoid interaction between religion and state. Even a state with a "hands-off" approach to religious doctrine can – and probably will – find itself interacting with, influenced by, and crossing boundaries with religious institutions and questions (Garnett, 2009). Politicians' and voters' basic ideologies and ethical guidelines are influenced and in some cases even dictated by religion (Barnea and Schwartz, 1998; Tatalovitch and Schier, 1993; Fastnow, Grant, and Rudolph, 1999; Djupe & Gilbert, 2008). Religious leaders serve as opinion leaders and have built-in public stages from which to exert authority and to influence public opinion and lobby leaders (Nteta & Wallsten, 2012; Boulay, Tweedie, & Fiagbey, 2008). Organized religious institutions can also serve as informal meeting places for exchange of ideas and political discussion. As we demonstrate in the next chapter in the case study of Chile and the Catholic Church, organized religions can function as lobbying agencies to promote policy, which corresponds with specific religious beliefs (Wood Jr, 1986; Yamane, 2005). Religious organizations can also use their status as communal service providers to negotiate policy with the state (Kortmann, 2018). As a source of identity and cohesion, religion may influence the preferences of voters and politicians in various areas, including even foreign policy (Blackman, 2018). We mention an example in the case of Chile in the next chapter.

Despite its potential for influence, as Fox (2001) observed, religion is often overlooked in the social sciences. Whether this is because modernization theorists reject its relevancy, methodologists find it hard to quantify, or liberal socialization has programmed researchers to disregard it, the fact remains that there is still much to explore in the relationship between religion and policy. This is doubly true for questions of reproductive rights, which, as we extensively discussed earlier, are strongly linked to religious questions. Indeed, in the context of exploring the effects of civil society on reproductive rights, religion is of particular interest.

Following Stepan's (2000) tradition of twin tolerations, Driessen (2010) argues that religious bodies can have an important role in the democratic state through civil society activity, rulers, and regime legitimization.[1] That said, how religion may influence a state varies based on regime type and constitutional framework as well as on various aspects of civil society within the specific state. In a theocracy, the influence is direct. In democracies, and perhaps to a lesser extent in non-democratic states, religion's influence may be more indirect in nature. We aim to capture some of the different ways in which religion interacts with policymaking in general and, in particular, with respect to the question of how religious elements in civil society influence reproductive rights. To that end, let us proceed now to the relations between religion and gender issues more broadly.

Religion, Women's Rights, and Gender Equality

The relationship between religion and women's rights is at the heart of our discussion. Organized religion is often perceived as associated with patriarchal structures and gendered role enforcement (Bakht, 2007). Historically, feminism and religion have had a rocky relationship. As early as the nineteenth century, first-wave feminists expressed views ranging from tempered criticism of patriarchal Church ideology and structure to outright rejection of religious institutions. Later, feminist waves reexamined the relationship between feminist ideology and organized religions. Some third-wave feminist thinkers paid respect to the complex relationship, even claiming that religion, with its appreciation for the role of the mother and the family, could be empowering for women (Woodhead, [2001], 2003). Woodhead claims, though, that despite this history of interaction, much of religious sociology remains "gender blind," leading to many unknowns in the relationship between religion and women's movements. Thus, despite the common wisdom that religion has a depressing effect on women's rights, which also dominates much of the feminist writing, even within feminist work there are reasons to think that there is more involved in the link between religion and gender equality.

For feminists, religion has often appeared as a source of oppression for a few reasons. Some would consider religion one of the pillars of a patriarchal

---

[1]   While Driessen's work refers to democracies, and our sample and theory include nondemocracies as well, his work is still relevant here.

system (Sultana, 2011). Within this school of thought, religion is commonly perceived as opposed to abortion and contraception. It is generally dominated by male leaders and often opposes even the possibility of female leadership. Religion – and especially the main Western denominations – also has gendered imagery, with a masculine God and a reverence for female virginity.

Critics of religious doctrine often claim that religion relegates women to the private sphere, and uses its texts and discourse to present the male standpoint as universal and to support male dominance (Taylor & Whittier, 1995). All of these features of religion are even more problematic for feminists because they are generally placed in the unconscious imagination, making them an inherent and embedded part of the patriarchy. This has made religious institutions obvious targets for feminist opposition (Obelkevich, Roper, & Samuel, 2013).

Even those who argue that it is not inherently patriarchal often see religion exploited as a tool to subordinate women. In their view, organized religion was hijacked and taken in a patriarchal direction (Sultana, 2011; Miller, 2013). Notwithstanding whether it is inherent or a result of exploitation, religion is often cited as a site of patriarchal oppression. This is true not just in academic scholarship but, in many ways, in public discourse.

Religion is often seen as a staunch supporter of traditional gender roles. Women and the family have a crucial role in constructing and maintaining religious group identity. This results in gendered images of women as mothers and caregivers – the moral guardians and teachers of culture and norms. As a result, law regarding the role of women, particularly as mothers and caregivers, can be especially sensitive to religious influence (Shachar, 2005). Strict gender roles are seen as necessary for the maintenance and reproduction of traditional symbolic order. Therefore, it is often necessary to control women to maintain the social and political order of religious fundamentalism (Yuval-Davis, [1992] 2005). In general, there is considered to be a significant and negative link between progressive women's rights and religious fundamentalism.

Often, different religions emphasize the role of men as workers and the role of women as mothers and caretakers. Women are encouraged to see themselves within the domestic sphere and emphasize their role as mothers over other sources of identity (Reynolds & May, 2014). Whether it is the Virgin Mary or "Mother Nature," women's primary identities relate to their roles as nurturers. This enforced role also affects the parts women can play outside of the private sphere. The degree of a woman's religious fundamentalism correlates with her likelihood to attain higher education, enter the labor force, and have elite careers. Women who hold fundamentalist religious beliefs are more likely to work fewer hours, leave the workforce after the birth of a child, and hold less-advanced academic degrees and lesser positions at work (Sherkat, 2000).

Sherkat (2000) gives examples of how a religion can build women's roles and identities around their job as mothers and keepers of the domestic sphere. She specifically focuses on Conservative Protestant texts on family dynamics:

> For many fundamentalist Protestants, women's roles are of paramount concern. The divine order of family relations relies on the headship of a Christian husband, the submission of the wife to her husband, and the subordination of children to their parents. Without this pattern of authority, many conservative Christians believe that the family cannot function properly, and a host of personal and social problems will proliferate. (pp. 345–346)

Sherkat further explains that in Judeo-Christian religions, those who advocate women's submission to men within the family structure find justification in sacred texts. In the story of creation, woman was made from man to serve a man's need. The first woman, Eve, then proves her frailty by defying God's orders and dooming women for all time. In New Testament texts, Paul writes that women should "teach the young women to be sober, to love their husbands, to love their children. To be discreet, chaste, keepers at home, good, obedient to their own husbands, that the word of God be not blasphemed" Titus (2:5). Of course, this reflects a very sweeping view of how religion defines and imposes upon the female identity. The extent of religious attitudes toward sex roles is also affected by the degree of religiosity and the specific denomination itself. Not all religions impose traditional gender roles to the same degree (McMurry, 1978).

These religious views on women's identity also direct religion's attempts to influence their welfare policy. There are different ways of viewing the relationship between religion and women's welfare policy. While some might adopt an approach that assumes that all religions and all women's welfare issues clash, not all scholars adopt such a sweeping position. Yet, even those with a more nuanced approach cite its role (Grzymala-Busse, 2012).

Htun and Weldon (2010) reject the notion of an all-encompassing effect for religion. Instead, they argue that religion influences only some types of gender equality policy. For them, the key distinction is between doctrinal and non-doctrinal policies. The former touch upon the core tenets of religious doctrine and codified cultural traditions. Non-doctrinal law, on the other hand, generally touches upon areas of life rarely addressed in religious doctrine. According to Htun and Weldon (2010), it is only in matters of doctrinal policy that we should expect to find major influence for religion. More often than not, abortion would fall within the doctrinal purview, which would lead us to believe even more strongly in the common wisdom cited above concerning religion's heavy influence on abortion policy. Before we delve into the influence of religion on such doctrinal policy issues, let us look some more into what the literature says about the topic of religion and abortion policy.

Religion and Abortion Policy

As we briefly mention above, abortion literature falls into one of two broad categories: U.S.-focused scholarship and comparative analyses. The first category typically applies quantitative methods to explore a wide range of variables that influence abortion policy. Firmly embedded within political science, this body of literature identifies the following critical predictors: religion, party affiliation, interest-group membership, presence of female legislators, income level, education level, and, most importantly, public opinion. In the context of religion, this research has addressed the effects of Catholic, Protestant, and Jewish voters on abortion policy. Yet, its findings are limited to a single country, the United States. As we discussed above, this literature is largely based on a public opinion perspective.

In this U.S.-based research, abortion stance is used as an indicator for possible effects on public policy. The underlying logic is that public opinion is a crucially important determinant of public policy and that abortion attitudes are a significant predictor of voter choice (O'Connor & Berkman, 1995). It is founded on the democratic nature of the United States, whose institutions are designed to translate public opinion into policymaking. This focus on the United States, with its single definition of Church-State relations, largely Christian population, and emphasis on public opinion, suggests that the external validity of this scholarship may be limited. It is hard to generalize from the American case to countries where the system of government is different, whose institutional design is not a democratic one, and where the denominational arrangements are different.

In the comparative literature, the connection between abortion and religion is also often discussed from an opinion perspective. For major world religions including Roman Catholicism, Protestantism, Eastern Orthodoxy, Buddhism, Hinduism, and Islam, attitude toward sexual morality was the strongest and most consistent predictor of opinion on abortion (Jelen, 2014). Comparative studies of abortion policy (rather than public opinion) have been limited to Christian denominations. In the handful of cases where this research goes beyond Christianity (e.g., Hildebrandt, 2015), Islam is found to be insignificant. Most other studies of the effects of religiosity or of religion-state relations have been limited to case studies within Christian states, and largely focus on

Europe and Anglo countries (McBride Stetson, 2001; Minkenberg, 2002, 2003; Knill, Preidel, & Nebel, 2014; Outshoorn, 1996; Engeli, 2009; Engeli, Green-Pedersen, & Larsen, 2013; Githens & Stetson, 1996).

In sum, despite the importance of religion and common understandings concerning its influence on policy, scholarship has explored only a limited number of religious variables with two major lacunas. First, our understanding of the effects of different religious denominations is limited. More specifically, do different religions have disparate effects or dissimilar levels of influence? The common wisdom holding that religion depresses women's rights would suggest homogenous effects for different denominations, but is this really the case? The second lacuna concerns the characteristics of religion within the state, and the religion-state relationship. For instance, we know little about how to compare the influence of religiosity, as distinct from a particular religious denomination, on policymaking in different countries.

In the next two sections, we present features of the religion-policy relationship, including religious denominations and formal and informal characteristics of religion-state interactions. We take up each of those in turn and theorize their effects on abortion policy. We do not aim to thoroughly explain the influence of a given religion or why one religious feature may be more influential than another. In the discussion section, we explore possible explanations for outcomes. The predictive variables we focus on allow us to examine the key ways in which faith in civil society and policy interact. Yet, they do not form an exhaustive list of all characteristics of religious groups and their state-religion interactions. Rather, they give insight into how religion and the state might interact and how religion, as a part of civil society, might influence reproductive rights.

THEORETICAL FRAMEWORK: PREDICTORS OF THE RELIGION-POLICY LINK

Religious Denominations

Both the U.S.-based and comparative literatures have given some attention to religion as a factor in the study of abortion policy. The U.S.-based literature finds anti-abortion public opinion to be associated with large Catholic and conservative Protestant constituencies. Non-conservative Protestant populations, on the other hand, increase support for permissive abortion policy (Berkman & O'Connor, 1993; Combs & Welch, 1982; Norrander & Wilcox, 1999; O'Connor & Berkman, 1995; Jelen & Wilcox, 2003).

In the body of quantitative comparative work, only Christianity and Islam have been analyzed and only in a limited number of countries. Comparative quantitative abortion studies have found that a higher number of Catholics was a significant predictor of restrictive abortion policy (Asal, Brown, & Figueroa, 2008; Hildebrandt, 2015; Pillai & Wang, 1999; Lovenduski & Outshoorn, 1986; Outshoorn, 1996). However, when controlling for other explanatory factors, a large Muslim population was insignificant in predicting abortion policy (Hildebrandt, 2015). This is in contrast to the claim by Norris and Inglehart (2002) concerning the role of gender in marking the new cleavages between Islam and the West. This lack of consensus regarding Islam makes it especially important to empirically test those claims using a battery of robust models. Additionally, none of these studies include any religions beyond Christianity (predominantly Catholicism) and Islam, despite the fact that the two denominations combined represent fewer than 40% of humanity.[2] Two of the world's largest organized religions, Hinduism and Buddhism, have been largely ignored in the literature. Hence, not only do we lack a clear theoretical understanding of the religion-abortion link but in fact we have, to our knowledge, no research that empirically tests it in any comprehensive manner. Notably, there is some indication suggesting that neither Hinduism nor Buddhism should have the kind of depressing effect on women's rights as we normally associate with religion in the West (Damian, 2010).

We theorize that Hinduism and Buddhism would have an insignificant or positive relationship similar to the one non-conservative Protestantism[3] has with abortion policy (Jelen, 2014). Buddhist texts are relatively silent on fertility practices and there is no consensus that abortion violates any standard Buddhist ethical teachings (Barnhart, 2009). Earlier Buddhist texts do not make any outright statements against abortion, although later texts do forbid nuns and monks from assisting in the procedure. Buddhism in general approaches abortion as a less polarized and polarizing issue, and this denomination does not employ a binary life or death approach (Perrett, 2000). Along the same lines, Gelb describes an ambiguous Buddhist position on abortion, in which religion sees it as "a necessary and regrettable evil" (1996, p. 131).

---

[2] Muslims represent about 23.2% of the world population, Catholics about 16%, unaffiliated 16.3%, Hindus 15%, Protestants approximately 11%, and Buddhists, the world's sixth largest religious denomination 7.1% (Pew Research Center 2012).

[3] Protestantism is presented as a single group in this study based on its categorization as a single religion in demographic studies, as well as its use as a single category in previous abortion studies (Minkenberg 2002; Pew Research Center 2012). Results should be treated with caution though, as Protestants can be considered a theologically diverse category (Jelen 2014).

In Hinduism, conflicts between religious texts and the modern development of the religion might neutralize any effect on abortion policy. According to Hinduism, from the moment of conception the embryo is a distinct life with both a spiritual and physical presence. However, modern Hindu religious leaders have been very tolerant regarding abortion and reproductive technologies in general (Allahbadia, Allahbadia, & Arora, 2009, p. 134). The cultural importance attached to having male children contributes to lenience toward abortion. Families may try to avoid having female offspring, who are often seen not only as an economic burden but also as incapable of fulfilling certain religious obligations (Allahbadia, Allahbadia, & Arora, 2009). Additionally, Jain (2003) explains that while abortion is a heinous crime in Hinduism, the religion also traditionally rejected absolutism. Therefore, as an organized religion, Hinduism is capable of recognizing situations in which an abortion is the lesser of two evils, for example, when the mother's life is in danger.

In sum, we expect to see a negative correlation between large Catholic or Muslim populations and abortion policy. The connection with Protestantism, Hinduism, and Buddhism should be positive or insignificant, given the ambiguous views these latter religions have presented in that matter. Accordingly, the following hypothesis applies:

H2.1: Muslim and Catholic population size will have a negative relationship with the degree of permissiveness of abortion policy. Other religions – specifically, Protestantism, Buddhism, and Hinduism – will not have a negative relationship.

Features of the Religion-Policy Relationship

We go beyond the effects of various religious denominations to consider the mechanisms by which religion interacts with and defines society: the state in general and women's rights in particular. Those mechanisms include legislation on religious freedom, separation of religion and state, levels of religiosity, and religious diversity. Minkenberg (2002) offers the only study to date that addresses some of these variables in the context of abortion policy. Focused on Catholic and Protestant European countries, Minkenberg examined whether state abortion policy is determined by religion type, level of religiosity, and institutional arrangements regarding the separation of church and state. Catholic countries were found to have more restrictive abortion policies than Protestant countries. Institutional impact was modest to low, meaning secularized institutions offered no guarantee of mitigated religious influence.

Religiosity was the best predictor of public policy, with low religiosity corresponding with permissive abortion policy. Yet, high levels of religiosity were only associated with restrictive abortion policy when paired with Catholicism. The study's small sample of countries, lack of statistical analysis, and limited representation of world religions leave much room for expansion. What Minkenberg does suggest is an interaction effect between religious denomination and religiosity. In other words, the effect of religiosity is contingent on the specific religious denomination dominant in the state.

More generally, various religious features will have their effects on abortion policy and may interact with the dominant denomination in the country regarding how reproductive rights are produced. But how does that happen? What are the causal mechanisms underlying such a connection? How does religion, as a civil society actor, manifest in the state-civil society relationship? To theorize on mechanisms, we distinguish between formal and informal devices that characterize the religion-state relationship. By formal relationship, we refer to the official laws and state policies that monitor the relationship between religion and the state, namely, laws on freedom of religion and on the separation of religion and state. By informal, we mean features of the religious population of the state. Specifically, we look at freedom of religion, separation of religion and state, religiosity, and religious diversity.

Freedom of Religion

Freedom of religion can be defined simply as "freedom of belief and freedom to act according to one's beliefs" (Robbers, 2001, p. 664). This definition is fairly sparse and leaves a gray area. Indeed, the very concept and basis of freedom of religion is debated, with some asking if its roots are in freedom of expression or freedom of association or movement, or if it stands on its own as a right (Nickel, 2005).

How it is defined, though, will also determine the shape this freedom takes. Offering a more detailed definition, McConnell defines religious freedom as "the right of individuals and groups to form their own religious beliefs and to practice them to the extent consistent with the rights of others and with fundamental requirements of public order and the common good" (2013, p. 772). Freedom of religion relates to the extent to which the state limits religious worship, practice, and expression.

We hypothesize that commitment on the part of the state to freedom of religion should contribute to more permissive abortion policy. Stance on abortion has been found to be determined by religion in general (O'Connor & Berkman, 1995; Minkenberg, 2002). Additionally, in the distinction we drew earlier between doctrinal and non-doctrinal policies, abortion falls into the former category (Htun & Weldon, 2010). Accordingly, a state that takes a more multicultural or liberal approach to religious freedom in general should also be expected to have a permissive abortion policy. If the state gives more freedom to a variety of religions and takes a more hands-off approach to dictating the practice of religion in the state, we hypothesize that this also means that in turn faith civil society would be less present as a part of national policy considerations. In other words, if the state does not use its powers to control religion, it is also not controlled by a religious doctrine. One possibility is that the state relegates religion to the private sphere, in which case, again, policy forums will be less influenced by religious doctrine. Another option is a general correlation between different types of rights and liberties. In other words, a state that adopts liberal religious freedoms also adopts a liberal approach toward women's rights. We, therefore, offer the following hypothesis:

H2.2: The degree of religious freedom will have a positive relationship with permissive abortion policy.

Separation of Religion and State

While the concept of separation of Church and state often includes freedom of religion, for the purposes of our discussion, we focus on how much the state allows itself to support religion and be entangled in religion in its various organs and functions. In other words, we distinguish between the establishment of religion and the exercise of religion. The establishment of religion refers to the extent to which the state may establish religion. The exercise of religion is understood and interpreted as pertaining more to the freedom of individuals to go about their religious practices and beliefs with minimum intervention by the state. Exercise matters are covered by the discussion of Freedom of Religion in the previous section.

The establishment of state religion relates to the support the state lends to organized religion and whether it bolsters religious institutions. Likewise, state-religion separation (or the lack thereof) will be reflected in the extent to which religious institutions are allowed to directly participate or influence the democratic process and the progression of policymaking. A thorough explanation of this idea touches on the spectrum of how a state defines the legal status of a religion; grants autonomy to religious institutions and religious communities; finances religion; and regulates and finances religious education, faith-based care, and social services (Bader, 2007).

Religious opposition to abortion is most apparent when religious denominations are institutionally built into politics (Lovenduski & Outshoorn, 1986, p. 3). The more intertwined the relationship between state and religion, the more influence we should expect. If religiosity and religious doctrine in general have a negative effect on women's status, then institutions enabling and facilitating religion's permeation into government itself could result in limitations on legal access to abortion.

The more the state is intertwined with religious institutions, the easier it is for those institutions to influence the state. For example, when the Catholic Church assisted in regime transition in Chile in the 1990s, it used this as an opportunity to encourage anti-abortion legislation. The Church's deep involvement in regime negotiations provided the opportunity to advance its agenda on reproductive health policy. We will explore the Chilean case study further in the following chapter. In cases such as this, we expect the boundary between state and religion to become less clear. Thus, the following hypothesis applies:

H2.3: Increased separation of religion and state will have a positive relationship with permissive abortion policy

Religiosity

Religiosity[4] has been found to be a strong determinant across a wide range of policy areas (Olson, Cadge, & Harrison, 2006; Brossard, Scheufele, Kim, & Lewenstein, 2009; Scheufele, Corley, Shih, Dalrymple, & Ho, 2009; Smidt, 2005). The definition of religiosity and its operationalization, however, have been debated extensively. Glock (1972) equates religiosity with religious commitment and measures it using five dimensions: experiential, ritualistic, ideological, intellectual, and consequential. Verbit (1970) built a 24-dimension scale, using four different dimensions each to look at six different components: ritual, doctrine, emotion, knowledge, ethics, and community. Clayton and Gladen (1974), though, stress that religiosity is in fact not multidimensional, but rather that all of these dimensions are different measurements of ideological commitment. Ideological commitment, or the strength of a person's acceptance of tradition, they contend, is the only true dimension of religiosity.

---

[4] While not completely overlapping, within this study the concept of religiosity will also stand in for the concept of religious fundamentalism. Altemeyer and Hunsberger define religious fundamentalism as "the belief that there is one set of religious teachings that clearly contains the fundamental, basic, intrinsic, essential, inerrant truth about humanity and deity" and that these teachings must be fought for and rigorously lived by (2004, p. 48). While religiosity and fundamentalism are not synonymous, they are correlated and we do not distinguish between them for the purposes of our discussion.

Greater religiosity would have a negative effect on abortion policy. In U.S.-based studies, a higher degree of religiosity consistently predicts anti-abortion public sentiment and more restrictive policies (Alvarez & Brehm, 1995; Cook, Jelen, & Wilcox, 1993; Wilcox, 1990). Voters who are less supportive of abortion tend to be more committed to organized religion and fall closer to the traditional (or conservative) end of the cultural spectrum (Shain, 1986).

Within a comparative framework, Castles (2003) explored the relationship between traditional assumptions about women's roles as a mother and home-maker on the one hand and workplace policy that supported women's integration in the public sphere on the other. Societies with traditional beliefs were less likely to have policies supporting women's activity outside of the private sphere and more likely to support policy that reinforced traditional gender roles. These societies were also more likely to see motherhood as the most important role for women and abortion as a threat to this identity (Berkman & O'Connor, 1993). Thus, exemplifying more traditional values, states with higher levels of religiosity would be less likely to adopt a permissive abortion policy, since it would threaten traditional gender roles. We, therefore, test the following hypothesis in the models estimated below:

H2.4: Higher levels of religiosity will negatively correlate with permissive abortion policy.

The consequences of religiosity for public policymaking may differ among denominations. That is, religiosity may interact with religion. For instance, Minkenberg (2002) found that degree of religiosity was relevant when the population was Catholic. In a Protestant state, on the other hand, a religious population was no more or less likely to have permissive abortion policies. We hypothesize that religions likely to have a negative effect on abortion policy (see H2.1) will also interact with levels of religiosity to affect such policy. In religious denominations that are expected to oppose abortions, levels of religiosity would accentuate this effect.

H2.5: There will be an interaction effect between religious denominations and levels of religiosity.

Religious Diversity

Lieberson defines population diversity as "the position of a population along a homogeneity-heterogeneity continuum" (1969, p. 850). Within the context of religion, this would be the diversity of religious groups in terms of number and size of religious denominations in society. Religious diversity can make it challenging for citizens and lawmakers to find a single conception of ethics

(Bader, 2007). Additionally, greater religious diversity can weaken the power of any given religious denomination and of faith civil society as a whole.

We offer two potential explanations. First, power would be distributed among a larger number of groups so that the influence of any one religious group is limited. Second, in order to avoid a precedent that allows any other religious denomination to do the same, each religious group would avoid pushing forward religious policy. Rather than risking that a different group may one day promote its own religious program, the Nash equilibrium for all groups would be to leave off the agenda any policy issue too tied to religious questions, teachings, or practices. Abortion would be such a policy issue. Accordingly, we propose the following hypothesis:

H2.6: Increased religious diversity will correlate with permissive abortion policy.

Let us now proceed to the empirical testing of the hypotheses. The approach in this book strives to provide theoretical developments side by side with their empirical examination. Do our theoretical predictions hold water when tested with data for the majority of world nations? Let us see.

RESEARCH DESIGN

Dependent Variables

In order to model abortion policy as the predicted variable, we created a comparative measure for state policy, the *CAI*. We take advantage of the coding scheme of the *Global Review of Abortion Policy*. The U.N. Department of Social and Economic Affairs has published the review periodically since 1992. For this study, scales were compiled based on the 2002 and 2007 reports. These reports contain up to 195 countries. The *Global Review of Abortion Policy* report offers seven criteria under which state law may allow access to abortion services: saving a woman's life, preserving a woman's physical health, preserving a woman's mental health, in cases of rape or incest, because of fetal impairment, for social or economic reasons, and on request.

For the coding protocol of the first version of the index, CAI_1, each criterion is given equal weight, and a country's score is a direct reflection of the number of conditions it accepts. The CAI_1 scale, thus, ranges from 0 (most conservative) to 7 (most permissive). A country where women cannot receive an abortion under any circumstances gets a CAI_1 of zero. A country in which a woman may access an abortion under all conditions, including on request, receives a score of 7.

For the purposes of robustness and to fix a potential measurement flaw in *CAI1*, we also generate a weighted index (*CAI2*; Forman-Rabinovici and Sommer, 2018a, 2018b). The first scale does not account for the different degrees of liberalism that each criterion represents. It would be imprecise, for instance, to suggest that the criterion of saving a woman's life is equivalent to (and thus carries the same weight as) allowing abortion on demand. The more liberal the criterion, the less likely it is universally accepted.

Accordingly, the weight of each criterion in *CAI2* is determined based on the percentage (*Pi*) of countries that allow that condition. In the weighted index, countries are given a score on a scale of 0–1. A score of zero represents countries in which there is no legal abortion, and a score of represents a country that accepts all criteria for abortion, including on request. The formula for the weighted index, *CAI2*, is therefore:[5]

$$CAI2_i = \frac{1 - P_i}{\sum_{j=1}^{criteria} (1 - P_j)}$$

As a form of discriminant validity, we estimate models with abortion policy as the dependent variable (the doctrinal policy area) side by side with models where women's political rights are the outcome variable (the nondoctrinal policy area). Unlike reproductive rights, which touch upon and are closely related to religious doctrine, political rights are more religiously neutral. We, thus, think of political rights for women as a nondoctrinal area of policy. The empirical distinction is, thus, between religiously laden women's rights in the realm of reproductive policy and religiously neutral political rights for women.

To specify models with nondoctrinal policy areas as the outcome variable, we employ Cingranelli and Richards' (*CIRI*) Women's Political Rights Index as our third dependent variable. This data set tracks the extent of political rights for women in 192 countries, indexing to what extent women enjoy political rights such as suffrage, right to run for office, and right to join political parties. Countries are given a score of 0–3 based on the degree of freedom. Zero represents a country where women are denied rights in both law and practice; 1, a country that gives rights under law but in practice greatly prohibits; 2, only moderately prohibits; and 3 offers rights in both law and practice (Cingranelli, Richards, & Clay, 2014; Jan et al., 2015).

---

[5] Certain features of abortion laws were not included in either version of the index. Abortion laws may also contain dimensions of time limits, spousal or parental consent, requirements for the mother to undergo counseling, and so forth. Yet, those additional characteristics are difficult to incorporate into a comparative index for reasons of data availability.

Estimating models with these dependent variables allows us to see to what extent women's rights policy can be viewed as a single type of policy, or if there are distinct types of rights that are dissimilarly affected by disparate variables. Such a design helps us examine whether divergent types of women's rights are affected differently by faith civil society, and to see to what extent reproductive issues must be treated as a policy category unto itself. Should women's welfare policy indeed be separated into doctrinal vs. nondoctrinal categories, with abortion falling into the former and political rights into the latter?

Independent Variables

The population shares of Catholics, Protestants, Muslims, Buddhists, and Hindus is specified for religious denominations (Maoz & Henderson, 2013; Pew Research Center, 2009). Religious freedom is indexed using the government regulation index developed by Grim and Finke. They define government regulation of religion as "the restrictions placed on the practice, profession, or selection of religion by the official laws, policies, or administrative actions of the state" (2006, p. 7). Grim and Finke place government regulation on a 10-point scale, with 10 being the most restrictive and 0 being not restrictive at all. The scale accounts for a variety of freedoms including if a state protects an individual's right to worship, engages in missionary work, and provides formal protection for freedom of religion.

To look at separation of religion and state, we also take from Grim and Finke, using their government favoritism index. This index measures the extent to which the government provides privileges or support to one or more religious groups. If a government provides any sort of aid or favorable treatment to a religious group, it is by definition not separating between itself and religion. This scale also ranges from 0 to 10, with zero representing a country with no religious favoritism and 10 standing for the maximum level of favoritism. This scale includes considerations such as government funding as well as historical legacy of separation between state and religion.

Degree of religiosity is indexed using the World Values Survey (WVS). The WVS includes the question "how important is religion in your life?" on a 4-point scale. As our religiosity index, we use the percentage of survey respondents in the country that gave religion the highest score, indicating religion to be very important.

To measure religious diversity, we calculated the sum of squares of each religious group in a country. This number reflects the chance of randomly picking out two people of the same religion from within the national population. The descriptive statistics for the different variables appear in Table 2.1.

TABLE 2.1 *Descriptive Statistics*

	Mean	Standard Deviation
Protestant	.127	.192
Catholic	.224	.300
Islam	.307	.401
Buddhist	.040	.148
Hindu	.021	.102
Government Regulation	3.88	2.97
Government Favoritism	5.35	2.9
Religiosity	.494	.313
Religious Diversity	.570	.246
Female Legislators	.185	.121
HDI	.735	.139
Polity	4.42	6.42
N= 71		

Controls

In all models, female legislators (as percentage of the lower house; Women in National Parliaments, 2015), the human development index (HDI; United Nations Development Programme, 2016), and the Polity index (Marshall, Gurr, & Jaggers, 2017) are specified as control variables. The rate of female legislators constitutes a control for societal attitudes regarding the status of women. It has been identified as a key independent variable and an important control in many previous abortion studies (Hildebrandt, 2015; Asal et al., 2008; Berkman & O'Connor, 1993). HDI allows us to control for modernization and economic development. As socioeconomic and development status can be associated with degree of religiosity, HDI allows us to identify whether faith civil society is truly the driving force in the model. Indicating the degree of democracy in a state, the Polity index allows us to control for system of government, civil rights and liberties, and the power of public opinion and elected officials. Controlling for those alternative effects gives further validity to the effects of variables rooted in civil society. A control for if a country has a communist legacy is included in religious denomination models (models 1–3). Communist tradition is a relevant control, as this tradition rejects religion-based moral standings and has often liberalized abortion law (Hildebrandt, 2015; Bélanger & Flynn, 2009). There is an overlap between countries with communist traditions and countries with large populations of certain religious groups (mainly Muslim and Christian Orthodox). This overlap makes it particularly important to add this control, particularly in the religious denomination models. It allows us to unpack the various effects at play here.

Model Specification

We estimate a series of ordinal regression models, pairing the three dependent variables with the predictors grouped by denominations (Hypothesis 2.1) and religious features (Hypotheses 2.2–2.6). Ordinal models were chosen, as all of our dependent variables are measured along ordinal scales. Half the models test the relationship between religious denomination and the dependent variables. The relationship between religious features and the dependent variables are tested in the other models. The first set of models specifies the world's five largest religious denominations[6] and tests their relations with the three dependent variables. CAI_1 and CAI_2 are the key outcome variables and $CIRI$ is specified for discriminant validity between doctrinal and nondoctrinal policy areas. In the second category, all of the religion variables concerning features of the state (religious regulation, religious favoritism, religiosity, religious diversity) are specified in three regression models (one for each of the outcome variables CAI_1, CAI_2, and $CIRI$). We estimate models with data for 71 countries representing 75% of the world's population from 2005 or 2010, depending on data availability. See full list of countries in our database in Table 2.2.

Testing the Interaction between Religiosity and Religious Denominations

H2.5 concerns the interaction between religious denomination and religiosity, which poses a challenge in terms of model specification. Given that both Islam and Catholicism were predicted to negatively correlate with abortion policy, we want to check how these religions interact with degree of religiosity. It is necessary to use countries with a significant majority group of the specific religion, because otherwise we could not really test the effect of that religious denomination. This limits the number of countries that can be included. While ideally we would only use countries with 100% Muslims or Catholics, no such countries exist. There are not even enough countries with a majority close to 100% to run a valid statistical test.

Since the small N makes it impossible to estimate any statistical tests, we plot the interplay among variables in an attempt to make statements based on

---

[6] These five denominations represent approximately 77% of the world population (Pew Research Center 2015).

TABLE 2.2 *List of Countries in Sample*

Algeria	Lebanon
Argentina	Libya
Armenia	Malaysia
Australia	Mali
Azerbaijan	Mexico
Bahrain	Moldova
Belarus	Morocco
Brazil	Netherlands
Bulgaria	New Zealand
Burkina Faso	Nigeria
Canada	Norway
Chile	Pakistan
China	Peru
Colombia	Philippines
Cyprus	Poland
Ecuador	Qatar
Egypt	Romania
Estonia	Russia
Ethiopia	Rwanda
Finland	Singapore
France	Slovenia
Georgia	South Africa
Germany	Spain
Ghana	Sweden
Guatemala	Switzerland
Hungary	Thailand
India	Trinidad and Tobago
Indonesia	Tunisia
Iran	Turkey
Iraq	Ukraine
Italy	United Kingdom
Japan	Uruguay
Jordan	Uzbekistan
Kazakhstan	Vietnam
Kuwait	Zambia
Kyrgyzstan	

their scatter. To this end, we need to set a minimum bar of what constitutes a meaningful majority. Setting the bar at 70% leaves us with enough countries to begin to see patterns in the relationship. It would also be the recommended threshold based on critical mass theory. Critical mass theorists commonly cite 30% as the minimum threshold for minorities to exert influence (Childs & Krook, 2008; Lovenduski, 2001; Joecks, Pull, & Vetter, 2013; Dahlerup, 1988,

2006). Therefore, a 70% majority allows us to test a country whose minority group has not yet passed critical mass. Among the countries appearing in the 2005 and 2010 data sets, there are 17 Muslim countries and 12 Catholic countries that satisfy the 70% criterion. A scatterplot also has the added advantage of visually confirming and demonstrating findings regarding religiosity and the influence of different religious denominations. If religiosity uniformly affects abortion policy across religious denominations, we would expect to see a correlation between abortion policy and religiosity, regardless of religious sect. There would be a correlation regardless of whether the country has a Catholic or Muslim majority of 70% or no religious majority at all. Under such a null hypothesis, a country with a religious Catholic and Muslim population would be just as likely to have a permissive abortion score as a country without any religious majority. With this research design in mind, let us now proceed to examine what the statistical analyses indicate regarding the empirical support for our theory.

RESULTS

Table 2.3 presents models estimated for the different religious denominations (Protestant, Catholic, Muslim, Buddhist and Hindu). Model 1 tests the effects of the range of predictors on our abortion index, $CAI1$. In Model 2, we test the effects on the weighted version of our index, $CAI2$. The dependent variable in Model 3 is the index for women's political rights. Regardless of the dependent variable, the effects of Protestant and Hindu populations are insignificant. The effects of Catholic, Muslim, and Buddhist populations were significant and negative in all models using an abortion-related dependent variable. No religious denominations were significant in the model with the CIRI dependent variable. This suggests support for our first hypothesis. There is a difference between disparate religious denominations insofar as their effects on abortion policy are concerned. In other words, the effects of religion on reproductive health policy are not homogenous. Let us now look at our tests for Hypotheses 2.2–2.6 concerning various religious features.

Models 4–6 in Table 2.4 test the effects of government regulation, government favoritism, religiosity, and religious diversity. Only religiosity is significant in abortion-related models. It is highly significant at a .001 level for both abortion models. In model 6, which specifies CIRI political rights as the dependent variable, government regulation has a negative and significant effect. No other religious variable, including religiosity, is significant in Model 6.

TABLE 2.3 *Religious Denominations as Predictors of Reproductive Policy and Women's Rights*

	Model 1 (CAI₁) (s.e. in parentheses)	Model 2 (CAI2) (s.e. in parentheses)	Model 3 (CIRI) s(s.e. in parentheses)
Catholics in	-4.88^{**}	-5.01^{**}	$-.552$
Population (%)	(1.73)	(1.77)	(1.3)
Protestants in	-3.11	-3.01	3.35
Population (%)	(1.74)	(1.84)	(3.52)
Muslims in	-3.97^{*}	-4.11^{*}	$-.885$
Population (%)	(1.88)	(1.9)	(1.1)
Buddhists in	-3.75^{*}	-3.68^{*}	$-.574$
Population (%)	(1.72)	(1.75)	(1.71)
Hindus in	$-.198$	$-.343$	-2.19
Population (%)	(1.69)	(1.77)	(1.93)
Communist	2.88^{***}	2.89^{***}	$-.602$
Tradition	(.901)	(.898)	(.865)
Female	4.44^{*}	4.18	24.65^{**}
Legislators (% of lower house)	(2.59)	(2.58)	(8.56)
HDI	5.39^{*}	5.45	$-.754$
	(2.56)	(2.65)	(1.87)
Polity	$-.058$	$-.059$	$.077$
	(.058)	(.058)	(.061)
N	71	71	71

$^{*}p<.05\ ^{**}p<.01\ ^{***}p<.001$

In Figure 2.1, levels of religiosity are on the x-axis; CAI_1, representing state abortion policy, is on the y-axis. Countries that have a significant religious majority (70% or more of the population) are denoted respectively by circles (Muslim) and triangles (Catholic). In line with the findings in Models 4 and 5 in Table 2.4, the scatter shows an overall negative relationship between religiosity and permissiveness of abortion policy. Furthermore, in line with the findings in Models 1 and 2 in Table 2.3, countries with Catholic majorities of 70% or more (triangles) are disproportionately found among countries with lower CAI_1 scores. In fact, only one Catholic majority country has a score higher than five (the Philippines, which is the triangle at the top left). Indeed, of the 12 Catholic majority countries denoted as triangles, 7 have a score of four or lower. It is also a Catholic country (Chile) that is the only country in the entire figure to have a score of zero, meaning abortion is not permitted under any circumstances (at the time the data was collected and true until 2017). We delve into the case of abortion policy in Chile in the next chapter.

TABLE 2.4 *Religious Features as Predictors of Reproductive Policy and Women's Rights*

	Model 6 (CIRI) (s.e. in parentheses)	Model 5 (CAI2) (s.e. in parentheses)	Model 4 (CAI1) (s.e. in parentheses)
Government Religious Regulation Index	.160 (.134)	.145 (.134)	−.424* (197)
Government Religious Favoritism Index	−.018 (.121)	−.016 (.123)	.136 (.184)
Religiosity (WVS)	−4.79*** (1.24)	−4.98*** (1.24)	.549 (1.32)
Religious Diversity	−.505 (.882)	−.596 (.882)	.160 (1.34)
Female Legislators (% of lower house)	−.517 (3.55)	−.808 (3.66)	26.2*** (8.64)
HDI	.325 (1.77)	.042 (1.74)	.332 (2.91)
Polity	−.035 (.045)	−.042 (.045)	.053 (.073)
N	71	71	71

Note. $*p<.05$ $**p<.01$ $***p<.001$

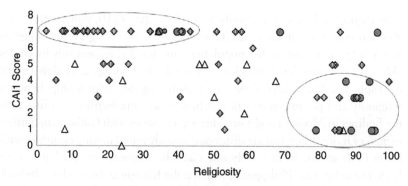

FIGURE 2.1: Effect of Religiosity on Abortion Policy (CAI1)

As for our interaction hypothesis, two main clusters are visible. The first is circled in the oval near the top left corner of the figure between 0% and 40% on the horizontal axis for religiosity. Here, countries exhibit permissive abortion policy. They all have a score of 7, meaning abortion is available on demand. This group is largely dominated by countries with no distinct religious majority (diamonds). Most countries found here are North American, European, and Asian. The Asian countries include post-Soviet states such as Azerbaijan and Kyrgyzstan, but also Eastern and South Eastern Asian states such as China and Singapore. The European countries in this group are also diverse and include Northern, Central, and Eastern European states.

The second cluster is in the oval near the bottom right corner of the figure located between 80% and 100% on the religiosity axis. It is in countries within this cluster, where the degree of religiosity is high, that we also find low levels of protection for reproductive rights. Countries with a Muslim majority (circles) are disproportionally represented in this group, constituting 11 out of 17 of the states within the oval at the bottom right. Of the other six countries, three have a Muslim majority, but do not reach our 70% threshold. These include Nigeria, Lebanon, and Qatar. They are indicated in the figure with blue diamonds. While clearly more restrictive in their abortion policies along the lines of the first hypothesis, Catholic majority countries (triangles) follow no apparent trend as religiosity increases. Muslim countries, on the other hand, do seem to closely follow the predicted trend.

DISCUSSION

There are forces in civil society that can act as strong influencers over state public policy, both in democratic and nondemocratic contexts. Religion can be a significant source of influence within that sphere. Scholarly understandings, public discourse, and feminist discourse often entertain the notion that religion is at odds with women's welfare and gender equality. Religion is often seen as an obstacle in the sense that it decreases the likelihood of permissive reproductive policy. The findings in this chapter, however, shed light on the complexity of this relationship and its underlying mechanisms. Disparate aspects of religion interacted differently with different types of women's welfare policy. Women's political rights on the one hand and abortion rights on the other reacted dissimilarly to various religious factors, which underscores the complexity of women's welfare policy.

Regarding the effects of different religious denominations on reproductive policy, Catholicism, Islam, and Buddhism are denominations that significantly and negatively correlate with abortion policy. Protestantism and Hinduism, which previous studies and theories implied might have an effect, were insignificant. Regarding religious features of the state, only religiosity was significant in abortion models. Likewise, the effect of religiosity is accentuated when the dominant religion is Islam.

Religious denominations

The effects for Catholicism and Islam were negative and significant in all abortion models. Our findings support previous scholarship showing that there is a negative relationship among Catholicism, Islam, and reproductive rights. Protestantism and Hinduism, on the other hand, were insignificant. Catholicism likely has a significant influence because of the Church's clear stance on abortion (Masci, 2016), paired with its highly organized, united, and hierarchal structure, which grants it unique lobbying abilities. In the following chapter, we discuss how the Catholic Church's structure grants it some unique political sway when we delve into the case study of abortion policy in Chile.

Among the different movements in Islam, there is no consensus on when life begins, nor is there a single authority dictating doctrinal inter- pretation. There is a range of views on when and under what circum- stances abortion is morally acceptable. This would imply that Islam should generate insignificant findings. Therefore, without running more tests, we might hypothesize that findings are a result of a correlation between large Muslim populations and traditional cultural norms regard- ing gender roles. While Islamic doctrine itself might not be clear on abortion, perhaps countries with large Muslim populations also tend to have more traditional cultures. If the culture advances traditional gender roles, it would be less likely to accept policy that allows women to separate themselves from their role of mother and caregiver. Indeed, as we show in the following chapter, there are examples of countries where Islam is the dominant religion, such as Bahrain, but reproductive health policy is relatively permissive. We attribute this to the loose institutional framework of Islam, particularly in comparison to Catholicism.

The insignificance of Protestantism makes sense when we look at where various Protestant communities stand on abortion. The Protestant movement is composed of a variety of Churches, which hold a range of opinions on abortion (Jelen, 2014). For example, branches of the Methodist and Lutheran movements oppose abortion with few or no exceptions. In comparison, some branches of the Presbyterian Church support abortion rights with few, or even no limits (Masci, 2016).

The insignificance of Hinduism might be caused by a clash between doctrinal texts and socioeconomic realities. Traditional Hinduism holds an anti-abortion stance (Masci, 2016). The modern realities of Hindu society, though, might balance out the doctrinal mandates. Tolerance for violation of religious doctrine, and cultural emphasis on the importance of male offspring, paired with the economic benefits of sons, might have a neutralizing effect on doctrinal texts.

Contrary to our hypothesis, and despite its unclear position on abortion, Buddhism was significant and negative. On closer inspection, Malaysia, Japan, and Thailand, three countries with significant Buddhist populations, have relatively restrictive abortion policies (*CAI1* scores of 4 or less). Explaining this outcome, given Buddhism's ambivalent stance on abortion would require further investigation. The case studies we focus on in the next chapter help shed light on the effects of Islam and Catholicism. As this book is not intended to be an exhaustive study of the effects of all religious denominations on reproductive health policy, we leave the discussion of Buddhism for future work.

The theoretical and empirical distinctions we drew among different religious denominations yielded interesting results regarding their effects on reproductive policy around the world. The effect of religion is not uniformly constrictive for reproductive rights. This effect is different between reproductive rights and other types of women's rights. In some cases, the effect of religion cannot be explained solely based on the principles of the particular faith.

Religious freedom

The presence or absence of laws regulating religion was insignificant in predicting abortion policy. Contrary to our hypothesis, degree of religious freedom did not correlate with permissive abortion policy. A country with many laws restricting religious freedom was no more or less likely to have lenient abortion access laws. That said, the variable was significant in the *CIRI* model. While religious freedom does not correlate with permissive abortion rights, it does correlate with women's political rights. This might just show that a country that restricts religious freedom is also likely to restrict other civil freedoms, such as political freedoms. In that case, our findings would represent a blanket limitation on civil rights and liberties, unrelated specifically to reproductive rights.

Separation of Religion and State

In all models – regardless of the dependent variable – separation between state and religion was insignificant. Contrary to our expectations, stronger boundaries between religion and state did not correlate with permissive abortion policy. The insignificance of both the religious-freedom variable and the

separation variable support Minkenberg's (2002) findings that institutionalization of religion and state attitude toward religion in general have little to do
with determining reproductive policy. Minkenberg found that formal institutional arrangements, whether separating or allowing Church-State interaction, were of little consequence in this context. Our findings show that neither
regulation nor aid toward religion correlate with how a country legislates
reproductive rights.

Religiosity

Religiosity is consistently significant and negative when specified in the *CAI*1
and *CAI*2 models. This effect is unique to abortion rights, as religiosity is
insignificant as a predictor in the model for the *CIRI*. Accordingly, we conclude that religiosity correlates with restrictive reproductive rights. A more
religious population will likely correlate with prohibitive reproductive policy.
Notably, this effect is unique to reproductive rights as opposed to other
women's rights such as political freedoms. Religiosity may affect policy related
to traditional gender roles, but does not affect a variable unrelated to women's
roles as mothers and caregivers.

We can think of several reasons why this connection exists. First, the more
religious a person, the more likely that person is to base decisions on religious
doctrine rather than competing secular doctrines or beliefs. Therefore,
a devout population would be more likely to turn to religious texts for
guidance than to ideologies of gender equality not generally based in religious
texts. As discussed earlier, the more religious a population, the more likely it is
to conform to traditional gender roles. Accordingly, women's identities are
more closely associated with their roles as mothers and nurturers. Abortion can
be interpreted as a rejection of this role, and thus as a violation of women's
natural calling and responsibility. Finally, religious populations might have an
overall less liberal approach to gender equality and women's rights. This
would mean that there is a lesser sense of urgency in advancing policy that
recognizes women's physical and political autonomy.

Interaction between religious denomination and religiosity

Figure 2.1 examined our theoretical contention concerning an interaction
between religiosity and certain specific religious denominations that negatively influence reproductive policy. We focus on Catholicism and Islam. The
scatter implies that the degree of religiosity in Muslim countries meaningfully
affects abortion policy. Muslim countries with a low level of religiosity are

consistently found to have permissive abortion scores. In fact, all Muslim countries with religiosity levels below 70% have a *CAI1* score of 7. Beyond this threshold, however, Muslim countries are disproportionately represented in the cluster of low-scoring countries on the scale of permissive abortion policy (11 out of 17 countries in this cluster are Muslim). Religious Muslim countries are more likely to have restrictive policies than non-religious Muslim countries.[7]

Catholic countries seem to follow no distinct pattern, with non-religious countries no more likely to have permissive policy than religious countries. While in a Muslim state the degree of religiosity will be significant, this relationship does not seem to hold true for Catholic countries. This throws into question any assertions regarding the interaction between Catholicism and religiosity (Minkenberg, 2002), which we suspect might be true for a limited number of observations but which loses significance once tested on a larger sample that goes beyond Europe and accordingly is more geographically diverse.

To account for this finding, we would look to the extremely structured and hierarchal nature of the Catholic Church on the one hand and the non-hierarchal structure of Islam on the other. The Church has a clear top-down structure of authority (Gill, 1998). Rome is not only the spiritual center of the Church, but also its political and bureaucratic core (Vallier, 1971). This means that even if national or local Churches exercise some degree of autonomy, Rome has ultimate control of political leverage, message, and stance on a range of policy issues (Hanson, 1987). By operating as a unified and cohesive organization, the Catholic Church can achieve results even in the absence of a thoroughly religious population. First, the message delivered throughout Churches worldwide is the same. If the Church holds a position banning abortion, it is unlikely that a local Church or individual leader will stray from the message. Second, the Church has power as a lobbying body (Warner, 2000). In particular, if there is a large Catholic population the Church can exercise more influence. Politicians would be influenced by the positions of the Church on certain issues given the Church's united front and its mobilization potential.

The same cannot be said for Islam. Islam does not have a centralized ultimate authority, such as the Pope. According to Richard W. Bulliet, Islam is a "faith without denominations, hierarchies and centralized institutions" (2002, p. 11). Bulliet stresses that while this has allowed Islam to adapt readily to

---

[7]   A scatter was also made at the 50% and 60% majority threshold. The results were substantively indistinguishable and thus reinforced what we found in Figure 2.1.

local contexts, and thus spread, it also represents a weakness that makes it hard for Muslims to present a united front on any given issue. Unlike the homogenous organization of Catholic communities, as dictated by Rome, Muslim communities can be organized based on sectarian, regional, or tribal divides (Abbas & Weir, 2005).

Based on the different types of communities, religious leaders may be more or less obliged to follow the religious teachings and doctrinal decisions of any higher authority. Failure of traditional leadership structures and the emergence of new types of religious and political leadership further fragments Muslim public opinion and interpretation of doctrine (Bulliet, 2002). In comparison to the Catholic Church, Islam as a religion would need a population whose religiosity pushes for the adoption of doctrine in public policy. If the population itself isn't particularly religious or dogmatic, it, unlike the Catholic Church, will not have the grounds, platforms, and organization on which to lobby for any given policy.

Additionally, it might even be misleading to think of Islam as a single religious denomination. Of the approximately 1.6 billion Muslims in the world, 85%–90% are estimated to be Sunnis; 10%–15% are Shia (Pew Research Center, 2009). Within these two groups can be found further sub-denominations. To consider Sunni and Shia Muslims as a single group, influenced by the same things, would be misguided. Not only are they two separate entities with distinct geographical distributions, cultures, religious practices, and so forth, but they are often engaged in violent clashes with one another over political power and doctrinal interpretations (Gonzalez, 2009; Mallat, 1988; Behuria, 2004).

Given that Islam does not inherently include the hierarchal structure and the lobbying machine that comes with faith civil society, as in the case of the Catholic Church, it is not surprising that in countries with less religious populations, it would have less sway over public opinion. A less-religious population would mean that politicians are also less inclined to deem Muslim doctrinal positions as important when considering public opinion, as the population itself is less dedicated to doctrinal rulings. Different religious leaders might also give different interpretations and rulings, splitting public opinion. This phenomenon is less likely in the Catholic Church, where doctrinal decisions are generated at the level of the Vatican. In cases where the Muslim population is strongly devout, this might imply a stronger religious influence or public opinion and potentially more uniform weight for religious doctrine.

Religious Diversity

Contrary to our hypothesis, religious diversity had no significant interaction with state abortion policy. While we cite a few mechanisms through which religious diversity might have an influence, in practice none of these seems to be relevant to policymaking in the realm of reproductive rights.

Doctrinal vs. Non-Doctrinal Policies

All in all, the connection between faith civil society and abortion policy is considerably more nuanced than scholarly literature as well as public and political discourse would have it. The only denominations that consistently and significantly correlate with abortion policy are Catholicism, Islam, and Buddhism, and even those do so to different degrees and under divergent circumstances. Of the denominations tested, only with Islam do we find an interaction between religiosity and religious denomination. Other features of religion, including degree of freedom of religion, separation of religion and state, and religious diversity, show no influence.

Whereas abortion policy was influenced by a number of religious factors, the political rights index was influenced by only one such factor: the government regulation index. Without looking into this further, we might hypothesize that a government that is very restrictive of religion would also have a tendency to restrict political rights. While we only measured women's political rights, perhaps a measure of general political rights of both men and women could shed new light on this question.

Our findings support Htun and Weldon's (2010) doctrinal model. In both the religious denomination models (Table 2.3) and the religious features models (Table 2.4), variables that had a significant effect on the abortion-dependent variables were insignificant in models estimating the effects on women's political rights. These findings support the idea that religion correlates with policymaking that pertains to areas that are at the core of the denominational doctrinal teachings. However, such impact may be considerably attenuated for nondoctrinal issues. The null findings in the CIRI models (models 3 and 6) demonstrate that the influences certain faith civil society variables may wield over abortion policy do not necessarily carry over to other aspects of gender discrimination.

The dissimilar findings for the abortion policy indexes and the political rights indexes bring us back to the discussion of whether or not women's welfare policy constitutes a single type of policy in its relationship with civil society generally and religion in particular. This would directly affect how we study and understand reproductive rights policy. There are those who claim that women's rights issues do not constitute a single category of policy (Htun & Weldon, 2010) while others tend to group all women's issues together.

Our findings support the former approach. Rather than a homogenous group of issues, women's welfare and gender equality policy constitute a collection of policies that are dissimilarly influenced by disparate variables. The key seems to be doctrinal vs. nondoctrinal policies. It is in the former category, within which reproductive policy falls, where we find a significant connection with the religious elements in civil society. This effect for faith civil society disappears when we examine the case of nondoctrinal policies, such as political rights for women.

CONCLUSIONS

This chapter aimed to illustrate how a key aspect of civil society could influence state abortion policy. Civil society is the sphere between the state apparatus and the family unit, in which large portions of the population's political activity occur. It is, therefore, critical to observe how players within this sphere ultimately affect state-level decisions. Civil society has the ability to be influential in both democracies and nondemocracies. We aimed to choose a civil society player that is ubiquitous in order to see how civil society interacts with the state apparatus around the world. For several reasons we elaborate on above, religion was ideal for this analysis.

Until now, research on religion and reproductive policy has largely been limited to Western Christian democracies and to a couple of denominations, neglecting the potential effects (or lack thereof) of a broad range of world religions practiced by substantial sections of humanity. Furthermore, we knew little about the effects of religion in a comparative perspective, despite the fact that it seems to have an effect when examined in the case of Western Christian countries. Additionally, simplified conceptions of religion in existing studies left some more gaps in our knowledge.

This chapter advanced our understanding of the religion-abortion link in several meaningful ways. We challenge previously held notions regarding the effects of religious variables on women's rights and gender issues. Regarding different religious denominations, while Catholicism and Islam behaved as expected, other religions surprised. Mostly overlooked in the reproductive policy literature, Buddhism consistently had a significant negative correlation with progressive abortion policy. Protestantism and Hinduism had no significant relationship. Accordingly, in the context of those religions it would be inaccurate to assume a religion-abortion link. Degree of religiosity, though significant, might be interaction dependent, specifically in interaction with certain religious denominations. This further challenges previous conceptions. Other religious variables such as religious freedom, separation of religion and state, and religious diversity proved to be consistently insignificant.

Juxtaposition of abortion rights with women's political rights clarified to what extent abortion as a variable represents women's rights and to what extent it should be treated as an issue unto itself. In our models, variables with a significant effect on abortion policy lost their significance when estimated in a model with the women's political rights index as the outcome variable. Faith civil society does not influence all types of women's rights policies to the same degree or in the same way, with policies that are at the heart of religious doctrine more heavily affected.

This distinction bears interest for scholars, policymakers, and international and grassroots NGOs committed to the promotion of women's rights. Such rights are a bundle of different fields, of which not all are affected and influenced similarly. Glossing over such disparities may blind the policymaker, activist, lobbyist, or researcher to critical distinctions, necessary in some cases to achieve a real understanding of this area and to make real progress. Additionally, those who address religion as an obstacle to women's advancement might consider re-evaluating such contentions. As our investigation of faith civil society suggests, the link between religion and abortion is missing in some cases and in others may be qualified and contingent on a set of political circumstances and institutions.

3

The Politics of Religion and Reproductive Health:
The Cases of Chile and Bahrain

Players from the sphere of civil society, even outside of democracies, are significant in shaping state public policy. Religious institutions are a classic example of players within this sphere, but religion's relationship with the state and the people is multidimensional. It cannot be analyzed without taking into account the numerous ways in which religion may influence the state. Earlier in the book, we isolated a few aspects of the state-religion relationship. In Chapter 2 we were interested in the relationship between women's rights and faith civil society in order to see how to characterize their interactions. The quantitative analyses based on data for most of the countries in the world suggest that when it came to state abortion policy, Muslim, Catholic, and Buddhist population size, as well as religiosity, negatively correlated with permissiveness of abortion policy. Other variables related to religion that we might otherwise expect to have an influence in this context proved to be insignificant. Additionally, in terms of divergent validity, abortion policy did not behave like other types of women's welfare policy (in particular, women's political rights). The production of reproductive rights was unique in how it interacted with religion.

The aim of the case studies in this chapter is manifold. First, by their nature, case studies allow us to examine more closely the causal pathways and mechanisms that underlie the effects of civil society, and particularly faith civil society, on public policy in the area of reproductive health. Second, the case studies bring the quantitative findings to life. They demonstrate how the numbers and regression results look in the day-to-day lives of real people. Last, such close inspection of particular cases provides insight into additional variables by providing a more complex picture of abortion policy. Quantitative methods such as the regression models estimated in Chapter 2 can overlook finer details of a story that we are better able to pinpoint using case study methodology. This adds to our appreciation of the complexity of the whole picture and allows for a more in-depth understanding of the political processes and institutional influences involved. We will analyze the Republic of Chile and the Kingdom of Bahrain as two countries that demonstrate the different ways in which the multiple dimensions of the state-religion relationship can correlate with state abortion policy.

This is not, nor does it intend to be, a book about either Chile or Bahrain. We limit ourselves to aspects of the case studies that shed new light on our specific discussion. By the nature of things, we omit certain aspects, some of which may be deemed important by other students of abortion policy in general and in those countries in particular. That said, even the partial detail offered within the scope of this project reveals interesting and surprising findings for anyone studying reproductive rights.

Chile is a South American country of approximately 17.5 million people (National Statistics Institute, 2018) and an area of 756,096 kilometers^2 (Instituto Nacional de Estadistica, 2006). Until 2017, Chile was one of the few countries in the world with a complete ban on abortion. As of the summer of 2017, state abortion policy is still extremely restrictive. Yet, it allows abortion in cases of threat to the mother's life, rape, or fetal impairment. On the books, state and church are legally separate in Chile. Freedom of religion is constituted in the state's legal code. In reality, however, the Catholic Church has been involved in politics throughout the state's history. How has the Catholic presence in civil society, despite having no official state protection, allowed this religious sect to be so influential in state politics? And what were the consequences for the production of reproductive rights?

In a different corner of the globe, Bahrain is an island kingdom in the Arabian Gulf. Considerably smaller than Chile, the country covers only 765.3 kilometers^2 (U.N. Department of Economic and Social Affairs, 2012) and has an estimated population of approximately 1.425 million people, including a very large number of non-nationals (Ministry of Information Affairs, Kingdom of Bahrain, 2014). Abortion is available on request. Women only have to pass a simple medical board in order to get approval from a licensed physician. This policy has been on the books since 1976.

State and religion are not separated. Islam is the official religion of the state and Islamic Sharia Law is enshrined in the Constitution as the primary source of state law. Furthermore, the majority of the population is Muslim. How is it that despite the large Muslim population and Sharia being constitutionally enshrined as a source of law, Bahrain still has one of the most progressive abortion laws in its region?

These two countries, Chile and Bahrain, demonstrate what prima facie would seem to be a surprising relationship between faith civil society and women's rights. A state with an official religion – and specifically one like Islam, some of whose teachings authoritatively ban abortion – does not have a restrictive abortion policy. With feeble religious institutions and a population that is not uniformly devoutly religious, the Bahraini case suggests it is possible to pass permissive abortion policy, even when Islam is enshrined as an official state religion. On the other hand, a country that technically separates state and religion and whose Catholic population is not religious is still being influenced by the powerful lobby of the Catholic Church. Those two case studies also demonstrate the disparities between different types of women's rights policy. The records of Chile and Bahrain on women's suffrage and political rights are almost as different as their records on abortion rights.

To introduce the two case studies and the background on each, we first provide an overview of recent political history, the status of women, religious characteristics, and record of abortion policy. This is followed by a discussion that ties in the empirical realities of each case with some of the findings in the quantitative models in Chapter 2, where we also examine the relationship between faith civil society on the one hand and abortion policy on the other. The case study methodology allows us to delve deeper into causal mechanisms and illustrate findings from the quantitative models. It significantly adds to the matrix of independent variables that define the influence civil society has on the production of reproductive rights.

THE REPUBLIC OF CHILE – STATE, THE CATHOLIC CHURCH, AND A PROHIBITION ON ABORTION

The Regime

Throughout much of the twentieth century, Chile enjoyed relative political stability. In 1973, however, a military coup, led by General Augusto Pinochet Ugarte, ousted President Salvador Allende (Dominguez, 1994). This marked the end of Chile's civilian rule and the beginning of close to two decades of dictatorship (U. S. Department of State, Office of the Historian, 2018; Valdivia Ortiz De Zárate, 2003). The first years of Pinochet's rule were marked by political disappearances, deaths, and systematic torture. It is estimated that at least 3,000 people were killed by the Pinochet regime and as many as 29,000 were imprisoned and tortured. Exact figures for some of these crimes are particularly hard to come by or even estimate, as during this time there were over 2,000 cases of political disappearances at the hands of the government (Warwick, 2014).

In 1980, Chile put a new constitution in place. This was followed by the election of Pinochet as president by referendum for an eight-year term. In 1988, Pinochet ran for re-election but was rejected by 54.5% of the vote, which marked the end of his rule and the beginning of a period of democratic transition. Presidential elections were held and in 1990 a democratically elected president, Patricio Aylwim, assumed office (Edwards, 2013; BBC Country Profiles, 2012; Barton & Murray, 2002). Since 1990 – when the new president was sworn in – Chile has experienced regular elections and a system of government categorized as democratic by independent agencies such as Freedom House and Polity.

As part of the transition to democracy – when President Aylwin was sworn in – the National Commission for Truth and Reconciliation was established ("the Rettig Commission" [Edwards, 2013]). The Rettig Commission investigated human rights violations under Pinochet. The conclusions of the Commission were documented in a report released in 1991, known as the Rettig Report. The report catalogued the killings, imprisonments, tortures, disappearances, and kidnappings of the previous 17 years (National Commission for Truth and Reconciliation, 1990).

The Status of Women in Chile

Article 19.2 of the Chilean Constitution (1980) states that "Men and women are equal before the law. Neither the law nor any authority can establish arbitrary differences." Nonetheless, the realities of Chilean society reflect a history of patriarchal culture that was gradually addressed only as the process of democratization continued (Power, 2004).

According to the World Economic Forum's 2017 Global Gender Gap Report, Chile is 63rd of the 144 countries ranked. Labor force participation for women is 57.9%, compared with 80% for men. The country has a gender wage gap of 21.1% (OECD, 2018a), ranking Chile 127 of the 144 in wage equality for similar work. There are no non-discrimination legal clauses in Chile for hiring, nor is there legislation mandating equal pay.

Chile's modern history of family law reflects certain patriarchal cultural tendencies as well as the influence of the Catholic Church. Within the Chilean civil code, in a married couple, parental authority rests with the father. This legal reality constitutes a gender-based discrimination of women's parental rights and privileges. In practice, such a provision means that the father's permission or presence is required for a range of legal procedures affecting a child. Indeed, the advantageous legal status for men goes beyond parental issues. For instance, the Civil Code provision that establishes the man as the head of a family household also means that husbands become the administrators of property inherited by their wives in the absence of a prenuptial property agreement (OECD, 2018b).

Divorce was only legally established in 2004, making Chile one of the last countries in the world to institute such a right (Rohter, 2005). A married couple has to prove that they have been living separately for over a year in order to be granted a divorce. During this year, the father maintains parental authority (OECD, 2018a). During the time that the divorce bill was making its way through the halls of the legislature, the Catholic Church protested and lobbied against the proposed law. The Church claimed it was a threat to the stability of the family and the institution of marriage. Despite the fact that the majority of Chileans are Catholic, the law had overwhelming public support (BBC News, 2004). The case of the divorce law already hints at some of the critical disparities in Chilean faith civil society. In particular, we focus on gaps between the public and the Catholic Church. Such cleavages between the Church and the people, especially as they become more substantial, are consequential for the type of political sway the Church can claim.

Some recent changes in the political sphere in Chile are notable and pertinent to our discussion. In 2015, Chile implemented a mandatory electoral gender quota. Before this, some parties had voluntary quotas. Yet, overall, Chile had never had more than 15.8% women in the lower house of its bicameral legislature. The 2015 quota determined that all party lists must have at least 40% representation of each gender. The expectation was that this new legislation would lead to increased political participation by women. As Schwindt-Bayer (2015) put it, "after a quarter century of relatively minimal progress moving women into the legislative arena in Chile, proponents of the new gender quota law hope that the quota will finally achieve what more traditional efforts to increase women's representation have failed to do" (p. 4). The election cycle of 2017 was the first one during which quotas were in place. Chile achieved an unprecedented share of 22.6% of women in parliament (Inter-Parliamentary Union, 2018; U.N. Women, 2018).

Religion and Society in Chile

In a 2017 survey, 59% of the population in Chile self-identified as Catholic. This is a marked decline from the beginning of the twenty-first century when the country was overwhelmingly Catholic and religious. Additionally, this was a drop of over 10% in only a decade; as recently as 2006, 70% of the population reported being Catholic (Encuesta Nacional Bicentenario, 2017). As of 2017, Protestants make up the second largest religious group, with 17% of the population. The remaining 19% of Chileans report as unaffiliated, Jehovah's Witnesses, Mormons, Jews, Orthodox Christians, Muslims, Baha'is, Buddhists, and members of the Unification Church (U.S. Department of State, 2008; Encuesta Nacional Bicentenario, 2017).

Apart from rates of religious self-identification, religiosity itself has also been in decline in recent years. As the results in Chapter 2 suggest, this variable is consequential for the production of reproductive rights. According to the Pew survey on religion, in 2007 46% of the population said that religion was very important to them. Only 10% said that religion was not at all important. Less than a decade later, in 2015, 27% said that religion was very important. The rate of those that said that religion was not important at all doubled, and was now one in every five Chileans surveyed (Pew Research Center, 2015).

Despite the fact that most of the population associates with the Catholic Church, for many Chileans professing belief in God is not synonymous with following Church dictates on social issues. For example, as mentioned earlier, despite the forceful objection voiced by the Church, there was overwhelming public support for the 2004 divorce legislation (BBC News, 2004).

Some of the reproductive statistics in Chile are surprising, particularly given the religious history of this country and the dominance of the Catholic Church. There is a high rate of clandestine abortions performed in Chile (Blofield, 2006). Some estimates also suggest that two out of every three Chilean children are born out of wedlock (OECD, 2016). This is largely the result of the choice of many Chilean parents not to marry (Power, 2004).

Public opinion does not rely on a dogmatic acceptance of religion. In the 2006 Chilean Encuesta Nacional Bicentenario survey, 75.3% of respondents felt that it was possible to carry out a morally good life without believing in God. Some 80.7% of participants in the survey said that they would prefer that their "children decide for themselves what their religious beliefs are and not try to influence them too much in this respect" (Celis Brunet, Castro, & Scroggie, 2009; Encuesta Nacional Bicentenario, 2017). Chileans are also less likely than other South American Catholics to attend religious ceremonies and festivals, marry in Church, or have their children baptized (Fleet and Smith, 1997).

The Church and the State

Chile has no official state religion. Its two recent Constitutions (in 1925 and 1980) guarantee religious freedoms. Article 19 of the 1980 Constitution states

The freedom of conscience, the manifestation of all creeds and the free exercise of all cults which are not opposed to morals, to good customs or to the public order.

The religious confessions may erect and maintain churches and their dependencies under the conditions of security and hygiene established by the laws and ordinances.

Concerning assets, the churches and religious confessions and institutions of any cult have the rights granted and recognized by the laws currently in force. Churches and their dependencies intended exclusively for the service of a cult will be exempt from any type of tax (. . .)

Freedom of religion is constitutionally enshrined for all citizens. All religions are equally entitled to tax exemptions. While freedom of religion is guaranteed by constitutional fiat, it would be inaccurate to say that there is a complete separation of Church and state in Chile. Chile recognizes religious Christian Catholic holidays and maintains certain religious traditions as national holidays (Celis Brunet, Castro, & Scroggie, 2009). Religious parties are allowed in the Chilean legislature and can be found on both the conservative and liberal wings of the political spectrum (Luna, 2013; Blofield, 2006).

In Chile, the Church has historically acted as a strong lobbying force and has actively tried to advance Catholic interests through political lobbying efforts (Gill, 1998). In Chile and around the world, the Church goes to great lengths to secure Catholic input in society. It does so through the establishment of schools, universities, newspapers, radio stations, and political parties and lobbies (Ryall, 2001; Warhurst, 2008). It acts as an interest group, aligning with political parties and lobbying parties and government to promote its positions (Warner, 2000). Since the transition to democracy, Chilean Church leaders have been particularly active in lobbying on issues such as divorce and reproductive right – much more so than other issues (Meacham, 1994). The Church has also fostered conservative interest groups, which have taken an active role in lobbying on divorce and abortion (Blofield, 2001).

Granted, no denomination is constitutionally defined as the state religion. Yet, the role of the Catholic Church in Chilean politics and society has been remarkable. The Church's political sway runs the gamut from helping broker international agreements to influencing regime transitions. For example, the Vatican helped broker a peace agreement between Chile and Argentina in the Beagle Channel Dispute. In 1984, the two countries signed the Treaty of Peace and Friendship at Vatican City, thus ending the conflict (Mirow, 2004; Lindsley, 1987; Alger, 2002).

As for the sphere of domestic politics, the Catholic Church in Chile was instrumental in making the transition to democracy after Pinochet. It played a crucial role in consolidating democratic rule and in protecting human rights (Hanson, 1987). One standout example would be the Vicariate of Solidarity, a human rights organization founded by Cardinal Silva of Santiago in 1976. The organization provided social services and legal aid for victims of the rampant regime violence. It also disseminated information internationally and, with the backing of the Vatican, publicly criticized and lobbied the Pinochet regime on issues of human rights violations.

The Church's involvement in regime transition can be seen in the close relationship between the Independent Democratic Union (UDI) and the Catholic Opus Dei movements. Throughout the transition, the Episcopal Conference put together informal meetings between the government and the opposition in order to form a dialogue. Bishops such as Juan Francisco Fresno and the Church as a whole were key in mediating between the dictatorship and the parties of the Democratic Alliance, eventually leading to the transition to democracy. The Church also played a crucial role in the acceptance of the Constitution and the neoliberal economic model.

The visit of Pope John Paul II in 1987 stands out as a significant moment in the country's transition. During his visit, the Pope stated that Chile needed "peace and national reconciliation." In response to violent anti-regime protests, the Pope said that "Chile's calling is of understanding and not of confrontation" (Strassner, 2018).

Participation in regime transition gave the Church meaningful political capital, which it used to influence policy. Once a democratic system of government was instituted, there were several cases where the Church partnered with the political right to lobby for certain policies and reforms. For example, the Church had an active role in lobbying on legislation related to divorce, sex education in schools, the morning-after pill, abortions, and the decriminalization of homosexuality (Pollack, 1999).

Indeed, the period of dictatorship revitalized the Catholic Church, not least because it established itself as a provider of social and psychological care services for those victimized by violence. The social activism of the Church helped recapture the affection of many Chilean Catholics (Fleet and Smith, 1997). Its history of supporting regime transitions and human rights also established the Church's image in the public eye as a progressive and liberating force, making it more difficult for left-wing or feminist groups to push back against Church policy as conservative or illiberal (Htun, 2003).

In recent years, however, the affinity between the Church and the public has plummeted to unprecedented levels. When Pope Francis visited Chile in

January 2018, public confidence in the Church had dropped to a two-decades low and ranked among the lowest in Latin America. Only one week before the pope's visit, vandals set fire to two churches and bombed another (PRI, 2018). Only 36% of the Chilean public showed confidence in the Catholic Church, according to Latinobarómetro[1], compared to Paraguay at 77% and even Argentina, where the popularity of the institution had never been high, at 55%.

Abortion and Reproductive Rights in Chile

In 1931, abortion was legalized in Chile when the life or physical health of the mother was at risk. Women needed the consent of two doctors in order to undergo the procedure. In 1989, Pinochet's regime outlawed abortion under any and all conditions. The Chilean Health Code was updated to say that "No action may be executed that has as its goal the inducement of abortion" (Law No. 18,826). With this Amendment, it became impossible to obtain a legal abortion, even in cases where the mother's life was at risk. One argument advanced by those drafting this legislation was that given recent advances in modern medicine, an abortion was no longer needed to save the life of a pregnant woman (U.N. Economic and Social Affairs, 2002). This was one of Pinochet's last actions in office (Reuters, 2017).

Since then, hundreds of women have been found guilty of having abortions, hundreds of thousands have had clandestine abortions, and many have been forced to carry on unwanted and at times dangerous pregnancies. Anyone who performed an abortion could be sentenced to a prison sentence of three to five years. A woman who performed her own abortion or consented to an abortion would receive the maximum-length prison sentence (U.N. Economic and Social Affairs, 2002).

The clandestine nature of abortion in Chile makes it hard to research. Yet, a national study from the 1990s estimated that approximately 160,000 abortions were performed annually. This is a rate of 45 abortions per 1,000 women aged 15–49. This statistic is considerably higher than the global average. The world average for developing regions is 36 per 1,000 and in developed regions only 27 abortions are performed for every 1,000 women. As we further develop in Chapter 8, these statistics for Chile are in line with World Health Organization (WHO) figures. WHO data indicates that rather than reducing the number of women seeking abortion, outlawing abortion leads to more clandestine and unsafe procedures.

[1] Based in Providencia, Chile, this nonprofit organization conducts an annual public opinion survey in 18 Latin American countries.

In the 1960s, Chile had a rate of 294 maternal deaths per 100,000 live births. As much as a third of these deaths were attributed to unsafe abortions. Today, there are less abortion-related deaths, mainly thanks to improvements in Chile's public health care institutions and the increased use of safer abortion methods. With that said, women from socioeconomically disadvantaged backgrounds are more likely to experience negative side effects of abortion and to seek post-abortion treatment in public health facilities (Prada, 2016; Casas & Vivaldi, 2014).

For many women, the risk of getting caught breaking the law is not an option. Rape victims as young as 11 years old have been forced to carry and deliver accidental pregnancies. In such cases, families often have no choice but to raise their teenage daughters alongside their infant grandchildren. The entire family unit – not just the pregnant girl or woman – is deeply affected by this legal state of affairs. In a rare interview, one mother told a Chilean magazine of the experience of raising her teenage daughter and infant grandson after her daughter was forced to carry a pregnancy as a result of rape:

> My daughter was in psychiatric therapy for seven years," she told The Clinic. "Whenever she came to my room after a nightmare, I let her sleep next to me in my bed. We all slept in one bed- my daughter, my grandson, and myself. We had lived like that for years.
>
> (Oyarce, 2015)

On August 21, 2017, President Michelle Bachelet, the first woman to occupy the position of President of Chile, passed a historic law allowing abortions in three cases: when the pregnancy is life-threatening for the woman, when the pregnancy is the result of rape, and when the fetus is unviable (BBC News, 2017). Six of the ten judges reviewing the constitutionality of the new provision upheld the new law as constitutional (Vivanco & Undurraga, 2017). The policy was widely supported by left and centrist parties as well as women's groups and human rights organizations (BBC News, 2017).

Opponents of the bill included the Catholic Church as well as other religious groups. Cristián Contreras, vice-president of the Episcopal Conference of Bishops, said the ruling was "a terrible decision, influenced by an ideology of death" (Kozak, 2017). In September 2017, in response to the new abortion law, Cardinal Ricardo Ezzati, the leader of the Catholic Church in Chile, said that "the value of human life is an inalienable right, and a woman's right to her body is not more important than the innocent child's right to live." He added that "it is now time for the church to double the efforts to accompany women who decide to continue their pregnancies. The church extends its arms to service all the people who need peace, support and comfort" (T13 Radio, September 18, 2017). Opposition has also been registered by some of Chile's conservative elite, as well as certain politicians. In 2018, the newly appointed Minister for Women and Gender Equality, Isabel Plá, and the incoming Health Minister, Emilio Santelices, were both vocal opponents of the landmark court ruling (Kozak, 2018).

The historic policy change in the summer and fall of 2017 represented a change in state reproductive rights, as Chile became one of the last countries to do away with a total ban on abortion. It came at a time of dwindling adherence to Catholic teaching and identification with the religion and the Church. As the abovementioned events leading up to the Pope's visit in January 2018 might suggest, the Catholic Church's sway over state politics is slipping as fewer and fewer Chileans identify as Catholic. With dwindling social support, the Catholic Church's power as a lobby declines further and further.

On October 5, 2017, an ambulance entered the gates of Hospital San José in Santiago de Chile. Inside was a 12-year-old girl clutching a teddy bear and her mother. The girl was a rape victim, arriving at the hospital to terminate her pregnancy. This would be the first case of legal abortion in Chile in the twenty-first century (El Desconcierto, 2018).

THE KINGDOM OF BAHRAIN - SUPPORTING ABORTION IN A MUSLIM STATE

The Regime

The Kingdom of Bahrain is a constitutional monarchy and has been ruled by the Al Khalifa dynasty since 1783 (Louër, 2013). Though the Al Khalifa family is Sunni, the majority of Bahrainis are Shia (Al-Rasheed, 2011; Yom & Gause III, 2012). Seven of every ten people in Bahrain are Muslim. Christians make up the second largest religious group, with Hindus and Buddhists following (Pew Research Center, 2010).

Throughout the nineteenth and twentieth centuries, Bahrain was subject to various degrees of British, Omani, and Persian rule. The country declared independence in 1971. Since that time, Bahrain has had a few attempted coups and popular uprisings, none of which resulted in a dramatic regime change (Bahry, 1997). Following a popular uprising in 1994, Hamad bin Isa Al Khalifa became the Emir. In a marked departure from past practice, the new Emir instituted elections for parliament, gave women the right to vote, and released political prisoners (Peterson, 2009).

Such reforms notwithstanding, Bahrain has been considered under authoritarian rule since its independence. Since 1971, it has achieved an average polity score of -9, on a scale of -10 to 10, with -10 being the most restrictive, least democratic form of government. Executive power is concentrated within the monarchy, which appoints the prime minister, commands the army, and chairs the Higher Judicial Council (Yom & Gause III, 2012). The king both appoints the higher house of parliament and has the power to dissolve the lower house (Karolak, 2010). Shaikh Khalifa bin Salman Al Khalifa, the uncle of the current king, has served as prime minister since 1971. Indeed, members of the royal family hold most of the key positions in government (Peterson, 2009).

While the king makes all appointments to the upper house of the bicameral legislature, the lower house is elected by popular vote once every four years. The upper house, however, has de facto veto power over the lower house (Louër, 2013; Peterson, 2009).

Bahrain has also been known for gross violations of civil and human rights. Though reforms were under way in the late 1990s and early 2000s, the regime once again began using methods of torture and suspending civil liberties leading up to and during the Arab Spring (Al-Rasheed, 2011). Systematic torture has been reportedly used against political protesters and more broadly against members of the Bahraini Shia population (Bahry, 1997; Yom & Gause III, 2012).

Technically, political parties are banned in Bahrain (Peterson, 2009). Rather than call themselves parties, political organizations term themselves "societies" and have used this status as an organizational platform for political activity and recruitment. These societies are often formed on the basis of religious association (Wright, 2010). Thus, de facto, political parties function within the Bahraini Parliament (Karolak, 2010). These societies are recognized under the 2005 Political Society law, which "Gives all citizens, both men and women, the right to form and join political societies in accordance with the provisions in the law (Art. 1). It sets out the conditions to be fulfilled in order to form or continue a political society."

The Status of Women in Bahrain

The status of gender equality in the Bahraini Constitution is somewhat vague. In the 2002 Constitution, Chapter 1, Article 1 states:

> Citizens, both men and women, are entitled to participate in public affairs and may enjoy political rights, including the right to vote and to stand for elections, in accordance with this Constitution and the conditions and

principles laid down by law. No citizen can be deprived of the right to vote or to nominate oneself for elections except by law.

Since 2002, women have had the right to vote and to run for office. One the other hand, Chapter 2, Article 5 states, "The State guarantees reconciling the duties of women towards the family with their work in society and their equality with men in political, social, cultural, and economic spheres without breaching the provisions of Islamic canon law (Shari'a)." This clause guarantees gender equality in a number of spheres. Yet, it allows interpretation of women's rights and gender equality to be based on, or be secondary to, Islamic religious law.

According to the World Economic Forum's 2017 Global Gender Gap Report, Bahrain ranks 126th in gender equality out of the 144 countries in the report. A total of 40.5% of women participate in the labor force, compared to 86.8% of men, although the pay gap for similar work is small. There are no non-discrimination laws for hiring, nor are there laws mandating equal pay. There are laws against sexual harassment in the workplace, although the rate of reporting is low, often because women fear tarnishing their reputation and that of their clan. There is also no job protection for women in the case of marriage, pregnancy, or birth (Al Gharaibeh, 2011). Certain labor laws, meant to protect women, essentially limit the type of work they can do and their overall employability (Kelly, 2009).

While women have a lower literacy rate than men by approximately 5%, they constitute the majority of those enrolled in secondary and tertiary education. Bahraini women are also served well by the Bahraini health care system. Women can receive free services in family planning and reproductive health, maternity services, and primary health care. These are freely available in government hospitals and health centers (Al Gharaibeh, 2011; World Economic Forum, 2017).

Women, however, are discriminated against in certain aspects of Bahraini law, reflecting certain religious and patriarchal cultural influences on national policy. Only since 2004 have women been able to transfer citizenship to non-Bahraini spouses. Women are not allowed to accumulate their own wealth. Rather, the male head of the family must hold their wealth. This creates significant complications, both legal and financial, for older unmarried women.

Domestic abuse and gender-based violence are frequent in Bahraini society and in some ways are protected by law. For example, while rape is punishable by life imprisonment, if the rape is of an unmarried woman, the man can escape punishment by marrying her. Generally, murder is punishable by life imprisonment or the death penalty. If a man murders his wife claiming she committed adultery, or his sister on the accusation of fornification, his sentence is reduced. The lack of legal protection for domestic abuse prevents many women from filing reports with the police. Judges often consider violence against women at the hands of a family member to be in accordance with religious and state law (Al Gharaibeh, 2011).

Unlike many other states in the region, despite lacking full civic rights, Bahraini women were involved in society and politics at an early stage. By the mid-twentieth century, the discovery of oil created a need for workers in the growing industry. Under the British administration, Bahrain developed trade relations with countries outside the Gulf. As a result, women often traveled abroad for work or for higher education. Returning home with their Western education, young Bahrainis, both men and women, called for trade reform and protested against the British administration (Seikaly, 1994).

In the 1960s and 1970s women's roles in political and social movements in Bahrain expanded further. A number of phenomena contributed to this. First, in the 1960s the numbers of university graduates in Bahrain reached new heights, creating a larger class of educated and politically active young people. Second, regional movements associated with Arab nationalism, liberation movements, and anti-colonialism in the Arab world prompted more political upheaval. Women were a part of this political mobilization and in the early 1970s they began to establish political organizations. By the mid-1970s – with oil controlling the economy in Bahrain – middle- and working-class women were firmly established in higher education and job markets. Women drove cars, took part in political demonstrations, and were involved in politics. Some joined existing political groups and others formed their own NGOs to further their political and social goals. Female branches of sports clubs, social societies, and professional organizations flourished.

Regarding formal political participation, as mentioned earlier, women have been allowed to both vote and run for office since 2002. Yet, it took until 2006 for a woman to win a seat in the legislature. In the 2011 election, 4 women were elected out of 40 members in the lower house of parliament. Bahraini women have held various appointed senior government positions including minister of health, president of the U.N. General Assembly, and ambassador to the United States (Kelly, 2009).

Religion and Society

Bahrain has a Muslim population of around 70%. Excluding non-citizens, the Muslim population is approximately 99.8%. The Muslim share of the total population has been dropping over time as a result of foreign workers coming in from Southeast and South Asia (Bahraini Census, 2010; Pew Research Center, 2010). The 2010 Pew Religion survey found that Bahrainis were considered to have low levels of social hostility toward religion. In other words, there are very few acts of religious hostility by individuals, organizations, or groups in society, and society is tolerant of different religious groups.

It is somewhat complicated to interpret the degree of religiosity of the population in Bahrain. On the one hand, in the 2010–2014 World Values Survey (WVS), only 40.6% of respondents said that religion was very important to them. Some 46.3% said that it was "rather important," and an additional 12.9% said that it was not very important or not at all important. Only 35.3% of respondents listed religion as an important value to teach their children. Almost 7 in 10 people agreed or strongly agreed with the statement "all religions should be taught in our public schools." Only 14.1% of respondents said that they were active members of a "church or religious organization," and 76.3% said that they were not members at all. On the other hand, 77.7% of respondents said that they attend religious services once a week or more. When asked if they consider themselves a "religious person," 76% answered in the affirmative.

Religion and the State

Islam is the official state religion of the Kingdom of Bahrain. Furthermore, it is enshrined in multiple parts of the Constitution as the ultimate source of state law. For example, the preamble states:

> The amendments to the Constitution proceed from the premise that the noble people of Bahrain believe that Islam brings salvation in this world and the next, and that Islam means neither inertness nor fanaticism but explicitly states that wisdom is the goal of the believer [and] wherever he finds it he should take it, and that the Qur'an has been remiss in nothing (...). Thus these constitutional amendments are representative of the advanced cultural thought of our beloved nation. They base our political system on a constitutional monarchy founded on counsel [shura], which in Islam is the highest model for governance.

Chapter 1, Article 2 of the Bahraini Constitution establishes Islam as the official state religion and source of legislation: "The religion of the State is Islam. The Islamic Shari'a is a principal source for legislation." The Constitution also emphasizes Shari'a law as the basis for the frameworks of Bahraini inheritance law and work law. Freedom of opinion and scientific research is allowed only to the extent that it does not violate Islamic law. The king is described as the "loyal protector of the religion and the homeland."

Chapter 2, Article 7 of the Constitution also mandates state teaching of religion in the public education system: "The law regulates care for religious and national instruction in the various stages and forms of education, and at all stages is concerned to develop the citizen's personality and his pride in his Arabism."

The Constitution ensures freedom of religion in several clauses. Chapter 3, Article 18, states that "[p]eople are equal in human dignity, and citizens are equal before the law in public rights and duties. There shall be no discrimination among them on the basis of sex, origin, language, religion or creed." Article 22 of the same chapter states that "Freedom of conscience is absolute. The State guarantees the inviolability of worship, and the freedom to perform religious rites and hold religious parades and meetings in accordance with the customs observed in the country."

The terms dictated in the Constitution are largely upheld by the state. Though religious groups are required to obtain permits to operate, and religious schools must get approval from the Ministry of Education, there are almost no instances of permits being withheld or denied. Non-Muslim minority groups are generally accommodated by the state. If any religious group is the subject of legal or bureaucratic discrimination, it is generally the Shia majority (Merriman, 2009).

The government has also taken steps to minimize religious intervention in politics. In 2016, the 2005 Political Society law was amended in an effort to minimize religious group influence in politics. The Amendment banned societies with sectarian or religious agendas, religious preaching in society activity, and religious figures from holding membership in political societies (Law No. 13 of 2016 amending some provisions of Law No. 26 of 2005 with respect to Political Societies, 2016; Toumi, 2016).

Abortion and Reproductive Rights in Bahrain

Abortion in Bahrain is legal. The procedure must be performed by a licensed physician, after being authorized by a panel of licensed physicians. Midwives cannot perform abortions, nor can women self-induce abortions. If an abortion is performed by anyone other than a licensed physician, the penalty is up to six months in prison, or a fine of up to 50 Bahraini Dinars (or approximately $130). In Bahrain, this is not a prohibitively high sum of money. Bahrain is a high-income country and its GDP per capita in 2017 was $23,655 (World Bank, 2018). In a comparison of purchase power parity, it ranks among the top-

10 countries in the world in per capita income. If an abortion is performed on a woman without her consent, the penalty is up to 10 years in prison (U.N. Economic and Social Affairs, 2002). Abortion costs are covered by the state when performed for medical reasons (Grossman, Grindlay, & Burns, 2016).

Reproductive policy in Bahrain is permissive overall. The state provides many of these services free of charge and as part of the national health care system (Al Gharaibeh, 2011). Along with its liberal abortion policy, Bahrain was the first state in the Gulf Cooperation Council to offer family planning services as part of the health care system, the first to offer free contraception, and the first to open a national family planning association (U.N. Economic and Social Affairs, 2002).

While abortion law in Bahrain is permissive – certainly by regional standards – some women still opt for clandestine abortions as a means of avoiding social stigma regarding female virginity and sexuality. Women on Web, a nonprofit organization that advises women on reproductive health, reported that an anonymous user from Bahrain told them, "I live in an Arab country and I'm alone here so I'm feeling so scared." Despite the legality of abortion, this woman still felt a stigma around the issue and could only seek counseling and guidance in the anonymous environment provided on the Internet (Rainey, 2018). Women seeking clandestine abortions often resort to abortion-inducing drugs. Indeed, it is not uncommon for doctors to see patients suffering the side effects of self-induced abortions, with primarily teenagers resorting to this option (Trade Arabia, 2010). The desire to hide an abortion, especially among teenagers, is rooted in the value Bahraini culture puts on a woman's virginity. A woman's virginity impacts not just her own future but the honor of her family (Kelly and Breslin, 2010). This ties into the same cultural value put on family honor that stands behind the abovementioned law minimizing penalties for a man who performs an "honor killing" of a female family member.

Despite societal hurdles, the legal and medical systems are hospitable to a woman seeking abortion, certainly by regional standards. What is more, there is even some recent effort to get legal recognition of abortion as grounds for sick leave in the labor market (Bahrain Mirror, 2018).

DISCUSSION

Earlier in this book, we surveyed various ways in which civil society – and, in particular, religious denominations, institutions, and groups – affect abortion policy. When it came to abortion policy, certain religious attributes of the state-society interaction had no effect. Specifically, religious freedom, separation of religion and state, and religious diversity showed no significant correlation with state abortion policy. Muslim, Catholic, and Buddhist populations did correlate with less permissive abortion policy. Protestant and Hindu population size had no effect. Religiosity in general correlated with more restrictive abortion policy, but also had an interesting interaction with different religious denominations. The size of the Muslim population was more significant when the population was also devout. A large Muslim population that was not religious did not have the same correlation with restrictive abortion policy as a Muslim population of the same size that was religious. This, however, did not hold true for Catholic populations. Regardless of degree of religiosity, Catholic populations correlated with restrictive abortion policy. That is to say, a large Catholic population would have the same effect on abortion policy, whether or not it was religious. Abortion policy interacted differently than women's political rights policy with the various religious factors. Though abortion was affected by Muslim, Catholic, and Buddhist population size and by religiosity, women's political rights only correlated with freedom of religion. The more restrictive a country was regarding religious freedom, the more likely it was to be restrictive regarding women's political rights.

The case studies presented in this chapter shed new light on underlying causal mechanisms and add some critical nuance. Until 2017, Chile was one of the only countries in the world that had a complete ban on abortion. Even with the passing of the 2017 legislation, the legal code continues to be fairly restrictive. With a strong presence of the Catholic Church in various aspects of informal social and political life, the official separation of Church and state seems less consequential. Whether or not the state officially embraces the Church is not a defining variable, at least not in the case of Chile. What seems important is that a large Catholic population (combined with a history of church involvement in politics) gives the Church a strong foothold in both society and government. The dominance of the Church in public life in general – and in policymaking and abortion policy, in particular – is not simply a function of constitutional arrangements. Rather, when, as in the Chilean case, the church has a long history of political engagement, its influence on policy may be far-reaching. This would be doubly true, as the Chilean case suggests, in areas that are of particular importance for the Church, such as questions about family and reproduction. As such, it is not surprising to find such substantial influence on women's rights and, in particular, in the context of abortion policy.

This is true even though the public in Chile is not particularly religious. A minority of Chileans today would say that religion has a defining role in their life, and this segment of the population has been waning for years.

Chileans often reject the idea that religion and Church guidance are necessary to lead a moral life. While they might identify as Catholics, certain tenants of the Catholic Church – such as premarital abstinence and pregnancy and children out of wedlock – are neither taboo nor uncommon within Chilean society.

Despite Chileans not being particularly religious, the share of the Catholic constituency did allow the Church to exercise significant influence. Let us look at the history of the Catholic Church in modern Chilean history – and the institutional design of the church – for reasons why. The Church has had a critical role as an arbiter for the state and the people during some of the most contentious times of Chilean modern history. The Vatican has brokered international agreements and treaties for the country. Its institutions and representatives in Chile helped the state transition to democracy after it experienced one of the darkest periods in its history. During the harshest years of the Pinochet regime, Church representatives spoke out against oppression and in support of human rights. The church provided services, support, and counseling for those affected.

A key feature of the Church that allowed much of this to happen was its united hierarchal structure and strong Vatican-supported institutions. The role the Church played guiding the population through this dark period in the country's history and bringing it to an end endeared it to many parts of Chilean society and granted it a foothold in the political arena.

The people's appreciation for the Church as well as its presence in state politics provided the church with influence over issues that were of particular significance to its agenda. One such case was reproductive rights. Were the church a less centralized body, and its institutions not as hierarchical, the citizens may not have necessarily associated the actions of this or that individual Catholic leader with the Church as a whole. It is possible that the church would not be able to exercise the influence that it did both among the people and within government.

The 2017 change in abortion policy heralded by President Bachelet correlated with a dramatic decrease in the Catholic constituency. In 2006, 70% of the population identified as Catholic. As mentioned above, only 11 years later, in 2017, the number plummeted to 59%, many of whom do not hold religion as critically important for their way of life. Those who would push for more permissive policy, and women's rights groups that advocate for better reproductive care, now find a less formidable adversary in a Church that is losing its political and social base.

The Kingdom of Bahrain is a profoundly different case. Throughout its history, Bahrain was defined as a Muslim state. This element in the nation's identity is entrenched in multiple places in its Constitution. The state identifies as Islamic and supports Islam and Islamic institutions. Though known to discriminate against and at times even oppress its large Shia population, the Sunni monarchy allows relative religious freedom for non-Muslim groups. Despite its strong identity as a Muslim state, Bahrain has a permissive abortion policy and certainly so by regional standards. As we find elsewhere in this book, the case of Bahrain shows that an official state religion does not automatically constitute a barrier to a permissive abortion policy.

The interaction we found between Islam and religiosity in Bahrain also demonstrates the statistical findings of the previous chapter. Though most Bahrainis are Muslim, they are not necessarily strongly religious. The WVS results discussed earlier suggest that large portions of the population do not feel strongly about religion in education or in various other areas of life. In fact, compared to other countries with similar-sized Muslim populations, Bahrain's population seems relatively non-religious. Out of the 14 countries in the previous chapter's samples that had a Muslim population of 70% or higher, on average 74% of 2010 WVS respondents said that religion was "very important" to them. In Bahrain, only 40.6% responded that way. In five countries (Algeria, Egypt, Jordan, Libya, and Tunisia) more than 90% of survey respondents said religion was very important to them. Only Azerbaijan, Kyrgyzstan, and Uzbekistan had less people identifying religion as "very important" than in Bahrain. If the Muslim population is not strongly religious, its size will not necessarily be a barrier to permissive abortion policy.

These findings are interesting also when compared to the case of Chile. In the latter, even though organized outside of state structures, the Catholic Church – with its high levels of organization and institutional hierarchy – traditionally exercised substantial influence. Islam in Bahrain presents no such united front. As mentioned above, the Muslim population is divided between the ruling Sunni minority and the Shia majority. In the case of Bahrain, thinking of Muslims as a single constituency is misguided. Because of this denominational rift, the Muslim state has even taken steps to minimize the influence of religion in politics. The 2015 law banning religion from political societies was motivated by a desire to remove Shia religious influence from the political sphere (Toumi, 2016). The fact that Islam as a religion is not centralized and its various factions are divided means that its civil society leaders are not in the same position to exercise political influence. Their political clout is largely jeopardized by this comparatively weaker position. Any religious movement's ability to impact policy or society is diminished further as state leaders try to block various Muslim sects from entering the political fray.

As we state elsewhere in this book, women's rights should not be seen as a single category. Some variables that correlate with abortion rights may not correlate with other types of women's rights policies. The women of Bahrain have had access to abortions since 1976, but were granted the right to vote and run for office only in 2002. This is a gap of 26 years between extending abortion rights and reaching full political participation. The various factors that might have allowed for permissive abortion rights did not translate into political rights. Clearly, the two were determined by different dynamics of the state. This fits in with the theoretical framework we will develop in Chapter 4. In an authoritarian state such as Bahrain, granting reproductive rights would be less likely to upset the regime stability. Political rights, on the other hand, might be much more carefully distributed and monitored. These two types of rights are not determined by the same factors. We will delve into this idea even further in the next chapter when we discuss how female politicians may or may not be allowed to influence politics in nondemocratic regimes.

There is much here that correlates with our findings in Chapter 2. The permissiveness of state abortion policy wasn't determined by whether the state had an official religion, religious diversity, or state support for restrictions on religion. Rather, it correlated with sect, and whether that sect had an interaction with religiosity. Catholicism, whose influence is independent of religiosity, indeed seemed to exercise a lot of influence in Chile. Chile has had and continues to have an extremely restrictive abortion policy. This is despite a constitutional separation of Church and state. That said, the Church exercises strong influence on civil society as a provider of social services and united identity. Bahrain, on the other hand, is officially a Muslim state, as enshrined in the state constitution. Islam, whose influence seems dependent on degree of religiosity, did not present a barrier to permissive abortion policy in Bahrain. It would seem that Islam's lack of a united front in civil society meant that religious leaders were limited in the influence they could exert.

These cases demonstrate the importance of observing the dynamics of religion in the sphere of civil society. In Chile, the power of the Church comes from a few sources. First is the shrinking but still considerable Catholic constituency. Second, the Church has been a key advocate for the people vis-à-vis the state, in particular in crucial moments in the state's history. Further, the Church provides social services, is often there when the state fails to respond to the needs of its citizens, and has advocated for civil rights and liberties when under attack.

The institutional strength of organized religion in Bahrain is nothing like what we find in Chile. We find no united Muslim front within civil society. Individual citizens identify with their sect within Islam. The state also goes out of its way to keep faith civil society players away from politics, as a means of keeping the Shia majority's religious leadership out of the political fray, to the extent possible. The analysis of Bahrain sheds light on several cases of Muslim countries' reproductive policy, including more religiously moderate countries such as Turkey. Levels of institutional robustness and strength are pivotal for the type of political clout organized religion would have within the state. When religion is a unifying and instrumental institution in civil society, such as the Catholic Church has historically been in Chile, it would be in a considerably better position to influence policy.

CONCLUSIONS

The two cases of Chile and Bahrain show how religion, as a key element within the sphere of civil society, has a complex interaction with state abortion policy. Whether or not a state has an official religion does not stand as a determining factor. What seems to matter more is the nature of faith civil society and how organized and hierarchical religious institutions are in general and in their interaction with the population. The degree of religiosity also matters, but is context specific. In some cases, it interacts with religious sect and may be less consequential in specific religions. Broad assumptions about religiosity and religion in their interaction with abortion policy miss the very intricate and multidimensional reality of such a relationship.

The two case studies also bring to light a variable that was not included in the analyses in the previous chapter. The level of unification, hierarchy, and organization of a religious denomination may be an important factor in determining its influences. It would seem that much of Catholicism's influence is derived from its highly structured, organized, and rigid hierarchy. It acts as a well-funded and well-organized civil society agent to exercise influence. Islam, on the other hand, lacks the organized structure of the Catholic Church. The lack of a centralized power to direct activity or unite citizens translates to diminished political sway. Indeed, this could serve as a barrier to political influence.

In Part II of the book, we move from a discussion of faith civil society to the influence on abortion policy from the sphere of state government. We focus on questions of representation and in particular the role of women leaders. Perhaps it was no coincidence that it was under President Bachelet, the first *woman* president of Chile, that abortion policy was liberalized. This was but one example of where women leadership may be consequential. In the next chapter, we go beyond specific cases to make a more theoretically developed argument about dimensions of representation in the context of translating descriptive representation into substantive representation. We strive to examine this connection not just through anecdotal case studies, but also through a comparative large-scale analytic scope. Part II takes us well beyond any specific category of systems of government, whether democratic or otherwise, to chart a global view of the power female leadership can achieve in influencing the production of reproductive rights.

PART II

STATE GOVERNMENT SPHERE

4

The Sphere of National Governments: Dimensions of Representation

How do dimensions of representation at the state level affect abortion policy? In this chapter we delve into the concept of representation within the state as a key factor in how policy in general, and specifically abortion policy, is made. Of the different spheres we examine in this book, the state is probably the most obvious and direct source of policy influence. It is there, at the level of the state, that policy is created. Indeed, the players and institutions that operate at this level are the ones officially tasked with deciding state policy. This is as opposed to actors in the other spheres, which try to influence policy and legal institutions but usually do not themselves legislate. While there are many state institutions that influence and make policy, in this chapter, we focus on the concept of representation – and specifically on female political representation – as a significant influence over reproductive health policy.

Women are leading the charge around the world to promote and address gender issues. Like Chilean President Michelle Bachelet, mentioned in Chapters 1, 3, and 8, Sweden's Margot Wallström is but one example of a woman leader who has used her political positions to advance unique feminist platforms. As Minister of Foreign Affairs she launched the first explicitly "feminist foreign policy" the world has ever seen. Her agenda put gender and women's rights at the center of Sweden's diplomatic efforts (Government Offices of Sweden, 2018; Vogelstein and Bro, 2019).

The importance of female leadership and representation in determining state abortion policy is based on the connection between descriptive and substantive representation. In other words, the key idea is that women are best suited to understand, and thus represent, the needs of women. Following this logic, the more that women are present in the legislature, the more likely it is that women's issues will get on the political agenda and be addressed.

Until now, such discussions in the literature of descriptive and substantive representation have been limited to the democratic state. Such influence, nevertheless, is not limited to democratic or Western states. As we show in this chapter, as well as in the in-depth analysis of the case study of Rwanda in the next chapter, the descriptive-substantive link pertains to developing nations as well.

As we are putting together a comparative framework, we want to understand abortion policy worldwide. Accordingly, we first introduce the interaction between women's representation and regime type. The nexus of national governments, questions of representation, women's leadership, and abortion policy is relevant to a range of governmental systems. In some cases, such as Sweden or Australia, a democratic system of government is in place. Yet, other cases, such as Kenya or Chile, are different in this sense. At least during extensive periods in their history in some cases, or their entire political history in others, such countries had a nondemocratic form of government in place.

Do women exercise the same powers of representation around the world and can their influence on policy survive beyond the sphere of developed democracies? This question, we argue, is critical for the comparative analysis of reproductive rights. On top of this, even within democracies, institutions influence forms of representation. In particular, there are certain institutions that may have direct bearing on questions of representation, and in some cases are designed to advance the democratic principle of equality and redress past inequalities. In the context of our discussion, gender quotas are one of the most notable of such institutions. How do quotas affect the interaction between women's representation and policy output in general and in the area of reproductive health in particular? The question of quotas is touched upon in the current chapter, as well as in the two chapters that follow. Chapter 5 complements the discussion here by delving into case studies, where part of the discussion revolves around quotas. Quotas are then addressed further in Chapter 6, where we analyze the effects of international institutions side by side with the effects of quotas.

Women's Representation in Different Political Environments

Let us start with the core question of women's representation in different regime types. There are a number of theoretical reasons why rates of women's representation might correlate with the permissiveness of abortion policy, even outside of democracies or developed countries. Indeed, literature suggests that this happens in other areas of policymaking. Swiss et al. (2012) use pooled time series analysis among 102 developing countries from 1980 to 2005 to examine whether an increase in women legislators leads to improvements in child health, as measured by immunization rates and survival rates of infants and children. Bhalotra and Clots-Figueras (2014) found that, in India, women politicians are more likely to build public health facilities and encourage antenatal care, institutional delivery, and immunization. Mavisakalyan (2014) examined women in cabinet positions and their views on public health spending in 80 countries. This study found that an increase in the share of women in the cabinet is associated with an increase in public health spending.

Particularly challenging, though, are the causal mechanisms that undergird the political impact that women politicians would have in places outside of the democratic sphere. While the above literature may provide some insight into other policy areas, here we offer some for the area of abortion policy. There are a few reasons why we think that when it comes to abortion policy, women representatives may have a real and substantive impact. First, countries with nondemocratic regimes might use a commitment to gender equality, in both political representation and public policy, as a means of pandering to international norms. This would be one way to gain acceptance within international forums, where democratic norms and institutions are often set as conditions for participation (Neumayer, 2005; Schwarz, 2004; Zwingel, 2012).

Second, a country, whose institutions are not democratic might still have a less-traditional approach to gender roles, resulting in both a high rate of female political representation as well as permissive abortion policy (Paxton, 1997; Welch & Studlar, 1996; Kenworthy & Malami, 1999). In both these scenarios, there would be a correlation between women's representation and gender equality on the one hand and abortion policy on the other. Yet, this correlation would not be as a result of substantive representation. In other words, what we expect to find under such political circumstances is the appearance of influence.

A third theoretical account, however, would suggest a much closer link between descriptive and substantive representation. In that account, nondemocratic states might allow political representatives to exercise influence in policy areas that do not threaten regime stability. It is in cases such as these that representatives would exercise substantive representation. Policy areas where we expect to see this freedom would overlap with the policy fields where women tend to exercise the most influence, such as health and education spending as well as women's reproductive rights. If indeed women were allowed to influence certain policy areas, this would imply a maintained connection between their descriptive and substantive representation, even in situations where political freedoms are otherwise compromised, and democratic institutions and norms are constrained. This would mean that female political representatives can influence abortion policy worldwide, even beyond the realm of democratic systems of government.

In order to understand the extent of women's influence around the world, in this chapter we build a series of models that differentiate among the various possible scenarios. Alongside abortion policy, we look at the relationship between women's representation on the one hand and public education expenditures and public health expenditures on the other. Previous studies of democracies have shown a correlation between the generosity of these three public policies and the rate of women's representation in democracies. By adding the additional two policies, which should not, according to our theory, be affected by international pressure or gender attitudes, we can identify what powers are at play. The juxtaposition of these areas would allow us to decide whether women can indeed have an influence or if they simply appear to do so. This comparison clarifies which of the three theoretical frameworks described above holds water when tested empirically with comparative data.

Before presenting those analyses, however, let us first discuss the sphere of the state and offer a general discussion of the concept of representation within different types of states. We will then delve into the relevance of women's representation and the theory behind it, including a discussion of female representation in the context of abortion law. This will be followed by a conversation about electoral gender quotas as a key factor in how women get elected, and a potential intervening variable in the relationship between women's descriptive and substantive representation. We next present a battery of empirical tests and multivariate analyses with data for a large number of states, which then leads us to our conclusions about the politics of representation and state-level institutions and their implications for the production of reproductive rights.

The State Sphere

What do we mean when we refer to the state level or sphere? There are multiple conceptions and definitions of the state (Vincent, 2001 [1992]). For the purposes of this discussion, we think of the state as it is classically defined – as the political organization with a monopoly on the legitimate use of physical force within a given territory (Cudworth, 2007; Salmon & Imber, 2008). This definition includes a few components. First, by political organization we are referring to the formal mechanisms of political power that operate within governing institutions. Second, through their legitimate claim to the use of force, these institutions can both make and enforce their decisions. Finally, the use of this force and the power of these institutions are limited by borders. Therefore, the state sphere refers to the geographically limited arena in which these institutions exist and function.

This sphere is perhaps the most critical for our discussion of how public policy on abortion is made because it is here that the laws themselves are formed and enforced. To a large extent, the other chapters of this book focus on spheres that interact with, and try to influence, the institutions in this sphere. Yet, it is within this sphere that we see the action of players directly generating policy.

There are numerous elements of the state that determine what public policy is made. At the broadest level, this includes the very character of the regime itself. Is the state a democracy? A dictatorship? A theocracy? Next, we may ask how the state is arranged. Is it a federal or a unitary state? How are the institutions of the state organized? How is the legislature designed? What are the powers of the executive? What is the role of the court? What is the size and power of the bureaucracy? We could even examine more minor details, such as the established arrangements and rules that govern a single institution within the infrastructure of the state. For instance, what kind of electoral system does the state have in place? All of these compose and define the nature of the state and its institutions. Furthermore, all of them affect the type of public policy generated. There are substantial bodies of literature in the fields of political science, economics, public policy, sociology, and public administration that examine and study these connections. We will therefore pick a theoretical concept that embodies certain aspects of the state sphere and allows us to zoom in on certain institutions for analysis. By choosing only a few institutions, we aim not to provide an exhaustive exploration of how state mechanisms influence abortion policy, but rather demonstrate the influence of certain key institutions that we deem particularly consequential in the context of reproductive rights.

We focus on the concept of representation as a defining feature of all states. Specifically, we will look at female representation and its effects on abortion policy. We place this discussion within a more elaborate framework of representation, looking at how it interacts with other aspects of political inclusion and related key institutions within the state sphere. This allows us to generate a nuanced discussion of how women's representation works in generating state abortion policy in different contexts and within varying institutional settings.

Representation and the State

The state is expected to represent its people, but different regimes claim various ways of offering representation. Some believe that representation is achieved through a democratic process, whereas others might see representation achieved through enforcing an ideology or religion that the regime feels best serves the people. This being said, the connection between democracy and representation is considered critically important. As Plotke (1997) observes, with the infeasibility of direct democracy in the modern state, representation is crucial in constitutional democratic practice. While the original Greek concept of democracy may have been unrelated to representation as such, the connection between the two concepts and the relevance of representation to democracy has long been accepted (Pitkin, 2004; Dovi, 2002, among many others). One of the great challenges for democracies today, however, has become the creation – or the maintenance – of representation. That is, how to ensure that elected politicians represent citizens and not just interest groups, businesses, and other elite groups (Pitkin, 2004).

The concept of representation is usually limited to discussions of democratic systems. States with this system of government are disproportionately located in the West (Waylen, 2008; Dovi, 2007; Devlin & Elgie, 2008; Matland, 1998). Though the connection between democracy and representation is important (Plotke, 1997; Pitkin, 2004; Dovi, 2002), we question the wisdom of limiting the discussion of this topic to the democratic sphere. Beyond democracies, there is a range of regime types that have legislative bodies with female representation. What is more, many of these legislative bodies – at least by name and even structure – mimic democratic state institutions (Levitsky & Way, 2002; Diamond, 2002; Morse, 2012; Carothers, 2002). Further, equally important is the fact that the majority of the people in the world live outside of a democratic system of government. To understand the political processes and institutions that determine public policy for those people, a more universal analytic framework is crucial. As abortion policy is relevant to women worldwide; it is vital to bring into the analytic fold cases beyond the democratic sphere.

Accordingly, the rationale guiding this book – and the analyses in this chapter and the next in particular – is that the discussion of women's representation should not be limited to democracies. If we did that, it would exclude a large number of states, some of which may even have certain democratic features. Thus, we should recognize and include the numerous regime types that exist in the state system and must explore how the concept of representation functions within them.

With the end of the Cold War, a new spectrum of regime types has emerged, along with a literature for how to understand and catalogue these states. With the fall of the USSR, democracy seemed to have emerged as the best practice in government, and rhetorically became the road to regime legitimacy (Diamond, 1999; Carothers, 2002; Ottaway, 2003). Diamond described this phenomenon as an ideological hegemony. While, stylistically, this ideal of democracy has been adopted, Diamond also pointed out that the number of countries implementing democratic practice while simultaneously limiting freedoms, falsifying elections, and violating liberal principles, proved the superficiality and weakness of this hegemony (1996, p. 30). These new regimes presented an anomaly for political scientists, who assumed that these states were merely in transition toward a familiar category, democracy.

At first, scholars predicted that these regimes, democratic in name but authoritarian in practice, would evolve into democracies; states that had adopted some characteristics of democracy were considered to be in transition. With time, a wave of scholars proposed that it was time to stop thinking of these regimes as in transition and to look at them for what they really were: hybrid regimes (Levitsky & Way, 2002; Diamond, 2002; Morse, 2012; Carothers, 2002). While not classically authoritarian, such systems of government certainly could not be categorized as democracies. These hybrid regimes, which fall along a gradient between liberal democracy and dictatorship, have demanded a new typology of regime types as well as a reconsideration of the theory of democratic transitions (Bogaards, 2009).

Various frameworks for regime classification have emerged based on where a state was positioned on the range between democracy and authoritarianism. Hybrid regimes have been described as flawed democracies, electoral authoritarianism, competitive authoritarianism, semi-democratic, semi-authoritarian and pseudo democracies (to name a few). Theoretical models focus on various features of the democratic system and procedure. Among others, those include freedom of elections, freedoms and restrictions of the legislature and the executive branch, freedom of the judiciary, restrictions on liberal freedoms including freedom of the press, freedom of speech, and freedom of assembly (Diamond, 2002; Levitsky & Way, 2002; Bogaards, 2009).

Since the beginning of this wave of literature calling for the end of the transition paradigm and for a new classification of regime types, an additional wave of research emerged to look at the electoral structures of these states as indicators of a state's chances of transferring into a democracy (Morse, 2012; Staffan, 2009; Magaloni, 2006; McCoy & Hartlyn, 2009; Mylonas & Roussias, 2008). This scholarship focuses on elections as the defining feature for the purposes of regime categorization. Elections, and hence representation, are present to varying degrees, even outside of democracies.

The Question of Representation

Accepting that representation is an important and desirable part of any state regime and that representation is not limited to democracy, we are then left to consider what constitutes representation. There are multiple models for conceptualizing and operationalizing representation. Pitkin's classic model of representation offers four dimensions: formalistic, descriptive, substantive, and symbolic. Formalistic representation refers to the legal authority to act for another. Descriptive representation denotes the representation of a group by virtue of shared characteristics. Substantive authority refers to a representative working on behalf of group welfare in policymaking. It assumes that members of a group have shared common experiences, and therefore have certain common understandings and interests (Grey, 2006). Symbolic representation refers to a representative standing for certain ideas, or having certain cultural meanings or ramifications (Krook, Franceschet, & Piscopo, 2009; Childs & Lovenduski, 2012; Pitkin, 1967; Schwindt-Bayer & Mishler, 2005). The four dimensions are interconnected, with no single one functioning independently of the other three (Schwindt-Bayer & Mishler, 2005).

Though Pitkin's may be considered the classic, there are additional models that contribute to our understanding of representation in general and of minority and women's representation specifically (e.g., Rehfeld, 2006; Grant & Keohane, 2005; Saward, 2006; Dryzek & Niemeyer, 2008). Williams' (1998) mediation model is particularly germane, as it looks specifically at the representation of historically disadvantaged groups. Williams advocates for a reconsideration of traditional electoral methods for the sake of inclusion of historically excluded perspectives. In her model, a representative offers three services: voice, trust and memory. Voice refers to the presence of representatives from the historically disadvantaged group. Trust refers to the faith the group can feel when represented by one of its own members, as opposed to a member of the historically privileged group. Memory refers to the shared past experience that defines the group. For democracy, Williams calls for institutional mechanisms that would guarantee representatives who can provide voice, trust, and memory. This theory is particularly interesting in a discussion of gender quotas, which we address later on.

Women's Representation and the State

Models of representation assume a connection between the attributes of the representative and that of the represented. As is true for any group, its members share characteristics, experiences, and struggles. Accordingly, it would be a group member who would have the most success representing the group and addressing its concerns and grievances. Such common issues unify the group as a political entity (Sapiro, 1998).

The desire to increase the number of female representatives is based on this assumed connection between the representation of women's issues and interests and the actual number of women in office. There is much literature on the connections between descriptive and substantive representation. The idea that electing women would lead to more policy and advocacy for women's issues is based on an assumed connection between the two (Mansbridge, 1999; Wangnerud, 2009). Mansbridge summarizes this connection by explaining that "legislators who themselves are members of a group respond to issues affecting that group with greater concern than do nonmembers" (2005, p. 625). Women will have distinct issues and interests, and female representatives will be most likely to understand these issues and advance pertinent goals (Bratton, 2005; Campbell, 2004; Childs, 2001). Women representatives have indeed been found to be a necessary (though not sufficient) condition for the advancement of women's issues (Sapiro, 1998, p. 183).

There are two parts to this connection. First, women have been found more likely to choose to advance women's issues and policy areas that have a disproportionate effect on women, such as child-related social services. Therefore, with more women representatives, there are more players advancing these issues. Second, the advancement of women's issues may require a critical mass. Critical mass theory implies that a particular proportion of women is required for change in political behavior, institutions, and policy (Celis & Childs, 2008). A minimum threshold of female elected officials is assumed to be necessary in order for women to start influencing and forming coalitions, and to reduce tokenism and minority isolation (Grey, 2006; Dahlerup, 1988; Childs & Krook, 2006; Wangnerud, 2009). While critical mass theory is neither straightforward – nor not without its critics (Diaz, 2005) – there is general support for the idea that more women will lead to the advancement of certain positions and agendas (Grey, 2002; Childs & Withey, 2004; Stockemer, 2009; Fallon, Swiss, & Viterna, 2012). Women have indeed been found to advance different issues than men. For instance, they are more likely to advance bills relating to women's rights, health, family welfare, and social issues (Paxton, Kunovich, & Hughes, 2007; Htun & Power, 2006; O'Brien, 2012; Westfall & Chantiles, 2016; Berkman & O'Connor, 1993; Chen, 2010; Wangnerud, 2000; Grey, 2002). The documented focus of women representatives on these policy issues directs some of our research design in this chapter.

Studies about female representation in varying regime types are largely limited to descriptive representation. Many have theorized that democracy should increase the number of female representatives for a number of reasons. Normatively, democracies should be interested in encouraging women for the sake of representation. Practically, women in democracies have more power to access information, form interest groups, and appeal to political leaders for policy change. However, studies have found levels of democracy to have no correlation with women's descriptive representation (Stockemer, 2009; Kenworthy & Malami, 1999; Paxton, & Kunovich, 2003; Reynolds, 1999; Stockemer, 2011). Women were no more likely to achieve any given rate of representation in democracies than in nondemocracies. Others have found women's numbers to relate to the democratization process, rather than the level of democracy at any given point in time (Fallon, Swiss, & Viterna, 2012). In short, the existing literature on female representation in nondemocracies is limited to the examination of descriptive representation. Research has yet to take the next step and fully study the connection between descriptive and substantive representation in less-than democratic regimes and to see whether, and to what extent, it is maintained in such settings as well.

In certain policy areas – especially those mentioned above where women are most likely to have an influence – there is no substantial difference between democratic and nondemocratic regimes (Mulligan, Ricard, & Sala-i-Martin, 2004). Therefore, perhaps even in nondemocratic regimes, female politicians can exercise substantive representation. This means that there is much room to explore how women's representation works in nondemocratic regimes and how women's welfare policy can be advanced in different political and institutional settings. Such questions are important, first, in order to justify national policies such as quotas, which have been politically contentious despite their presence in a multitude of nations and over long periods of time (Sommer & Asal, 2018). Clayton and Zetterberg (2018) indeed found that substantial quota reforms are followed by increased government expenditures in public health.

Second, programs for advancing women leaders are common in various countries and are also promoted by transnational and international organizations. For example, U.N. Women, a United Nations' agency focused on women's rights, is broadly active in advancing female leadership. For instance, prompted by a 2011 U.N. General Assembly resolution on women's political participation, U.N. Women initiated a variety of international programs aimed at political leadership and participation for women. Ranging from training for women political candidates to voter and civic education, U.N. Women backs gender equality advocates and calls for legislative and constitutional reforms around the world. Analyzing the efficacy of women representatives and its antecedents is critical for such programs. Lastly, analyzing women's representation is important for our understanding more generally of the nature of representing the demos.

The influence of female legislators on abortion policy has been examined extensively within the United States (O'Connor & Berkman, 1995). In U.S.-based literature, more female politicians lead to more permissive abortion policies, which holds true across party lines (Berkman & O'Connor, 1993; Norrander & Wilcox, 1999). Hildebrandt (2015) also included this variable in his comparative study of regime types and abortion and found this to hold true in comparative cross-sectional cases.

The idea that more female legislators would lead to more permissive abortion policy is based, of course, on the hypothesized connection between descriptive and substantive representation, which we discussed above with respect to the work of Pitkin (1967), and others (Schwindt-Bayer & Mishler, 2005; O'Regan, 2000). Let us now take a moment to look at a specific institution that has been making a meaningful impact on the rate of women's representation, electoral gender quotas.

Electoral Gender Quotas and Representation

A large body of literature shows that institutional design is one of the determining factors in the chances of women and minorities to reach political office (Iversen & Rosenbluth, 2008; Fortin-Rittberger & Rittberger, 2014; Joshi, 2013; Matland, 1998; Carey & Shugart, 1995; Kenworthy & Malami, 1999; Asal, Sommer, & Harwood, 2013; Solodoch & Sommer, 2018; Sommer, 2017; Sommer, 2018; Sommer & Frishman, 2016; Rosenbluth, Salmond, & Thies, 2006; Forman-Rabinovici & Sommer, 2018a; Htun & Weldon, 2018). Institutions that allow for greater pluralism and diversity are particularly important, as democracy is also defined by the extent to which a system reflects society and represents its various demographics (Dovi, 2002).

One of the key ideas behind quotas – and electoral quotas in particular – is that for a country to be democratic, it should offer representation to its population, minority and historically oppressed groups included. Not just the democratic process matters but also the final makeup of the elected body. Elections are insufficient if certain segments of society cannot participate equally. Quotas and affirmative action in general are based on the premise that historically oppressed groups continue to experience barriers to equal participation. To redress past injustices and inequalities, society must offer remedies to these barriers. Electoral gender quotas are part of a larger category of minority quotas and an even larger category of affirmative action policies (Dovi, 2002; Sommer & Asal, 2018).

Electoral quotas specifically aim to apply affirmative action to legislative and elected bodies. They aim to compensate for past oppression and to ensure "power sharing," which will safeguard democratic stability in divided societies (Krook & O'Brien, 2010). Minority and gender quotas are based on a modern idea that any single social segment should not monopolize political power, at least not in democracies (Htu, 2004).

Multiple groups have been the subject of quota legislation, including groups defined by their language, religion, ethnicity, nationality, race, caste, age, and profession. These are often done through reserved seats that only group members may contest (Krook & Zetterberg, 2014). Electoral quotas exist in both democracies and authoritarian regimes. They may allocate a share of the seats in parliament, define how party lists must be formed, or decide the distribution of all seats in the legislature (Bird, 2014).

Voluntary party-level electoral gender quotas have existed for over 80 years (Franceschet, Krook, & Piscopo, 2012; Pande & Ford, 2011). Since 1991, the trend of mandatory quota adoption has been on the upswing. In 1991, Argentina became the first country to adopt a mandatory national electoral gender quota and the first to use gender quotas for national legislative elections (Jones, 2008). Since then, quotas have been adopted throughout the world in dozens of countries.

The increased use of quotas represents a shift from a discourse of incremental change to that of fast-track change. According to Dahlerup and Freidenvall (2005), feminists and women's movements are no longer willing to wait for change, nor are they willing to trust that the change will eventually come on its own. A discourse of fast-tracking, or introducing speedy change, is one of the key catalysts driving the wave of quota adoption. This institution aimed at achieving faster representation and equality takes three main forms: reserved seat quotas, legislative quotas, and political party quotas.

In a reserved seat system, a certain number of legislative seats are put aside for women in chambers of the legislative branch. In other words, only women may compete for these seats. As of 2011, 20% of countries with gender quotas adopted the reserved seats type (Pande & Ford, 2011). Such reforms typically are specified in the state Constitution or are a part of electoral law. They may create designated electoral roles for women, designate special districts for female candidates, or distribute a number of reserved seats for women to parties based on election outcome (Krook, 2006; Krook, Franceschet, & Piscopo, 2009; Franceschet & Piscopo, 2008; Jones, 2008).

Legal candidate or legislative quotas are the most recent type of quota policy. As of 2011, such quota policies were in place in 38% of the countries with quotas. Legislative quotas aim to regulate the number of women elected, usually by requiring parties to nominate a certain percentage of women on their electoral slate (Franceschet, Krook, & Piscopo, 2012). The success of legislated candidate quotas is very sensitive to accompanying mechanisms. The presence of placement mandates and enforcement policies, for instance, has a significant effect on the efficacy of legislative quotas (Pande & Ford, 2011).

Lastly, the most popular type of quotas is a party quota. Quotas of this sort aim to increase the proportion of women on a party list. Unlike reserved seat and legislative quotas, individual parties usually adopt party quotas on a voluntary basis. They are not mandatory under law and can exist simultaneously with other types of quotas (Krook, 2006; Krook, Franceschet, & Piscopo, 2009; Franceschet & Piscopo, 2008; Jones, 2008).

Quotas are a tool meant to enhance the relationship between democracy and representation (Franceschet & Piscopo, 2008; Zetterberg, 2008), but they are not just found in democratic states. They can be found in non- and developing-democracies as well. This raises the question of what the purpose of quotas is in these contexts, and of how varying political contexts affect the ramifications of quotas generally and in the context of reproductive rights in particular.

Abortion is a type of policy that the introduction of gender quotas would be expected to influence. As quotas increase the number of female legislators, greater substantive representation should lead to more permissive abortion policy. That said, when you consider the fact that quotas exist in a variety of regimes – and scholarship does not fully understand how female representation functions in these different regimes – we are left with a very interesting question: What is the substantive effect of quotas on policymaking across varying regimes? Though we do not empirically test this question in this chapter, we return to it in the discussion, and in a case study in the next chapter as well as later on in Chapter 6. Thus, the quantitative empirical analyses in this chapter focus on female elected officials, and on varying regime types and their interaction in the context of abortion policymaking. We empirically deal with questions concerning the effects of quotas later on in the book.

THEORETICAL FRAMEWORK – TESTING WOMEN'S REPRESENTATION IN DIFFERENT REGIME TYPES

There are two givens in how the literature conceives of questions of representation. First, in democratic countries, women's descriptive representation contributes to their substantive representation. In the context of reproductive health, this would translate into more permissive abortion policy. The presence of female representation leads to the advancement of women's issues and interests on the public agenda and a more permissive approach to women's welfare and autonomy. Second, it is taken as a given that representation in nondemocracies overall is of diminished significance (Malesky & Schuler, 2010). In such systems, the argument would be, the policy generated by the representatives is not necessarily designed to reflect the will of the people, nor can one assume that there is a connection between descriptive and substantive representation in this type of political environment.

The question that we pose, though, is how various aspects of the state-level sphere, and representation at the state level in particular, interact to affect abortion policy. We isolate women's representation as a crucially important state-level variable that should correlate with abortion policy. Given the prevalence of nondemocratic and semi-democratic regimes worldwide, we want to see how women's ability to provide substantive representation fluctuates as a function of regime context. We want to move beyond democracy so as to offer a more thorough explanation of forces that exist within the state-level sphere. In order to do so, let us offer several reasons why women's representation might correlate with permissiveness of abortion policy, even under less-than-democratic conditions.

First, we may look at incentives that go beyond the domestic politics of the nation state. In a globalized world, some of the chief motivations for political activity and for policymaking stem from international sources rather than political dynamics within the state. In the case of women representatives in nondemocracies, increasing certain types of women's rights may be a method of pandering to international organizations and powerful democratic countries, without actually relinquishing any regime control. States can agree to international treaties and protocols on human and women's rights as a way to appease international organizations and other states (Neumayer, 2005; Schwarz, 2004; Zwingel, 2012). This might grant these states access to better trade conditions, loans from international institutions such as the International Monetary Fund, relief from sanctions, and a host of other benefits in the international arena, some of which we discuss in other sections of the book (Hafner-Burton, 2005; Bush, 2011). Based on this premise, nondemocracies might simultaneously adopt policies to increase women's numbers in parliament (such as quotas), as well as policies that demonstrate a liberal gender attitude.

For example, in 2003 King Abdullah II of Jordan adopted a small reserved seat quota for women in parliament. He was motivated by a desire to improve Jordan's international image and to improve relations with the United States, Britain, and the European Union (Bush, 2011). In this case, there would appear to be a connection between women's descriptive and substantive representation in Jordan. Yet, rather than substantive representation, it is the international effect that lead to both the increase in women representatives and other changes in policy. In this case, descriptive and substantive representation might correlate, but causality stems from a third variable – the motivation to adhere to international norms and the range of benefits such conduct would bequeath on the Kingdom. We go into a much more in-depth discussion of the effects of international organizations in Part III of this book in Chapters 6 and 7.

A second reason why we might see a correlation between descriptive and substantive representation in a variety of regimes is that regimes that accept gender equality would accept it in all fields, regardless of the level of democracy. Even in nondemocratic countries, the ability of women to achieve descriptive representation might imply a certain societal acceptance of gender equality, which would also be carried over to the realm of policymaking (Paxton, 1997; Welch & Studlar, 1996; Kenworthy & Malami, 1999). Therefore, even if the regime restricts certain activities, usually those related to democracy and civil rights, it does not specifically target women's welfare. In the presence of largely progressive societal values and attitudes toward women – even in the absence of a complete set of democratic institutions and norms – we would see a correlation between women's representation and permissiveness of other women's welfare policy. Because of general regime and cultural ideology, there could appear to be a correlation between women's descriptive representation and some substantive policy outcomes. Yet, it is nothing more than that – a correlation. Those societies hold favorable attitudes toward liberal gender equality, as reflected in both voting patterns and the policy produced in the area of reproductive health.

Finally, the third theoretical account we offer would be that nondemocratic regimes might have less interest in monitoring certain types of policy. It would be in these policy areas that the regime would allow some measures of substantive representation. These regimes may focus more attention on limiting civil rights and other activities perceived to endanger regime survival. As we discussed earlier, there is abundant evidence in the literature suggesting that women's political presence tends to influence certain policy fields such as health, social services, and education spending. Such policy areas do not necessarily threaten the regime. Hence, there is reason to believe that female representatives would be able to exercise influence in these fields even in less-than-fully democratic settings. Indeed, studies have found that there are differences in public policy between democracies and nondemocracies in areas such as maintaining public office, military spending, or freedom of the press. Yet, in areas of economic and social policy, democratic and nondemocratic regimes largely resemble each other (Mulligan, Ricard, & Sala-i-Martin, 2004). Thus, it is the policy areas where women generally exercise influence that will probably be more amenable to representative influence and less susceptible to regime control.

The regime – democratic or not – might have less interest or no interest at all in monitoring these policy areas. Therefore, it would not restrict the connection between women's descriptive and substantive representation. Further, the regime might allow free reign in these policy areas so as to claim democratic tendencies at home and abroad and thus gain legitimacy without relinquishing significant control. By allowing freedom in certain areas it perceives as benign or politically harmless, the regime can save resources and gain legitimacy at home and abroad to enforce stricter controls in other areas, which the regime would perceive as essential to its survival.

In nondemocratic regimes, female representatives might be especially keen on influencing non-threatening policy areas. In such regimes, the strategies of women activists depend largely on whether they are considered a threat to the regime. This relates both to whether gender equality is considered in line with or in contradiction to the authoritarian nation-building project, and whether female activists frame their activism in regime-friendly or regime-hostile terms (Muriaas, Tønnessen, & Wang, 2013). Women and women's movements can "feminize" their cause and focus on traditionally feminine issues (health, education, child care) as a way of advancing the movement without appearing threatening to the regime (Johnson & Saarinen, 2013). Female political representatives might take their cues from women's movements or, unrelatedly, adopt similar strategies or agendas. We therefore want to see if women's descriptive representation does indeed correlate with women's welfare policy and with policymaking in areas where women tend to wield influence. If it does, it would mean that there are unexplored democratic features even within such nondemocratic political environments and that, as far as abortion policymaking is concerned, the sway of women representatives will extend beyond purely democratic regimes.

All three of these scenarios would result in the appearance of statistical correlations between descriptive and substantive representation in certain policy areas. The first two theoretical frameworks offered here, though, would only indicate the appearance of a connection, when in reality a third variable is causing both high levels of female representation and progressive women's rights policy. Conversely, within the third theoretical account offered here, there is a real connection between descriptive and substantive representation, even in nondemocratic regimes. In the next section, we delve into this logic.

The Logic of the Proposed Research Design

Whether or not female politicians were behind the policy, in all three theoretical frameworks developed in the previous sections, women's representation would correlate with more liberal abortion policy. Thus, in order to gain some insight into which of these explanations is the most appropriate, we juxtapose abortion policy with other policy areas. These would be policy areas where the predictions of the three theoretical frameworks differ. This way we can undo the behavioral equivalence that is predicted for the policy area that is at the core of our investigation – abortion policy.

Thus, in our empirical tests we include two additional policy fields: state education spending and state health spending. In order to better gauge what determines abortion policy at the state level, these two fields help us differentiate between the influences at play. Health and education are not a women's welfare issue, but are policy areas where women tend to exercise influence. Therefore, a correlation between women's representation and health and education spending wouldn't imply a commitment to women's rights, or a pandering to international norms, but rather a presence of substantive representation by female politicians. It would be a case where, the democratic nature of the regime notwithstanding, female elected officials deliver for their designated constituency. This would shed important light on the issue at the core of this chapter – the process of policymaking at the level of the nation-state and, more specifically, the effect of female representatives on this process. Such findings would suggest that it is not only a matter of general gender equality, but that women's representation is consequential in democracies, non-democracies, and developing democracies.

If the first or second explanations were correct, we would expect women's descriptive representation to correlate positively with abortion policy only. It would not, however, correlate with policies that are not gender specific but tend to be influenced by women, such as health or education spending. Put simply, if the link between descriptive and substantive representation just appears to be there, it would not materialize in policy areas beyond abortion policy. This is why the juxtaposition of abortion with other policy areas is so important.

Conversely, if the third explanation were correct, we would expect all of these policy types to correlate with greater female representation. We would expect to see not only a correlation between women's representation and women's welfare policy, such as reproductive rights, but also with policy areas where women tend to have influence, such as health or education spending. In addition to the discussion in the text, the logic in our research design is laid out in Table 4.1. At this point, we put the discussion of quotas

TABLE 4.1 *Explaining the Connection between Descriptive Representation and Substantive Policy Outcomes in Non-Democratic Regimes*

Reason for connection	Explanation	What we'd expect to see	Hypothesis
1. Pandering to norms of international organizations and the international community	States can adopt international norms of human and women's rights, as a way to appease international organizations and other states. This improves their access to better trade conditions, loans from institutions such as the IMF, relief from sanctions, and so forth.	Women's representation will correlate with permissiveness of other women's welfare policy areas. It will not necessarily correlate with policy areas not directly related to women.	H4.1: Rate of women's representation will correlate positively with more permissive abortion policy. H4.2: Rate of women's representation will have no correlation with education spending. H4.3: Rate of women's representation will have no correlation with health spending.
2. Liberal view of gender roles and acceptance of gender equality	Regimes that accept gender equality will accept it in numerous fields, regardless of level of democracy. Even in nondemocratic countries, if women are able to achieve descriptive representation, it might imply a certain societal acceptance of gender equality, which would also be carried over to other policy areas.	Women's representation will correlate with permissiveness of other women's welfare policy areas. It will not necessarily correlate with policy areas not directly related to women.	H4.1: Rate of women's representation will correlate positively with more permissive abortion policy. H4.2: Rate of women's representation will have no correlation with education spending. H4.3: Rate of women's representation will have no correlation with health spending.

| 3. Political representatives can exercise political will in policy areas that do not threaten the regime | Women's political presence tends to influence policy fields that do not necessarily threaten the regime (health, social services, education spending), so there is reason to believe that they would be able to exercise influence in these fields even in less-than-fully democratic settings. The policy areas where women generally exercise influence will probably be more amenable to representative influence and less susceptible to regime control. The regime might simply have less or no interest in monitoring these policy areas and therefore, they do not restrict the connection between women's descriptive and substantive representation. | Women's representation will correlate with permissiveness of other women's welfare policy areas, as well as in policy areas where women commonly have influence in democratic regimes (e.g., reproductive rights, health, education). | $H_{4.1}$: Rate of women's representation will correlate positively with more permissive abortion policy.
 $H_{4.2}$: Rate of women's representation will correlate positively with education spending.
 $H_{4.3}$: Rate of women's representation will correlate positively with education spending. |

aside in order to focus on the interaction between women's representation and regime type in their effect on abortion policymaking. We want to thoroughly test one phenomenon and not overly complicate an already multilayered statistical model. We will return to the topic of quotas in the discussion at the end of this chapter, as well as empirically in the following chapters.

METHOD

We develop a series of multilevel linear regression models aimed at testing the correlation between the rate of female political representation and a number of policy fields under different regime conditions.

Key independent variable

Our main independent variable is the rate of female legislators. We want to see if more female legislators correlate with different policies under a variety of regime conditions. Rate of female representation is therefore measured as the percentage of seats of the lower house of parliament occupied by female legislators (Women in National Parliaments, 2015).

Outcome Variables

We use three different dependent variables to observe disparate areas where female representatives might exercise substantive representation: abortion policy, national education expenditures, and national health expenditures. In order to measure permissiveness of state abortion policy, we apply the CAI described in Chapter 2. The scale utilizes the U.N. Department of Social and Economic Affair's periodic report, *Global Review of Abortion Policy*. It offers 7 criteria under which the state may allow access to abortion: saving a woman's life, preserving a woman's physical health, preserving a woman's mental health, in cases of rape or incest, fetal impairment, for social or economic reasons, and on request. The scale ranges from 0 (abortion is entirely illegal) to 7 (abortion available upon request) and gives each country a score based on the number of criteria accepted as grounds for abortion.

The second dependent variable is rate of government spending on public education. For this variable, we use government expenditure on education as a percentage of total GDP. These data have been collected by the World Bank Group since 1980 and cover 177 countries (World Bank Group, 2015b). Our third outcome variable is the rate of government spending on health. Data are taken from the World Bank Group's data on public health expenditures as a percentage of GDP (World Bank Group, 2015a). These data have been collected since 1995 and cover 191 countries. For both the education and health variables, the data do not cover every country for every year. There are gaps in the data; years with missing data were left out of the pool.

Controls

Two controls were included in the models: adjusted GDP per capita purchase power parity (PPP) and the KOF Globalisation Index (Cygli, Haelg, Potrafke, & Sturm, 2018; Dreher, 2006). GDP PPP reflects the purchasing power of individuals in a given country, controlling for exchange rate. This variable was included as a control, as general development status and economic strength are often associated with both gender equality and level of democracy.

The KOF Globalisation Index includes economic, social, and political dimensions of globalization, and tracks development in over 200 countries and regions over time. This was included to account for variables arising from a few of our explanatory hypotheses, which refer to a country's desire to integrate and participate in the international community.[1]

Models

For each dependent variable, we create a set of four models, for a total of 12 models. Each set includes a pooled model of all countries, regardless of regime type. In addition, there are three models for each set that group countries based on regime type. We use the Polity index of each country for regime classification. The Polity IV data series (Marshall and Gurr, 2017) assigns country scores ranging from −10 to 10, with −10 being a totalitarian regime and 10 being a consolidated democracy. Scores are made up of multiple components that reflect characteristics of executive recruitment, constraints on executive authority, political competition, civil rights and civil liberties, and institutionalized qualities of governing authority. Based on Marshall and Gurr's (2017) own scale application, scores of zero or less are considered nondemocracies. Scores greater than 0 and less than 7 are categorized as developing democracies. Countries with scores between 7 and 10 are considered democracies. As a result of state-level changes, a country might not fall into the same regime-type for every country-year observation. If a country

---

[1]   The Human Development Index and a gender parity index were also considered as controls. These variables, though, are highly collinear with each other, other control variables, and the independent variable. They were therefore ultimately excluded from the models.

has undergone a democratic transition, for example, it might be coded as a non- or developing democracy for some years and as a democracy for others.

Our models cover the years 1995–2013. This 18-year span was determined by the combined availability of our dependent, independent, and control variables. Data sets include between 166 and 178 countries; again, this is contingent on availability of data. For example, a given country might have data available for abortion policy, but not necessarily for health expenditures. Given the large number of states included in all models, there are no country selection issues within any of the sets. Data for the different models are comparable. Because our data set encompasses different countries over time, we use multilevel nested linear models. The multilevel models account for issues arising from the repeated measures in the data set that are not accounted for when standard fixed effects models are estimated (Quené and Van den Bergh, 2004; Hofmann, 1997; Gelman, 2006).

Scatter plots with trend lines are also generated for each dependent variable, examining its relationship with female political representation. The scatters use data from 2010. Every country is represented, with those categorized as non-democracies marked as circles, developing democracies as triangles, and developed democracies indicated by Xs. Trend lines are added to reflect simplified relationships. The aim of the figures is to allow us to detect general trends with the naked eye, which offers a useful visual representation of the data.

RESULTS

Table 4.2 presents the findings for abortion policy, separated by regime type. In the pooled model, as well as in the models for all three regime types, there was a significant and positive correlation between the rate of female legislative representation and the permissiveness of state abortion policy. This is confirmed in Figure 4.1. In the graph, all three regime types follow a visible positive trend, though the trends are stronger for some regime types than others. The linear trend lines confirm this.

Table 4.3 presents the findings for state education expenditures as a percentage of the total budget, based on regime type. As in the abortion models, there is a positive relationship between women's representation and education expenditures in all regime types and in the pooled model. This is reflected in Figure 4.2, which plots the scatter and trend lines between female representation and state education expenditures by regime type. For all three types of regimes examined, the scatter shows a positive relationship that can be seen with the naked eye. The trend lines reinforce this impression.

Table 4.4 presents the findings for state health expenditures. In a pooled model, there is a positive and significant correlation. When broken down by

TABLE 4.2 *Abortion Models*

	All	Non-Democracies	Semi-Democracies	Democracies
Female Legislators (%)	.008 (.001)***	.005 (.002)*	.006 (.003)*	.011 (.002)***
PPP	$7.95e^{-6}$ $(2.28e^{-6})$***	$4.15e^{-6}$ $(3.90e^{-6})$	$4.96e^{-6}$ $(6.54e^{-6})$	$.000$ $(3.03e^{-6})$***
Globalization Index	.008 (.002)***	.011 (.004)**	.004 (.003)	.002 (.003)
Number of Observations	2,793	709	521	1,563
Number of Groups	178	71	60	110
Constant	3.17 (.205)***	2.67 (.319)***	2.94 (.321)***	

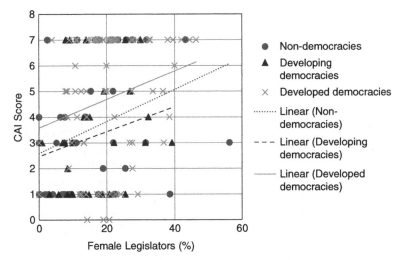

FIGURE 4.1: Women's Representation (%) and State Abortion Policy by Regime Type

regime type, there is a positive and significant correlation for nondemocracies and developing democracies. The relationship for democratic states is positive but not statistically significant. This is also reflected in Figure 4.3. The scatter for democratic countries does not reveal any clear pattern. The other two regime types also follow a less obvious pattern than found for the other two policy areas. The positive relationship found in the regression analysis is perhaps a result of effective controls. It might be visible outliers that affect the trend lines in the scatter.

TABLE 4.3 *Education Expenditures Models*

	All	Non-Democracies	Semi-Democracies	Democracies
Female Legislators (%)	.027 (.004)***	.015 (.007)*	.024 (.0123)*	.018 (005)***
PPP	$-6.69e^{-06}$ $(4.55e^{-6})$	$-.000 (7.55e^{-6})$	-.000 (.000)	$.000 (5.31e^{-6})$
Globalization Index	.01 (.004)	-.003 (.007)	.044 (.012)***	-.000 (.006)
Number of Observations	1,642	336	288	1,018
Number of Groups	166	57	47	104
Constant	3.76 (.259)***	4.35 .409)***	1.98 (.588)***	4.45 (.357)***

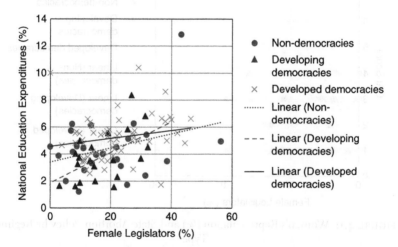

FIGURE 4.2: Women's Representation (%) and State Education Expenditures by Regime Type

There is no detectable pattern among the three dependent variables in terms of size of coefficient. The comparative size of the coefficient of the relationship between female representation and the outcome variables is not consistent. In other words, at least for the policy areas under consideration here, the number of female representatives in a democracy is not consistently more influential than in other regime types.

TABLE 4.4 *Health Expenditures Models*

	All	Non-Democracies	Semi-Democracies	Democracies
Female Leg (%)	.007 (.002)***	.012 (.003)***	.023 (.007)***	.000 (.002)
PPP	1.42e^{-6} (2.57e^{-6})	-8.05e^{-6} (4.36e^{-6})	.000 (000)	8.97e^{-6} (2.90
Globalization Index	.005 (.002)	.006 (.005)	-.005 (.006)	
Number of Observations	2,775	704	509	1,565
Number of Groups	177	70	59	110
Constant	2.2 (.165)***	2.28 (.277)***	2.79 (.358)***	2.02 (.227)***

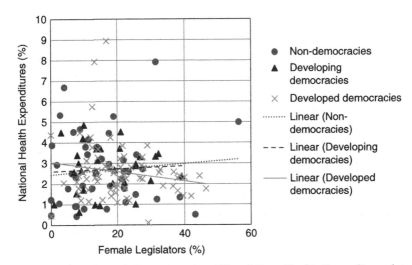

FIGURE 4.3: Women's Representation (%) and State Health Expenditures by Regime Type

DISCUSSION

As predicted by the third theoretical framework we developed, in all three of the outcome variables – abortion policy, education expenditures, and health expenditures – there was a correlation between the rate of female political representatives and policy output. The literature has often found that female

TABLE 4.5 *Significance of Coefficient on Number of Female Legislators*

	Abortion model	Education expenditures model	Health expenditures model
All Countries	*Significant*	*Significant*	*Significant*
Non-democracies Category 1 (Polity<0)	*Significant*	*Significant*	*Significant*
Developing Democracies Category 2 (Polity b/w 0–6)	*Significant*	*Significant*	*Significant*
Democracies Category 3 (Polity>6)	*Significant*	*Significant*	*Not Significant*

* Results are robust whether democracy is defined this way or based on Categories 1 (Polity<0), 2 (Polity b/w 0–6), and 3 (Polity>6).

legislators in democracies are likely to engage in policymaking in specific fields including health, education, and reproductive rights. They offer substantive representation in areas that disproportionately affect women or are traditionally considered "women's issues." Of course, reproductive rights disproportionally affect women as child bearers. Health and education policy disproportionately affect women as those who bear a disproportionate number of childcare tasks and those who are more likely to spend disposable income on childcare, including health and education (Tzannatos, 1999). There are no surprises or digressions from existing literature here.

The answer to our question emerges, though, when we separate countries by regime type. In nondemocracies and developing democracies, again, all three dependent variables significantly correlate with the rate of female political representation. There is some variation in results in democracies. In democratic regimes, there is a correlation between the rate of female representation for abortion policy and for education expenditures. There is no correlation for health care expenditures. As Table 4.5 summarizes, in 11 of the 12 models we estimated, the rate of female elected officials in parliament shows a statistically significant connection to the policy area examined. The significance is also in the anticipated direction.

We proposed three different theoretical frameworks explaining why women's political representation would at least appear to be leading to substantive representation. First, countries outside of the family of democracies may encourage female representation, and allow access to reproductive rights as a means of pandering to international norms promoted by IGOs such as the United Nations or the European Union. This might mean the simultaneous adoption of electoral gender quotas and more permissive abortion policy. Under such circumstances, we would see a correlation with abortion policy, but not necessarily with the other two variables of education and health. If this had been the pattern reflected in the results of our empirical models, we would have concluded that substantive representation was not truly maintained for women living outside of a democratic form of government. Yet, the results do not reflect such a pattern.

Under the second theoretical account developed above, even in non- or developing democracies, a general acceptance of gender equality and women's advancement would lead to a correlation between female representation and certain policies. Again, we hypothesized a correlation between female representation and abortion policy, but not education or health spending. This is because female representation and reproductive rights would be a direct reflection of attitude toward women and gender equality. Health and education spending are not directly related to women's welfare attitudes. Rather, they would reflect the extent to which female politicians were actually able to be influential. Therefore, if women were achieving political representation, but this representation was not in correlation with increased spending in these areas, again, we would have concluded that substantive representation was not truly the case for women outside of democracies. Again, such a pattern was not evident in the results of our models.

This brings us to the third theory proposed, which seems to gain the most support from the data and models estimated. As we theorize above, women may achieve substantive representation even in non- and developing democracies. If this were the case, we would expect a correlation between the rate of female representation and all three of our outcome variables for all three regime types examined. This indeed is what we find.

Given that our findings are significant for the three outcome variables in different regime types, we believe that even outside of democracies, women are indeed exercising substantive representation. The literature has found that women's representation correlates with policy outcomes in democracies, and we are able to show that the case for nondemocracies and developing democracies is similar. Of course, this does not eliminate the possibility of the first two explanations also being correct. They might exist simultaneously with substantive representation, hence strengthening the effect.

By including the education and health variables, though, we were able to better differentiate between disparate types of influences that might be at work over abortion policy in both democracies and nondemocracies. While abortion policy is affected by international norms (as we will further elaborate in Chapter 6), the findings here would imply that women representatives, in all regime types, have a significant effect on abortion policy. While Plotke (1997) originally related to representation only as a necessity of direct democratic regimes, we see that dimensions of representation can also have great significance in introducing democratic practice into nondemocracies.

This also speaks to the relevance of Pitkin's (2004) and Williams' (1998) models in all regime types, nondemocracies included. In the case of Pitkin, it implies that the connection between descriptive and substantive representation is maintained, even in non- and developing democracies. As for Williams' theory, the empirical patterns we identify emphasize the relevance of voice in providing memory. The importance of the representative in providing a voice relates directly to the fact that the representative also has the collective group memory. In this case, female representatives understand and express the importance of reproductive rights and access for women, because they are aware of its impact. This connection between voice and memory is maintained not just in democracies, the context Williams originally refers to. Rather, this connection seems to also exist beyond the realm of democracies.

Bringing quotas back into the discussion, it would be interesting to see how the introduction of electoral gender quotas might affect this connection between descriptive and substantive representation, and voice and memory, in different regime types.

There are reasons to believe that quotas might hinder the connection between the two types of representation. Women elected in a system with quotas may not associate their success with the constituency with whom they share characteristics, or may feel less likely to represent these constituent interests upon taking office. Put simply, when gender quotas are in place, having more women in decision-making positions should not necessarily be taken to mean that they made it through the support of a sympathetic electorate or an overarching societal belief in gender equality. The election of women representatives may not reflect constituents who are particularly sympathetic to the causes of women's rights. Rather, their election is a result of remedial policies. These representatives might not feel the obligation to provide substantive representation, nor will they necessarily associate their voice as political representatives with their identities as women and the memories entailed. We explore these ideas further in Chapter 6.

Quotas would also be a significant intervening factor in determining which of our three scenarios is at work. Within Williams' (1998) model of representation, for example, quotas are the first step in ensuring the necessary voice for the historically oppressed group. Quotas can be adopted by nondemocratic states, and indeed are often found in such countries. This begs the question of why nondemocratic countries would feel the need to introduce a democratic mechanism to improve representation. The answer often is that these countries adopt such democratic mechanisms as a means of signaling commitment to women's advancement or democracy, although largely at a symbolic level.

This corresponds directly with our first scenario in which nondemocratic states pander to the norms of the international community to gain benefits. If we separated regime types by countries that do and do not have quotas, might we get different results? Might the presence of quotas indicate that different scenarios are at play in different contexts? Though we chose not to include them in our models in this chapter, so as to more clearly focus on and elucidate the relationship between regime type and women's rate of representation, we return to this question in one of the case studies in the following chapter.

CONCLUSIONS

In order to identify a connection between descriptive and substantive representation and test the theoretical models developed, we estimated a battery of models juxtaposing abortion policy with other policy fields. We chose two types of policies that were commonly influenced by female representation in democracies, though they do not relate directly to gender equality or women's status: national education expenditures and national health expenditures. All three policies were tested for their correlation with the rate of women's political representation in nondemocracies, developing democracies, and developed democracies.

The findings in this chapter imply that even outside the context of democracies, a key variable at the level of the nation-state in the formation of abortion policy is the question of women representatives in government. All three policy areas – whether related directly or only tangentially to women's welfare – were significant in their correlation with women's representation. The policy areas where women generally exercise influence in democracies appear to also be sensitive to their influence in non- and developing democracies. This also implies that by paying attention to such dimensions of representation, we can identify opportunities for the democratic concept of representation, even in nondemocracies. This has important implications, as we show here, for the production of reproductive rights.

5

Reproductive Rights and the Nation-State: The Cases of New Zealand and Rwanda

Within the sphere of the state, we focus on the concept of representation as a critical factor in determining public policy in general and reproductive policy in particular. The extent to which political representatives promote the interests of different demographics and interest groups within the population depends on both regime type and the representatives themselves. Is the regime democratic? In other words, are its institutions designed to encourage political representatives to make policies that reflect the will of the people? Second, to what extent do the representatives reflect the demography of the state? The logic linking substantive and descriptive representation would suggest that representatives from various parts of society would be necessary in order to capture the desires and needs of those varied groups. Because of an expected connection between women's political incorporation and the promotion of women's issues, this is of particular importance for those looking to promote women's rights. The worldwide average for women in parliament in 2018 is 23.8% (IPU, 2018). In other words, women – who make up half the population everywhere – are heavily underrepresented in politics. It has always been this way. Indeed, the share of women representatives is better today than it ever was in the past. Still, levels of underrepresentation are staggering. If descriptive and substantive representation are indeed linked, as we would argue – and as the results of the previous chapter would imply – then the implications of this underrepresentation for women's agendas and issues are severe.

In Chapter 4, we looked at how the two factors of representation, regime type and substantive representation, were linked in their effects on state abortion policy. Were the abilities of the representatives to provide substantive representation connected to the nature of the regime? We found that even in nondemocracies, female representatives seem to provide substantive representation in the areas that are commonly of concern for women. Though this was left out of the empirical analysis, we also wanted to know if or how gender quotas might intervene in this relationship.

In the current chapter, we delve into two case studies. These case studies provide illustrative examples of many of the findings presented in Chapter 4. They also allow us to go deeper into the causal mechanisms underlying some of the political phenomena we are interested in, and thus go well beyond illustrating assertions from previous chapters. The case studies present our quantitative analyses and their results from a fresh perspective and in more detailed political, social, and economic contexts. They also address the issue of quotas, mentioned at several points in the book from a theoretical perspective, which has yet to be examined empirically.

First, we explore the case of Rwanda. Rwanda has the highest rate of female representation in parliament in the world. This is linked to quotas enacted in 2003. Nine short years after the implementation of quotas, and the ensuing monumental increase in female representation, Rwanda updated its abortion law, granting women much greater access to the procedure, at least on paper. In reality, a woman's access to abortion in Rwanda is still restricted. What can we learn from this discrepancy between de jure and de facto rights and from the Rwandese case more generally? Is there a connection between Rwanda's female representatives and its new laws? How does the Rwandan context as an authoritarian regime affect the production of reproductive rights in this country?

Our second case study in this chapter is New Zealand. New Zealand has, for almost 200 years, been a leader in promoting women's political rights. In fact, it was the first country, in 1893, to extend suffrage to women. For the last 20 years, it has also had far more female politicians than the global average, and has even had a handful of women serving as chief executives. That said, the state abortion policy has not been updated since 1977 and has been restrictive compared to the policy of states with similar political institutions, cultures, and social structures. In practice though, women in New Zealand seem to have little difficulty accessing abortion when necessary and there are virtually no incidents of clandestine abortions. Abortions in New Zealand are also free when deemed necessary. What does this de facto access to abortion tell us about the status of women in New Zealand? How might the presence of women in the legislature be dictating the outcomes on the ground?

The juxtaposition of these two cases is particularly instructive since they differ so dramatically in their contexts. Rwanda is an authoritarian state, characterized by a history of unstable regimes and conflict. Recently though, it has achieved an unprecedented number of female politicians thanks to electoral gender quotas and has made big changes in its state abortion policy.

New Zealand is a stable democracy that has had a gradual, though progressive, history of female leadership. With that in mind, there has been little change in this country's rate of female representation in the last three decades, and even less change in its state abortion policy. Access to reproductive health as well as the rate of illegal abortions in each country dramatically diverge.

As this is a book neither about New Zealand nor about Rwanda, we limit ourselves to aspects of the case studies that shed light on our specific discussion of state-level influences on abortion policymaking. Inevitably, we omit some facets. We believe, nonetheless, that even without going through the entire stories of the two countries, they can provide engaging and insightful case studies for our purposes.

These case studies will provide theoretical insight into the significance of top-down vs. bottom-up change, the significance of female leadership, and the impact of electoral gender quotas and fast-track vs. incremental change (Dahlerup & Freidenvall, 2005). They will also bring to life our findings from the previous chapter, regarding women's ability to influence even in less-than democratic contexts. To lay the groundwork, we will first look into the nature and history of the regimes, the countries' histories of women's political representation, and their modern practices of reproductive rights. We will then discuss how these historical and cultural contexts both reflect (and at times contradict) findings from previous chapters.

RWANDA: A REVOLUTION OF REPRESENTATION IN A CULTURE OF PATRIARCHY

Rwanda makes for a dramatic case study when discussing the impact of regime type and women's representation on public policy. Since declaring independence from colonial rule in 1962, Rwanda has experienced a chain of conflicts on the basis of ethnic divisions. Hutus and Tutsis – composing 84% and 15% of the Rwandan population, respectively – have fought for control of political institutions and resources throughout modern Rwandan history (Mutisi, 2012). Conflict reached its peak in the 1990s, with a civil war between 1990 and 1993, closely followed by a campaign of ethnic cleansing and genocide of the Tutsi population in 1994.

With the establishment of a new regime after the conflict of 1994 came a most dramatic turnaround regarding women's representation. For our purposes, we ask if and how all of this interacted with state abortion policy. Let us first understand the history of the regime and the conflict that led to the seeming revolution in women's political participation. This will lead to Rwanda's modern reproductive rights policy.

The regime

After years of European colonial intervention and U.N. involvement, in 1961 Rwanda declared itself a Republic. Its first democratic government was elected in 1962. Grégoire Kayibanda and the party for the Emancipation of Hutus, known as the Parmehutu party, ruled from 1962 to 1975, following an agenda of Hutu emancipation from the Tutsi aristocracy (Newbury, 1998; Mutisi, 2012).

In 1975, General Juvénal Habyarimana, who was then serving as chief of staff, staged a coup, seized power, and established the Hutu-dominated National Republican Movement for Democracy and Development (MRND). The MRND was established as the only legal party in Rwanda and governance was retained through continuous electoral fraud and totalitarian rule. Habyarimana largely continued the anti-Tutsi discriminatory practices implemented by his predecessor (Peter & Kibalama, 2006). The totalitarian order left the majority of Rwandans in extreme poverty (Gourevitch, 1998).

With the implementation of discriminatory legislation, Rwanda saw a mass Tutsi exodus. Most of these Tutsi exiles became refugees contributing to the gradual power consolidation of the Hutu majority. By the beginning of the 1990s, around 480,000 largely Tutsi Rwandans were said to have become refugees in neighboring Burundi, Uganda, Zaire, and Tanzania.

The Rwandan Patriotic Front (RPF) was established within the community of Tutsi exiles in Uganda. This group had the stated goal of reforming the Rwandan government, with an emphasis on enforcing political power sharing. In October 1990, the RFP sparked a civil war when it launched an extensive attack from Uganda, sending more than 7,000 fighters into Rwanda. Along with military action, the Hutu government responded with a propaganda campaign labeling all Tutsis – inside and outside of Rwanda – as enemies of the state (U.N. Outreach Programme on the Rwanda Genocide, 2007).

A peace agreement was signed in 1993 and the United Nations Assistance Mission for Rwanda (UNAMIR) was sent into the country with the mandate to assist with peacekeeping and humanitarian activities. These efforts were quickly abandoned when President Habyarimana was killed after his plane was shot down in April 1994 (BBC Rwanda Profile, 2018). Though it was never discovered who was responsible, the event triggered a highly organized government-backed genocide and ethnic cleansing campaigns against all Tutsis, as well as moderate Hutus (Peter & Kibalama, 2006). In response, the RPF, under Paul Kagame, entered Rwanda in full force and by July had regained control over the entire country. Within four months between April and July, an estimated 800,000 people were killed, an estimated 150,000 to 200,000 women were raped (although by some estimates the number of women raped is significantly higher – as many as 400,000 [Buvinic, Gupta, Casabonne, & Verwimp, 2013]), and 1.4 million people, both Hutus and Tutsis were displaced (U.N. Outreach Programme on the Rwanda Genocide, 2007; Tadjo, 2010; Schabas, 1996). At the end of this horrific period, Kagame established a unity government, including a Hutu president.

Despite some continued tension, the Kagame regime has largely succeeded in maintaining political and civil stability. The regime has initiated economic stabilization and recovery programs, with the nation's gross domestic product steadily climbing since 1994. That said, Kagame has been accused of a range of civil right violations, including oppressing dissent, corrupting election practices, controlling private media, suppressing independent civil society organizations, and destroying potential opposition parties (Tadjo, 2010; Uvin, 2001; Reyntjens, 2011; Bauer and Burnet, 2013).

Since its inception as a state in 1962, Rwanda has never been a democracy. Instead, it has always found itself under some form of authoritarian rule. During the Kayibanda period (1962–1975), Rwanda had an average polity score of −5.[1] In the Habyarimana period (1975–1993), it consistently had a score of −7. Post-1994 Rwanda has been inching toward greater democratic practice, but progress has been slow. The average score between 1995 and 2017 has been −4, although since 2000 Rwanda has more commonly been given a score of −3. Especially after 2003, when the new constitution was instated, Rwanda has consistently received a score of −3. While still far from a democracy, Rwanda has been steadily moving away from extreme authoritarian structure and practices.

Rwanda's post-genocide politics and the changing roles for women

In part because of changing norms but also because of substantial demographic changes, the role and position of women in post-genocide Rwanda has had some marked differences from the pre-1994 era. Rwanda underwent a significant demographic shift within 100 days during the genocide in 1994.

---

[1]   The Polity IV data series (Marshall and Gurr, 2017) assigns countries scores ranging from −10 to 10, with −10 being hereditary monarchy and 10 being consolidated democracy. Scores are made up of multiple components that reflect characteristics of executive recruitment, constraints on executive authority, political competition, civil rights and civil liberties, and institutionalized qualities of governing authority. Based on Marshall and Gurr's (2017) own scale application, scores of zero or less are considered nondemocracies. Scores greater than 0 and less than 7 are categorized as developing democracies. Countries with scores 7–10 are considered democracies.

Of the estimated 800,000 people killed, men were disproportionately targeted. With the end of the conflict, many of those involved with the killing were either jailed or fled the country. Of these military and paramilitary figures, again, most were men. While initial claims that up to 70% of the post-genocide population was female were most likely exaggerated, it is clear that the number of men in the population was, post-1994, significantly less than the number of women (De Walque & Verwimp, 2009). This was especially true within the age demographic of 20- to 29-year-olds, a population critical for the rebuilding of the state and its economy. According to Hamilton (2000), there were only 69 men for every 100 women in the age group of 25 to 29.

Besides the extreme disproportion between men and women, there was another demographic dimension to the genocide: it disproportionately affected the urban and educated. The main victims of the genocide, the Tutsi, came from a higher socio economic, urban background (De Walque & Verwimp, 2009). The genocide and mass flight also left Rwanda's political elite a skeleton of its formal self. For example, only 20 of the country's 785 judges remained after 1994 (Hamilton, 2000). Thus, faced not only with the loss of a great number of men, but with the loss of the country's most highly educated human capital, Rwanda's women were pushed to the front to take on a more significant part in rebuilding their country. This meant taking on many traditionally male roles (Devlin & Elgie, 2008). Out of necessity, women became household leaders and filled many of the multitudes of vacancies in the labor market (Buvinic, Gupta, Casabonne, & Verwimp, 2013; Schindler, 2010). This was a radical change for Rwandan women, few of whom had higher education or career experience. In pre-genocide Rwanda, it was rare for a woman to carry on a profession other than running the house or working in subsistent agriculture. Before 1994, women's general societal status was low, and their lives were defined by poverty, lack of education, and poor health.

Along with their new roles in the family and labor market, women also had to fill the political sphere. The former political elite was in jail, exile, or banished from political circles. The lack of men in the general population meant that there were few promising male candidates to take such positions.

Representation of women and quotas in Rwanda

In 2003, nine years after the genocide, Rwanda elected a new national parliament. After the election women occupied 49% of seats, and Rwanda took Sweden's place as the country with the highest percentage of women in its legislature (Doan, 2010). In fact, every year since 2004, Rwanda has topped the list of states for highest number of female parliamentarians (Devlin & Elgie,

2008). In 2018, 49 out of 80 (61.3%) seats in the lower house, and 10 out of 26 (38.5%) seats in the upper house were held by women. This amounts to a combined 50% of all seats in parliament for women (Akwei, 2017). For comparison, the worldwide average in 2018 is 23% of women in national parliaments. This also represents a major leap compared to women's representation in Rwanda pre-2003. Although women had been allowed to run for office since state emancipation in 1961, female parliamentary participation was at most 18% before 1994. Between 1994 and 2003 it reached a maximum of 25.7% (Powley, 2006).

What happened in those nine short years between 1994 and 2003? How did a country characterized by a traditional patriarchal society – and ravaged by one of the most horrific genocides in history – seemingly construct the most gender-equitable and emancipated political system in the world?

The answer lies largely in shifts occurring at some of the highest echelons of state government in the early 2000s. While Rwanda's transition to democracy is said to have started as early as 1989 – and its first female prime minister, Agathe Uwilingiymana, was appointed in 1993 – sweeping political pro-women reforms were only implemented in the aftermath of the genocide. These reforms were initiated by Paul Kagame, the president of Rwanda since 2000 and its de facto leader since the end of hostilities in 1994. They were part of wider reconstruction efforts of his ruling political party, the RPF. Efforts by Kagame and his administration to forge a new national unity and to build a "New Rwanda" that would leave behind the genocidal ideology of the past were the key motivation. In its effort to integrate women, the RPF created a ministry of gender, organized women's councils throughout different levels of government, and instituted electoral gender quotas, canonized within the 2003 Rwandan Constitution (Burnet, 2008; Powley, 2006).

Drafted by an RPF-dominated government in 2003, the state's new Constitution slated 30% of seats for women in all decision-making organs, including the bicameral parliament and political parties. Women were chosen through a special electoral college of voters from women's councils at the local and district levels (Burnet, 2011). Chapter 2, Article 9, of the Rwandan Constitution of 2003 states that "building a state governed by the rule of law, a pluralistic democratic government, equality of all Rwandans and between women and men reflected by ensuring that women are granted at least thirty per cent of posts in decision making organs." Article 75, Subsection 2, states that of the 80 members of the lower parliament, there will be "twenty-four (24) women elected by specific councils in accordance with the State administrative entities." In the Senate, the upper house of parliament, Article 82 states,

"The Senate shall be composed of twenty-six (26) Senators serving for a term of eight (8) years and at least thirty per cent (30 %) of them shall be women."

In addition to their role in electing women for parliament, women's councils were tasked to "promote women's interests in development, to advise local governance structures on women's issues and to teach women how to participate in politics" (Burnet, 2008, p. 368). As a result, already in 2003, the set minimum quota of 30% was exceeded by an additional 18%. In 2013 it was exceeded by an astounding 34%. The government also announced that it would advance education for girls and that women would be given main leadership roles in government and other high-ranking state positions (U.N. Rwanda, 2013).

Mr. Kagame has been a leading force in integrating women and mainstreaming gender into Rwandan politics (Burnet, 2008; Powley 2006). However, this top-down introduction of gender equality has had trouble finding footing within Rwandan society. This development toward greater gender equality was not spearheaded by emancipated women, as is often the case in societies undergoing transition in gender roles. The enforcement of Kagame's dramatic policy changes was more a testament to his strong leadership, broad popular mandate, and authoritarian regime (Wallace, Haerpfer, & Abbott, 2009). While grassroots movements and civil society women's organizations predating the 1994 genocide did exist, they did not seem to play a significant role in advancing the will of women or advancing female representatives in politics (Burnet, 2008).

In fact, given that the change was top-down, with reform initiated by leaders and not society, there has been a certain degree of societal backlash. As men in Rwanda fight against changing gender roles, there has been an increase in domestic violence and sexual and physical partner abuse (Finnoff, 2012; La Mattina, 2017). While it is rare that the state is the one that initiates a campaign for greater democratic values, rather than the people, it is predicted that popular acceptance of such policies will be hard to accomplish (Wallace, Haerpfer, & Abbott, 2009). Such a phenomenon can be found in a National Public Radio interview with Rwandan researcher Justine Uvuza:

> Justine Uvuza (. . .) worked for a while for the Kagame government promoting Rwanda's pro-women policies. She was curious how much progress had been made. So when she was getting her Ph.D. at Newcastle University, she returned to Rwanda to interview female politicians about their lives – not just their public positions but their private lives, with their husbands and children. She found with rare exception that no matter how powerful these women were in public, that power didn't extend into their own homes.

"One told me how her husband expected her to make sure that his shoes were polished, the water was put in the bathroom for him, his clothes were ironed," Justine says. And this husband wanted not only his shoes laid out in the morning, but his socks placed on top of the shoes. And he wanted it done by his wife, the parliamentarian.

Justine heard countless stories like this – women were still expected to perform even ceremonial domestic duties. It was rarely an option to out-source such tasks to a maid or get your husband to shoulder more work at home. Some women feared violence from their husbands if they didn't comply with these expectations, and one said that she had felt so trapped, she had contemplated suicide.

Justine says that for some of these women, the very real strides that they were making outside the home could feel less like liberation and more like a duty to be fulfilled. Being a "good Rwandan," as she termed it in her research, meant being both patriotic – serving her country through her public work and career – but also being docile and serving her husband. As a result, Justine said, a female politician could stand up in parliament, advocating for issues like stronger penalties for sexual violence and subsidized maxi-pads for the poor, but find herself scared to speak out about the oppression in her own home.

And so Justine would end each interview asking these female legislators what seemed to her to be an obvious question: Would they support a Rwandan women's movement? A movement to change not just the public roles for women but to re-evaluate gender relations on all levels? Would these powerful Rwandan women be willing to stand under the banner of feminism?

Almost all of the women said no. Feminism? "That's not Rwandan," they told her. "That's for Westerners." (January 10, 2018)

Though within the Kagame government and RPF-dominated state institutions these women may have found power and acceptance, in the private sphere and civil society gender expectations have not changed. As mentioned above, female leaders have seen a backlash. In sum, political incorporation of women is a complicated story in Rwanda, one which mere statistics for numbers of representatives would not divulge.

Beyond political incorporation and its acceptance, the next big question that interests us concerns the translation of descriptive representation into substantive representation. Were the women who achieved power able to exercise influence? One clear alternative would be that they turned into puppets of the political party appointing them. Indeed, most of the female MPs are members of the RPF. That said, the vast majority of MPs are RPF members as well. The political system in Rwanda is such that it functions almost entirely as a single-party state. Outside of the RPF, women find limited ability to influence. The following excerpt, brought by Marima (2017) from an interview with Rwandan politician Diane Shima Rwigara, provides some illustrations of women's limited ability to exercise independent influence within the Rwandan state structure:

> Diane Shima Rwigara, 35, was the first Rwandan woman to run for president as an independent before she was disqualified. The fact that Rwanda has the world's highest proportion of women in Parliament does not mean the country is comfortable with women in power, she says. Kagame may be credited with ending a horrific genocide and improving the country's economic growth and maternal mortality rates, but Rwigara warns that the president's increasingly authoritarian stance could further oppress women, rather than empower them.
>
> "I don't believe in the lie being sold to the world that Rwandan women have a voice – we don't," she says. "We're only allowed to do or say certain things as dictated by the ruling party. If you don't, you pay a high price."
>
> For Rwigara, that price was her bid for the presidency. Her nomination was excluded when the electoral commission said she didn't have enough names to endorse her candidacy, a charge she rejects. "When I finally submitted my papers, the number of signatures was almost double the required number of 650 – I had over 1,100 signatures," she says. "If Rwanda was a place fair to women I would not have been treated the way I was while trying to run."
>
> The harassment didn't end there. Rwigara says the ruling party tried to discredit her by releasing fake nude pictures online, but Kagame's RPF denied any involvement. Some of her family's businesses have been shut down and bank accounts frozen without justification, she says, while members of her movement have been temporarily jailed and threatened by the police.

History and Development of Abortion Rights in Rwanda

Until 1977, it was illegal for women in Rwanda to have an abortion unless the woman's life was at risk. This law originated in Rwanda's colonial heritage. Rwanda's Criminal Code was based on the 1940 Penal Code of the Belgian Congo under which abortion was illegal unless the women's life was in danger. A new, somewhat liberalized Penal Code was enacted in 1977, stating that if two doctors certify that a women's health is at serious risk through the pregnancy, an abortion performed by a state physician in a public hospital can be granted (U.N. Economic and Social Affairs, 2002). The new code made it somewhat easier to access abortion, but still limited it to cases of risk to the mother's life or serious risk to health. Illegally performed abortions carried heavy penalties, ranging from 5 to 15 years in jail for any health professional who assisted or performed an abortion, and 2 to 5 years for any woman who induced or consented to an abortion. The code stated that "every child has the right to live from the time of conception. Deliberate abortion is prohibited except in circumstances provided for by law" (Kimenyi, 2011, para 2). The code mandated that any individual involved in conducting an abortion, including the woman, health professional, or even family members who encourage abortion, is subject to punishment by law (Basinga, Moore, Singh, Carlin, Birungi, & Ngabo, 2012). Over the years, pressure to maintain strict abortion laws has come from pro-natalist and religious groups (U.N. Economic and Social Affairs, 2002).

In the wake of the civil war and genocide of the 1990s, the national perspective on abortion was re-evaluated. There were estimated to be between 2,000 and 5,000 "unwanted children," or children born as a result of rape at the time of the conflict. There was also a massive increase in the number of women seeking abortions or suffering from the outcomes of clandestine abortions (U.N. Economic and Social Affairs, 2002, p. 61). On the other hand, the country was also reeling from the loss of hundreds of thousands of lives. The nation was torn between the demographic aftermath of the war, the need to replenish the population, and the need to recognize the recent history of unprecedented sexual violence against women. Side by side with the realities of the aftermath of war, Rwanda has long had to deal with a rapidly growing population, partially as a result of low rates of contraceptive use. This was an additional source of pressure on religious and pro-natalist groups to relax any stances against contraception and abortion. The ground was shifting, however, not just from within. At the regional and international levels as well, changes were taking shape.

In 2004, Rwanda signed and ratified the Protocol of the African Charter of Human and People's Rights on the Rights of Women in Africa, also known as the Maputo Protocol. This African Union treaty is the main legal instrument for the protection of women's rights in Africa (Wandia, 2004). We discuss the Maputo Protocol in great detail in Chapter 7 of this book. In a nutshell, though, among other things, this treaty obligates ratifying countries to legalize abortions in cases of sexual assault, rape, incest, and where the continued pregnancy endangers the mental and physical health of the mother or the life of the mother or the fetus. When Rwanda signed the treaty in 2004, they issued a reservation concerning Article 14(2)(c) concerning abortion. No official written explanation was provided so as to why the reservation was stipulated (Nabaneh, 2012).

For Rwanda, the reservation on Article 14(2)(c) in practice meant that the national law on abortion remained highly restrictive, only permitting the procedure when two doctors certified that the pregnancy poses a threat to a woman's life or causes serious danger to her health. In other words, there was little change between the mandates of the 1977 Criminal Code and the legal reality after signing the Maputo Protocol as far as reproductive health was concerned.

In 2012, however, Rwanda updated its criminal code on abortion. Women are now able to access abortion under conditions of rape, incest, forced marriage, or threat to the health or life of the mother (Guttmacher Institute, 2013). Despite this substantial de jure change, in practice, access to abortion is still extremely restricted. It is not enough that a woman and her doctor agree that an abortion is necessary and that the legal criteria are met. An intermediary court must give final approval. This introduces red tape and techno-bureaucratic challenges into the process of seeking an abortion. For example, in 2017 a 14-year-old girl was gang-raped and became pregnant. Because she did not file her case in time (within 15 days of the rape) she was denied an abortion. Another recent teenage rape survivor filed on time, but it took eight months for the court to return an answer. Needless to say, by that time it was too late. In both cases, the teenage rape victims were forced to deliver the child (Rwirahira, 2018). Since 2015, the Rwandan government has debated further revisions to the penal code in general and specifically on the issue of abortion. Yet, no further modifications have been made (Rwirahira, 2018; Kwibuka, 2017).

The correlation between an increase in women's representation and the change in abortion policy makes a strong case for the argument tested in the quantitative analyses in the previous chapter. This is a case for the relation between descriptive and substantive representation. In the context of women's rights and the production of reproductive health, an increase in the number of women representatives, even as a result of the implementation of legislative quota policies, would translate into substantive improvement for women. More progressive abortion legislation would pass in a legislature, like the Rwandan bicameral house, where more women legislators are present. The fact that Rwanda ratified the Maputo Protocol but submitted a reservation only strengthens this conclusion. Even when the country is less influenced by the constraints of international law, its women members of parliament would carry the political sway leading to progressive abortion policy. Indeed, our findings suggest that the change in Rwandan law did not come as a result of international pressure or ratification of an international treaty. With its reservation, Rwanda's government relieved itself of the pressure to adopt the protocol's position on abortion. It seems that substantive representation could be key for the liberalization of abortion policy.

The anecdotal evidence also strongly points away from changes in society as accounting for this new stance on reproductive rights. It is not that a sudden embrace of equality in Rwandan society led to this change. The society continued to be patriarchal and due to the backlash mentioned above, in certain ways women became more subject to traditional gender roles and patriarchal power dynamics. Yet, the Kagame regime, with its pro-women position, may very well have left women room to practice substantive representation at least in the political arena.

The case study of Rwanda leaves some important questions open. First, the authoritarian nature of the regime as reflected in the interview with Ms. Diane Shima Rwigara raises questions about how much power politicians have in Rwanda and the extent to which state policies are dictated by the party. Perhaps not all female leaders can exercise substantive representation. Instead, it might be the case that only those associated with the RPF are free to do so in any meaningful way. While this does not stand in direct contrast with our key contentions, it does imply that we need to look more closely at the makeup and nature of the political inclusion of women before declaring that they can exercise substantive representation. Second, this case study underscores the importance of the historical context. In the case of Rwanda, the move to change abortion policy was also influenced by the history of sexual violence. The large number of children born as a result of wartime rape may have been the tipping point behind the government's move to liberalize abortion policy. This does not refute the argument about substantive representation, as the presence of female politicians certainly brought additional attention to this issue. What it does, however, is introduce more complexity into an already complicated story.

NEW ZEALAND: LEADING THE CHARGE IN WOMEN'S REPRESENTATION, LAGGING IN PERMISSIVENESS OF ABORTION POLICY

New Zealand has stood as one of the most stable continuous democracies in modern history, as well as a state that has led global trends in women's political rights and representation. It was the first state to grant women suffrage and to allow women to run for office. New Zealand has had numerous female prime ministers. It reached a rate of 30% of women in parliament in the mid-1990s and has consistently maintained this rate for most of the last two decades.

Parallel to this history, though, abortion law in New Zealand has not always advanced with its rate of women's representation. Until the 1970s, New Zealand's abortion law was extremely restrictive. Indeed, to this day, it lacks the on-demand accessibility typical to most developed Western democracies. While there are legal limitations on abortion, de facto legal conditions in New Zealand leave considerable room for access. Indeed, resort to illegal abortion is very rare.

The Regime

New Zealand was first inhabited by ancestors of the indigenous Maori, who arrived by canoe sometime between 1,200 AD and 1,300 AD. In order to focus on the institutions that laid the basis for the modern New Zealand government, let us fast-forward to the eighteenth century. Throughout the 1760s and 1770s, British explorer James Cook traveled the country and mapped the New Zealand coastline. By 1815, the first British missionaries had arrived to establish a colonial British presence. By 1840, British colonial rule was officially established in New Zealand. In 1907, New Zealand became a dominion within the British Empire and, 40 years later in 1947, it gained independence (BBC News, 2018).

The institutional design of the New Zealand government was shaped in 1856. Other than changing its status regarding British rule, there have been few major changes in the system of government in New Zealand since the middle of the nineteenth century. While there is a governor-general who represents the queen, de facto political power is vested in the prime minister and Parliament. Established in 1854, the New Zealand Parliament is one of the oldest continually functioning legislatures in the world. New Zealand had a bicameral legislature until 1951, when it was replaced by a unicameral legislature consisting of the House of Representatives only (Martin, 2015). New Zealand is, and has for most of its modern history been, considered a democracy. That said, the country's policies toward and treatment of indigenous people have often compromised its standing as a full democracy for all of its people. Since 1869, Parliament has had 4 reserved seats for Maori representatives, which was expanded in 2002 to 7 out of 120 seats.

Women's Representation in New Zealand

New Zealand has been groundbreaking in its history of women's political participation. The history of women in politics in New Zealand can be traced back to the year 1893, when governor Lord Glasgow signed a new Electoral Act that granted universal suffrage. With this Act, New Zealand became the first state to offer women the right to vote. At that time, it observed limited self-rule under the New Zealand Constitution Act of 1852, which established a system of representative government. Before 1893, only male British subjects over the age of 21, who were land owners or paid a given amount a year in rent, and who were not serving prison time for serious criminal offenses were allowed to vote. While this officially did not exclude Maori men, they were de facto excluded, as communal landholding did not count toward the criteria of landownership (Grimshaw, 1972; New Zealand Ministry of Culture and Heritage, 2016).

The campaign for women's suffrage in New Zealand was part of a worldwide movement for the right of women to vote, as part of the first-wave feminist movement. Civil society leaders and organizations played critical roles in the campaign for suffrage. For example, the Women's Christian Temperance Union (WCTU) had 10 local branches set up in New Zealand by 1885, with more than 600 women enrolled as members. As a force for women's suffrage, this organization argued that women could bring morality into democratic politics and protect not only women's rights but also children and the family. Rather than contradict the prevalent notion that politics was "outside women's 'natural sphere' of the home and family, it changed the rhetoric by framing politics as a legitimate forum for women's role as mother and caretaker. It placed women's activity in politics as a part of 'moral motherhood'" (Grimshaw, 2000, p. 555). Civil society leaders such as Kate Sheppard and Mary Ann Müller were also critical in the New Zealand suffrage movement. Already in 1893, the first year women exercised their right to vote, their voting turnout was 85%, 15% higher than that of their male compatriots. This reflected women's enthusiasm for their newly gained right, which came after almost two decades of campaigning by women's organizations and leaders (Tribble, 2018b; Grimshaw, 1972).

As a result of this massive movement toward political incorporation of women, in 1893 Elizabeth Yates was elected to become the first-ever female mayor in the British Empire. Yet, in the years after suffrage was granted, little changed concerning the way parliament was run. The same was true for the status of women in New Zealand overall. Gradual change was only observed after the National Council of Women (NCW) was founded in 1896. The council aimed to build upon the achievement of women's suffrage, and to continue their political agenda. Here, multiple accomplishments were achieved including, though not limited to, raising the age of consent from 14 to 16 in 1896 and securing women the right to run and serve in the House of Representatives in 1919. While several women ran for office, it was not until 14 years later, in 1933, that the first female MP, Elizabeth McCombs, actually took her seat in parliament (Brookes, 2016). While this was followed by minor ceremonial changes in the functioning and procedures of the House, the sweeping reforms and drastic changes that many suffragettes envisioned failed to materialize (Tribble, 2018b).

In 1941, state law was changed to allow women to become members of the Legislative Council, and the first woman was appointed five years later in 1946. The first female Cabinet minister was appointed in 1947. Despite these early achievements, throughout the 1950s and 1960s there was little growth in the rate of female political representation.

Scholarship is divided on the reasons why it took so long for women in New Zealand to take advantage of such unique political freedoms, certainly in a historically comparative perspective. Sir Lady Stout, wife of New Zealand's thirteenth prime minister, Robert Stout, wrote in 1914 that "New Zealand women were emancipated before they realised the great power and responsibility they now had on their hands." The women of New Zealand failed to recognize their monumental political achievements in legislating for political representation. Along the same lines, Grimshaw (1972) stresses that women

> . . . did not enter public life in large numbers, they failed to compete favorably with men in the professions and industry, or to assume their share of responsibility in government and political life. They opted instead to retain the private family structure, to rear their children in their own homes in which increasingly high standards of living absorbed the free time which modern appliances afforded. (p. 122)

Such perspectives fail to account for social and practical obstacles that often stand in the way of women's political participation. The reality, though, was still such that only in the late twentieth century did women more vigorously take advantage of their political privileges in New Zealand, at least as far as elected positions in government were concerned.

In the 1980s, women increasingly started taking on senior positions in parliament and in the Cabinet. In 1989, Helene Clark of the Labour Party became the first female deputy prime minister. In the mid-1990s, women MPs occupied 30% of the seats in parliament. In 1997, 104 years after women gained suffrage, New Zealand had its first female prime minister, Jenny Shipley. In comparison, the culturally similar Australia – where the Commonwealth Franchise Act enabled women to vote in 1902 – elected its first woman as prime minister more than a decade later in 2010. In 1999, Shipley lost the race for prime minister to Helen Clark, who became the country's first elected female prime minister (Curtin, 1997).[2] Clark served three consecutive terms until 2008.

Since 1996, the rate of female parliamentarians in New Zealand has hovered around 30%. It reached a record high of 38.4% in 2017, with the election of the 52nd Parliament. This included the appointment of Jacinda Ardern of the Labour Party as prime minister (Hurley, 2017). Like Rwanda, New Zealand's rate of women parliamentarians is consistently above the global average.

History and Development of Abortion Rights in New Zealand

Before 1977, abortion was a criminal act in New Zealand. Until that point, the New Zealand law was based on the United Kingdom Offences against the Person Act 1861, whose text New Zealand adopted in 1866. Sections 58 and 59 of the Act specify the offense of self-abortion or providing abortion services (Naughton, 2017). Articles 58–59 of the Person Act (1861) state:

> 58. Every woman, being with child, who, with intent to procure her own miscarriage, shall unlawfully administer to herself any poison or other noxious thing, or shall unlawfully use any instrument or other means whatsoever with the like intent, and whosoever, with intent to procure the miscarriage of any woman, whether she be or be not with child, shall unlawfully administer to her or cause to be taken by her any poison or other noxious thing, or shall unlawfully use any instrument or other means whatsoever with the like intent, shall be guilty of felony, and being convicted thereof shall be liable to be kept in penal servitude for life.
>
> 59. Whosoever shall unlawfully supply or procure any poison or other noxious thing, or any instrument or thing whatsoever, knowing that the same is intended to be unlawfully used or employed with intent to procure the miscarriage of any woman, whether she be or be not with child, shall be guilty of a misdemeanor, and being convicted thereof shall be liable to be kept in penal servitude ..."

In 1893, the law was altered and the updated Criminal Code Act reduced the punishment to a maximum seven-year prison sentence. The Crimes Act of 1961 slightly altered abortion law, allowing abortion to save the life of the mother. Section 182- "killing unborn child" states:

(1) Everyone is liable to imprisonment for a term not exceeding 14 years who causes the death of any child that has not become a human being in such

---

[2] Shipley was not elected directly but rather became prime minister by becoming the ruling National Party's new leader.

a manner that he or she would have been guilty of murder if the child had become a human being.

(2) No one is guilty of any offence who before or during the birth of any child causes its death by means employed in good faith for the preservation of the life of the mother.

Public debate in New Zealand increased after a more liberal law on abortion was passed in the United Kingdom in 1967 and Australia in 1969. The permissive abortion law of Australia also made it possible for New Zealand women to travel to Australia for an abortion (n.a., 2014).

A significant change came about in 1977, when the Crimes Acts 1961 was reformed. Abortion was then permitted up to 20 weeks on the grounds of threat to the mother's life, threat to the mother's physical or mental health, in the case of an impaired fetus, in case of rape or incest, or if the mother had any pre-existing mental impairments. All of these considerations could also be put in the context of the age of the mother, considering whether she was near the beginning or the end of "child bearing years" (U.N. Economic and Social Affairs, 2002). These conditions were further established in the Contraception, Sterilisation and Abortion Act 1977. The new laws created a system in which a woman would need the approval of a three-person committee, which could confirm that she fit the criteria set by law for an abortion. With such approval, abortions could be received for free at national public hospitals.

Since 1977, little change has been made in New Zealand's abortion legislation, which is still largely based on the 1961 and 1977 Acts. In 2012, The U. N. committee overseeing the implementation of CEDAW, which New Zealand ratified in 1985, recommended that the country look to simplify abortion laws. In 2016, the same committee called New Zealand abortion laws "convoluted" (Edmond, 2016). According to Terry Bellamak, president of Abortion Law Reform Association of New Zealand (ALRANZ), at present the three biggest obstacles to safe abortions are "lack of accessibility, poor integration of medical abortions, and delay in accessing care" (2018, para. 3), which in her opinion are all a result of outdated abortion laws in the country. It should be noted that many women are able to access abortion pursuant to the Mental Health Clause in the legislation by claiming that the pregnancy and birth would cause mental stress and illness. Anti-abortion groups have lamented this use of the clause, claiming it to be an abuse of the original law (Singh, Remez, Sedgh, Kwokand, & Onda, 2018; Family First Lobby Press Release, 2008).

In 2017, abortion also became a platform issue during the elections when Prime Minister Jacinda Ardern declared she would aim to remove abortion from the Crimes Act, which had remained unchanged since 1977 (Roy,

2017). Since then, a law commission has been established to review alternatives to the current law and how abortion can be treated as a health issue in the future. Various interest groups from both the pro-life and pro-choice camps, religious groups, as well as other members from civil society have been encouraged to provide their input (Te Aka Matua o te Ture, 2018). The director of Family First NZ, a conservative national Christian lobby group, stated that legalizing abortion "denies the humanity of the baby and creates inconsistency with other legislation which clearly recognizes the rights of the unborn child" (Picken, 2018). This was in line with the statement submitted by the country's Catholic bishops, who stressed that life began at conception. On the other hand, organizations such as Family Planning NZ and ALRANZ released statements in which they label the current law as outdated as well as morally wrong and dangerous to women's lives (Picken, 2018).

The New Zealand case study raises interesting questions about the quantitative findings in the previous chapter. As New Zealand is a democracy, the connection between descriptive and substantive representation is taken as a given. However, the increase in women's representation since the 1990s has not correlated with change in abortion policy. In fact, there has been little liberalization in abortion policy in New Zealand since 1977. This has been the case despite pressure from international organizations and changes made in countries with similar cultural and socioeconomic profiles. Does this leave New Zealand as an outlier in the theoretical framework we develop in this book?

Rather than being an outlier, this case study demonstrates several additional variables that need to be taken into consideration. Overall, rates of abortion in New Zealand are low. In developed parts of the world, the average rate is 27 to every 1,000 women ages 15 to 44 in the population. In New Zealand, the rate of abortion in 2017 was 13.7 per every 1,000 women ages 15 to 44 in the population, and overall rates of abortion have been in decline since 2007 (Davison, 2018; Stats NZ Tatauranga Aotearoa, 2018). The rate of unsafe abortions in New Zealand is negligible (Haddad & Nour, 2009).

These low numbers might be related to the availability of contraception in the state. Contraceptive rights in New Zealand are extensive for both women and men, and government funding and subsidies make contraception widely available (Smyth, 2000). One possible explanation for the lack of policy change is that permissive abortion policy is not high on New Zealand women's agenda, as relatively few women have a need to resort to this option. Indeed, a 2015 U.N. report titled *Trends in Contraceptive Use Worldwide* found that levels of contraceptive use in New Zealand were high by Western standards[3].

The lack of pressure to change abortion policy might be compounded by the fact that despite a policy that is technically restrictive, the interpretation of this policy has been quite liberal (Singh, Remez, Sedgh, Kwokand, & Onda, 2018; Family First Lobby Press Release, 2008). The clause that allows women an abortion on grounds of mental health concerns has been used and accepted quite liberally. While de jure there are restrictions on access to abortion, de facto it would seem that every woman can access abortion if she so chooses. While we do not see the expected correlation between the rate of female politicians and the permissiveness of abortion policy, certain evidence does point in this direction. For instance, Prime Minister Jacinda Ardern and her Labour party campaigned in 2017 on a platform that included abortion law reform. They proposed that abortion be treated as a health issue and removed from the Crimes Act. A proposal to such an effect is likely to reach the New Zealand Parliament in 2019 (Davison, 2018; Moir, 2018).

DISCUSSION

The case studies of New Zealand and Rwanda illustrate the quantitative findings presented elsewhere in this book, and in particular in the previous chapter, and allow us to delve into the causal mechanisms that underlie these phenomena. At the same time, however, the findings for each of those two countries separately and certainly their juxtaposition raise new and interesting questions relating to our discussions thus far.

The case studies of Rwanda and New Zealand raise interesting issues that need to be considered when addressing the correlation between representation and regime type and the production of reproductive rights in those two countries as well as more broadly. First, these cases demonstrate the relevance of the forces of change. Shifts may happen as top-down or as bottom-up. In Rwanda, the call for greater gender equality came from government leaders and, specifically, from President Kagame himself. The Rwandan case adds complexity to the question of representation, in particular in the case of the political efficacy of female politicians that come from outside the authoritarian regime's ruling political party. Our theoretical framework did not directly account for cases such as these, but what the case of Rwanda suggests is that impactful representation for women is contingent also on their political party

---

[3] https://www.msd.govt.nz/about-msd-and-our-work/publications-resources/journals-and-magazines/
social-policy-journal/spj13/review-new-zealands-contraceptive-revolution.html

and its relation to those in power. It seems that this is at least true in authoritarian regimes. Even if women's participation in politics is encouraged with means such as powerful legislative quotas, their ability to substantively influence abortion policy is limited if they are not affiliated with the dominant political party.

Another question concerns the translation of female leadership into substantive representation. The fact that in Rwanda female leaders are not backed by a supportive society is reflected in the difficulty in accessing abortion policy within the Rwandan legal and health systems. This is particularly salient in comparison to New Zealand. In the latter, the demand for female leadership came from civil society groups and women's movements. The efficacy of female leadership and women's ability to reach office is not dependent on the whims of an authoritarian ruler and is backed by a truly supportive electorate. This is reflected in the ease with which New Zealand women access abortion services, despite a relatively restrictive law. The difference between top-down and bottom-up change in the ability to translate policy into actual services is significant.

The de jure-de facto gap seems to be closely related to female leadership and societal acceptance of gender equality. This is particularly evident in the institutional design in place. It is interesting to note that where women gained leadership positions through quotas, actual access to abortion services is poor. This relates to our earlier discussion in Chapter 4, where we asked if perhaps the presence of a truly sympathetic electorate was important to the efficacy of female leadership. Though female politicians of Rwanda may have achieved equality in government, it is not clear how successful they have been in generating effective policy. This is in comparison to New Zealand, where the large number of female politicians seems to correlate with a sympathetic electorate that supports women's welfare and gender equality. Despite a relatively restrictive policy on the books, especially by Western standards, the medical and legal systems all seem to support free access to abortion services in New Zealand.

This takes us back to the broader theoretical debate around a fast-track to women's representation. One key institution in this context is quotas. Dahlerup and Freidenvall (2005) describe different approaches to achieving female political leadership. The incremental track describes a scenario in which equality of representation will be achieved over time as an inevitable process of progressive gender equality. The fast-track approach to representation, though, suggests that eventual gender equality is not a given and it is therefore legitimate to take proactive measures to "fast-track" gender equality. Electoral gender quotas are one such measure. Of course, our case studies demonstrate the strengths and weaknesses of both scenarios. The incremental approach, such as the case in New Zealand, ensures that when female leadership is achieved, a necessary condition is a supportive electorate. General public support for women's rights seems to be essential. The fast-track approach to change, as is the case in Rwanda, suggests that quotas can be a very strong tool in bringing women into a sphere that they otherwise might not enter. That said, their presence in that sphere might not translate into change in other spheres, in policy or within the general culture. This affects the ability of female leaders to provide meaningful substantive representation.

In sum, in Rwanda we saw the correlation between an increased number of female representatives and more permissive abortion policy. Complex aspects concerning the efficacy of female leaders came up when we considered what party they were from and how effective the policy actually was. In New Zealand, on the other hand, we did not observe the correlation we might expect in policy, at least at the level of de jure law. The law on the books does not seem to reflect the type of progressiveness we would expect in light of the almost-unmatched share of women representatives. Yet, in reality, legal loopholes seem to be widely used in relation to how abortions are accessed in New Zealand. The two case studies raise the relevance of political context, the importance of drawing analytical distinctions (as well as empirical ones) between de facto and de jure policy application, and the idea of the fast-track vs. incremental approach in regard to electoral gender quotas. Those case studies demonstrated the interplay between different aspects of state-level representation in their effect on abortion policy.

CONCLUSIONS

Within the state-level sphere, our theoretical framework focused on representation as a critical concept in examining how state characteristics define public policy. In this chapter, we focused on two case studies: Rwanda and New Zealand. Those two countries provide much room to explore these concepts. Rwanda represents an authoritarian regime where, theoretically, descriptive representation might be hard-pressed to translate into substantive representation. That said, the introduction of electoral gender quotas following the tumultuous years of the civil war and its demographic, economic, and political ramifications has made Rwanda the world leader in female legislative representation. Its harsh history of conflict and violence, and specifically gender-based violence, only makes the case study more relevant.

As far as regime types are concerned, New Zealand represents almost the exact opposite of Rwanda. New Zealand has been a stable democracy for close to 200 years, historically being a leader in allowing female political participation (yet, with incremental change in this respect). Like Rwanda, New Zealand also boasts a rate of female leadership far above the world average.

Gaps between abortion policies on the books and what exists in reality are true for both countries. As of 2012, Rwanda has had a considerably more permissive abortion policy. That said, legal and bureaucratic requirements limit the true permissiveness of the law as it is implemented on the ground. Given its well-developed political and socioeconomic profile, New Zealand has a surprisingly restrictive abortion policy. In reality, however, free and safe abortion services are widely available, and a relatively small number of women resort to the procedure. Both countries highlight the significance of women in politics and female political leadership, while at the same time also highlighting a host of other variables that are necessary to fully understand the impact of female representation.

PART III

THE INTERNATIONAL SPHERE

6

The International Sphere: Efforts for Global Norm Standardization

As other chapters in this book discuss, it is the national government that forms reproductive health policy. Yet, while domestic politics are a crucial part of the picture, there are influences which, in order to fully capture the complexities of abortion policymaking, need to be considered. One such crucial influence is international politics.

Some of the key intergovernmental organizations have incorporated women's rights and gender equality into their agendas. Most prominent among recent examples is the United Nations' SDGs. Set by the U.N. General Assembly, these 17 goals are a part of U.N. Resolution 70/1: Transforming our World: The 2030 Agenda for Sustainable Development. Encompassing a broad range of interrelated objectives, the SDGs cover issues of social and economic development running the gamut from gender equality, water, health, education, and global warming to poverty, hunger, sanitation, energy, environment, social justice, and urbanization. The aim of SDG5 is to achieve gender equality and women and girls' empowerment. It is composed of nine target goals, one of which directly addresses reproductive rights and health: "Ensure universal access to sexual and reproductive health and reproductive rights as agreed in accordance with the Programme of Action of the International Conference on Population and Development and the Beijing Platform for Action and the outcome documents of their review conferences."

This target articulates universal access to reproductive health and the safeguarding of reproductive rights, and mentions specific international agreements, platforms, and provisions that address this issue. As we know, however, from the statistics presented in previous chapters, abortion is far from being recognized as a given part of reproductive health. Many states, even those committed to U.N. goals, do not necessarily see abortion rights as a part of the package. In other words, hundreds of millions of women around the world do not enjoy such rights, lacking free access to abortion because of the policy of the state in which they reside.

Part III of the book focuses on how transnational players and the international sphere as a whole influence domestic abortion policy. While intergovernmental organizations such as the United Nations have been able to encourage cooperation and coordination of hundreds of states, and to facilitate their joint decision making, the translation of provisions into actual policy is a different ball game. Dozens of countries still limit access to reproductive health services, including abortion. The rights of women and men to reproductive health services differ substantially between countries. How, then, does this international agenda, set as a part of a universal agreement between U.N. member states, influence reproductive health and abortion policy at the level of the nation-state?

The extent to which state policies are influenced by powers beyond the state has generated a range of debates in the literature. Some of the questions are empirical and focus on positivist questions such as the extent to which such influence exists and the mechanisms that drive it. Others are normative in nature, and pertain, for instance, to questions of legitimacy and state sovereignty. How legitimate is it for international bodies and norms to influence policy within the nation-state? Naturally, such debates may become particularly pernicious when the policies concerned raise moral questions, which more often than not is the case with abortion policy. In this project, we focus on the empirical-positivist questions and largely stay away from the normative, leaving it for another time.

States, in their desire to be part of – and reap the benefits of membership in – the international community, are often open to the influence of international organizations. For example, in 2003, the African Union adopted the Protocol to the African Charter on Human and Peoples' Rights on the Rights of Women in Africa, also known as the Maputo Protocol (throughout Part III of this book, we interchangeably call it the Maputo Protocol, the Protocol, or the African Charter on the Rights of Women in Africa). This Protocol was the first instance an IGO defined abortion as a woman's right (under certain circumstances). Countries that wanted to gain legitimacy in the AU forum and signal commitment to women's rights to the international community felt pressure to sign and ratify the Maputo agreement. We go into the groundbreaking significance of this particular document in more detail in both this chapter and Chapter 7.

There may be a number of causal mechanisms linking transnational actors to policymaking at the level of the nation-state and in the context of abortion. We first look at how transnational players may encourage change in state reproductive rights. For the purposes of this examination, we will choose one type of player in the international sphere – IGOs – as an example of a key actor. IGOs strive to influence state policy on women's rights, and, more specifically for our purposes, on reproductive policy.

The international sphere is the stage on which sovereign states interact with one another (Jackson & Sørensen, 2016; Carlsnaes, Risse-Kappen, Risse, & Simmons, 2002). Beyond nation-states, the international sphere also includes a large number of non-state players including non-governmental organizations (NGOs), transnational corporations, and IGOs. We focus our discussion on one element within the international system, namely IGOs, as players actively striving to influence the domestic policy of sovereign states – especially in the field of gender equality and reproductive rights – and who have concrete and measurable tools with which to do so. The United Nations and the African Union, both mentioned above, are two examples. Given the discussion in previous chapters of the effects of the national sphere on abortion policymaking, in this chapter we also consider, side by side with international effects, the effects of institutions in the national sphere. More specifically, and as a continuation of the discussion in Chapters 4 and 5, we incorporate the discussion of gender quotas into the discussion here.

Gender quotas are a key institution for equal representation of women and women's interests at the state level, which is often associated with international and regional trends. By including quotas in the analysis, we control for a key institution in the state government sphere. Showing the effects of IGOs, while controlling for the effects of domestic institutions such as gender quotas, highlights the advantages of the multi-sphere theoretical framework developed in this book and increases the overall validity of the empirical findings. But before we get to consider the simultaneous effects of those various spheres, let us consider carefully the international sphere itself. In order to understand the value of looking at the international sphere, we briefly delve first into theories of norm and policy diffusion.

NORM AND POLICY DIFFUSION

Theories of diffusion ask how norms and policies travel among states in the international system. Given its focus on international actors, this research touches on the debate between policy diffusion theory on the one hand and World Society theory on the other. Both theories are based on an assumption of interdependence between players in the international sphere (Gilardi, 2012) but differ on who these players are and how they generate this interdependence. These perspectives cite external actors as influencing local state policy.

Yet, they differ in how they understand this process and its underlying causal mechanisms.

Policy diffusion theory describes a process in which pressure for policy innovation comes from outside the polity, spreading from one state government to another (Braun & Gilardi, 2006; Shipan & Volden, 2008). In the World Society paradigm, on the other hand, policy diffusion is IGO-driven (True & Mintrom, 2001). Within this latter framework, many features and norms of the nation-state are derived from global culture as mediated and determined by IGOs. International organizations are often at the forefront of campaigns to author, codify, and validate international norms (Khagram, 2004), which in turn inspire and influence state-level policymaking. The abovementioned SDGs are one such example. As we will explain below, we believe that the World Society framework better accounts for the international spread of policy norms in the area of reproductive health.

THE INTERNATIONAL SPHERE AS A DOMAIN OF INFLUENCE OVER DOMESTIC POLICY

The international sphere is composed of the international state system, the stage on which sovereign states interact with one another. The system is by definition anarchic, as no one state has formal governing authority over the entire system. There is no world government, either. While many states pursue peaceful relations with one another, the uncertainties inherent to the system leave all countries in constant pursuit of security and stability. States are required to interact with each other because of their inevitable dependency on one another for economic, strategic, and security purposes. Resource swapping, economic interaction, human migration, tourism, conflict management, and diplomatic efforts are at the heart of interactions among states. How those issues are handled defines the interactions in the international sphere, which can range from peaceful cooperation to interstate conflict (Jackson & Sørensen, 2016; Carlsnaes, Risse-Kappen, Risse, & Simmons, 2002).

The international sphere is not limited to sovereign states. Any entity that spreads beyond the borders of a single state – or with the specific goal of functioning beyond the borders of a single state – can be defined as operating in the international sphere (Risse, 2007). This includes players such as NGOs, IGOs, transnational companies, and multinational corporations, to name a few. NGOs include organizations such as the International Red Cross on the one hand and terrorist groups such as Al-Qaeda on the other. Both see their activity as transnational in nature, of international relevance, and not limited to any one state. Commercial entities, such as multinational corporations, produce, invest, and sell across multiple national markets. Such players increase the unpredict-ability of the international sphere but also support its interdependency (Jackson & Sørensen, 2016; Mimiko, 2012). IGOs such as the United Nations, the African Union, and the European Union exist for the purpose of coordinating activity and meeting common goals of states. Such IGOs combat the inherent anarchy of the international sphere. They are composed primarily of sovereign states and derive their authority from treaties formed by those member states.

Players of the international sphere can exert considerable influence on domestic politics affecting policymaking at the level of national and local governments (Carlsnaes, Risse-Kappen, Risse, & Simmons, 2002; Simmons & Martin, 2012). IGOs and NGOs can lobby, embolden civil society movements, prompt policy creation, educate, and also influence the rights of minority groups (Asal, Murdie, & Sommer, 2017). For example, Oxfam may prompt policy change by educating the public concerning possible methods to combat issues of poverty and hunger. Al-Qaeda's terror attacks on the United States on September 11, 2001 prompted a wave of new policy regarding surveillance, security measures, and privacy law. Multinational corporations influence policy, as they lobby for more hospitable conditions in a country or prompt the country to change economic conditions in order to attract or deter business activity. IGOs directly and indirectly influence policy by serving as a site for the creation of treaties, brokering of pacts, and influencing and educating on evolving norms and standards. IGOs are also often the source of international legal provisions.

In this chapter, we isolate IGOs as a player within the international sphere that actively strives to influence domestic policy of sovereign states, especially regarding gender equality and reproductive rights. While many international players can influence policy in general, we have chosen IGOs as players who can be influential and often try to use their influence specifically in the field of gender equality and reproductive rights. IGOs make a particularly good test case for our purposes for a few reasons. First, they have a history of leading the charge on gender equality issues. Second, their activity is highly bureaucratized, and thus traceable. The international treaties and agreements that they generate make for highly visible and relatively measurable actions. For these reasons, they make for a good type of actor to analyze within the broader international sphere as an influencer on the production of reproductive rights.

A Brief History of IGOs

Emerging in their modern form in the nineteenth century, the number of IGOs increased dramatically at the beginning of the twentieth century

(Kingsbury, Krisch, & Stewart, 2005; Boli & Thomas, 1999). A number of international organizations emerged throughout the nineteenth and early twentieth centuries dedicated to both professional standardization in communication, transportation, and so forth, as well as multinational peacemaking and arbitration campaigns. These laid the basis for one of the first major intergovernmental efforts at the beginning of the twentieth century known as the League of Nations (Smith, Chatfield, & Pagnucco, 1997).

The League was established in 1920, in the aftermath of World War I. As the dust settled from the Great War and its horrific upshots became clear, the stated goal of the League of Nations was to maintain world peace. After failing to prevent the rise of the Axis Powers and World War II, the League was ultimately deemed a failure. It did not achieve its top priority of preventing another global war. That said, it laid the philosophical and bureaucratic groundwork for the largest IGO yet to emerge, the United Nations (He, 1996).

The United Nations was established in 1945, as a result of peace negotiations that took place at the end of World War II (He, 1996). Today, the United Nations is the largest IGO in the world. It is composed of 193 sovereign member states and numerous departments and bureaucratic wings (United Nations, n.d.). After the United Nations, some of the largest IGOs include OPEC, NATO, the European Union, and the African Union. These different bodies address a variety of issues such as trade, security, human rights, and international crime. One of their roles is to establish international norms for a range of issue areas, including, but not limited to, gender equality and the protection of women's rights and reproductive policy.

IGOS AS NORM CREATORS

Theories of norm and policy proliferation

To begin our discussion of IGOs as norm creators, let us first review some literature on global trends in policy and norm change. The discussions of international norm proliferation and international policy spread are intimately connected. Laws and policies are often the statutory expression of norms. Laws and policies codify what is considered acceptable and desirable behavior, or encourage the acceptance of new standards of conduct. This connection is especially salient for our discussion of abortion law, because abortion is seen as a morality policy. Thus, we argue that change in policy reflects a change in norms concerning women's autonomy, secular definitions of gender equality, and the common view on the question about the beginning of life.

Norms are guides for conduct. They dictate behavior and imply what ought to be and what one ought to do (Hage, 2005; Martinsson, 2011). In other words, norms are the interpretation of normative assessments of scenarios and behaviors. They exist to guide behavior and are essentially a group expectation of behavioral standards (Hage, 2005; Katzenstein, 1996; Shannon, 2000). Global norms are the shared normative frameworks that exist among a large enough number of states and other international actors. Norms can be applied to states, intergovernmental organizations, and a variety of non-state actors (Khagram, Riker, & Sikkink, 2002)

There are competing theories of why and how norms and policies diffuse. Some believe that states comply with international norms only when it is consistent with their material and security interests, or when compliance is not particularly burdensome (Martinsson, 2011; Hyde, 2017). States are unlikely to adopt a norm at a high price nor are they likely to legislate a standard that does not already correlate with national positions (Guiraudon, 2000). Others hypothesize that states will actually accept burdensome norms imposed by the international sphere as a means of signaling their commitment to the norm. This is done to send credible signals to other states and international entities and to increase the share of and access to internationally allocated benefits and resources. The costlier the norm adoption, the stronger the signal. This in turn sends a message about the acceptability of the norm, the cost of its adoption, and the material benefits – real or potential – involved (Hyde, 2017).

Given our focus on international vs. domestic actors, this project touches on the debate between policy diffusion and World Society diffusion. As discussed above briefly, these are two competing theories of how norms and policies spread. Both theories are based on an assumption of interdependence (Gilardi, 2012). Yet, they differ on where this sense of interdependence is communicated and how pressure is applied to and by different actors. Both theories cite external actors as influencers of local state policy, yet differ in how they see the process and its underlying mechanisms unfold.

Policy diffusion theory describes a process in which pressure for policy innovation comes from other polities, spreading from one state government to another (Braun & Gilardi, 2006; Shipan & Volden, 2008). Some types of policies, such as economic policies, have been found to cluster in time and space, implying such patterns of diffusion (Simmons & Elkins, 2004). Policy diffusion could be caused by numerous mechanisms including changing conditions in one country altering the benefits of a certain policy in another, regional influences and trends, or more information becoming available because of an experiment in a neighboring state (Simmons & Elkins, 2004;

Shipan & Volden, 2008). Within the state-based theory, social hierarchy, as defined by international standing and rank of influencing and influenced states, can play a critical role (Towns, 2012).

The alternative theory is World Society theory, in which policy proliferation is IGO-driven (True & Mintrom, 2001). Within this framework, many features and norms of the nation-state are derived from global culture. International organizations are often at the forefront of campaigns to author, codify, and validate international norms (Khagram, 2004). This is true in particular to intergovernmental organizations.

The culture of World Society defines the boundaries and norms of the nation-state. The nation-state's desire to conform to World Society encourages diffusion. Within this theory, bodies such as the United Nations and the African Union serve as the "organizational frame" for World Society. Procedures defined in these international bodies can strongly influence practice at the nation-state level, even when a nation may resist influence initially or even later on in the process (Meyer, Boli, Thomas, & Ramirez, 1997; Stone & Ladi, 2015).

We offer three main reasons why the World Society framework – rather than the policy diffusion one – is appropriate and useful to explore abortion policy in the context of the international sphere. First, abortion policy is considered highly susceptible to religious and cultural influence. Yet, since states may not have religiously or culturally similar countries in their vicinity, such policy is less likely to diffuse. It is IGOs that would be the forums where such policy emulation may originate.

Second, the economic considerations that are often at the root of policy diffusion theory are irrelevant for abortion policy. Given that abortion is a moral issue, it does not fit into the market-driven considerations prevalent in the policy diffusion literature (Sedge et al., 2011).

Third, the supply-driven explanation for World Society is particularly appropriate for the study of abortion, since international agreements and protocols both normalize a given policy position and provide grounds and support for local movements to further entrench them in various national systems (Finnemore, 1993). Thus, when juxtaposing world society and policy diffusion, we expect the former to better explain the spread of abortion policies. In the empirical analyses that follow, we test whether the World Society theory holds water with data for the majority of the countries in the world and present evidence for the systematic effects of IGOs. In the following chapter, we will delve into the processes underlying IGO influence on the production of reproductive rights around the world.

IGO Mechanisms for Influencing Norms

Within the World Society theory, IGOs provide fruitful forums for global public policymaking (Mamudu, Cairney, & Studlar, 2015). They serve a number of purposes, function through a number of avenues, and have multiple tools at their disposal to influence states. These include their powers as forums of socialization and education; their ability to provide material, economic, and financial incentives; their methods of creating legal obligation; and their ability to empower international and local NGOs. Let us examine each of those mechanisms more closely.

IGOs serve as forums for state socialization. In the process of socialization, norms and ideologies are internalized (Clausen, 1968; Goodman & Jinks, 2004). In this case, states and their leaders are exposed to discussions, debates, projects, and research about a given topic. This offers the exposure necessary for socialization to occur (Macionis & Gerber, 2011). Whether or not the norms originated in the IGOs, the IGOs are the ones to transfer them and teach them to the international community (Finnemore, 1996; Park, 2005). Such a forum of socialization allows new topics to be brought into the public discourse, exposing players and states that might otherwise not have been exposed to certain ideas and issues, or might not have been aware of how other states internalize particular norms (Martinsson, 2011; Greenhill, 2010).

IGOs also provide forums for education, for mutual learning, for best practice mentoring and for exposure to practical policy solutions (Finnemore, 1993). Through this function as forums for education, IGOs not only socialize states into norms, but educate for the spread of policy initiatives (Finnemore, 1996; Abbott & Snidal, 1998). Within IGO forums, states can see what other states have chosen. This allows them to analyze what best fits their own countries, learn from successes and failures, emulate certain practices, and analyze incentive structures for a range of policy alternatives (Elkins & Simmons, 2005).

IGOs often also have the power to provide material, economic, and financial incentives for norm and policy adoption. IGOs are a source of positive incentives such as loans, aid packages, and development and research grants. For example, preferential trade agreements can be a means of enforcing standards of human rights (Hafner-Burton, 2005). The International Monetary Fund (IMF) practices conditional lending, imposing IMF-defined good practices as conditions for loans (Vreeland, 2006). In its research funding programs, the European Commission defines priorities, some grounded in values such as gender equality or diversity in research teams. The Commission then uses these as criteria to assess research proposals and allocate funds.

In addition, there is also the option of negative material incentives. The quintessential example here would be the imposition of sanctions. In the past, the U.N. Security Council has resorted to economic sanctions in order to encourage behavior change at the state level and in an attempt to avoid armed conflict (Reinisch, 2001). This generally involves bans on trades and loans that all member states are expected to adopt. For example, in August 1990, the U. N. Security Council imposed sanctions on Iraq after it invaded neighboring Kuwait. All exports from Iraq as well as certain imports were banned. The country's assets abroad were frozen. The hope was to force an immediate withdrawal from Kuwait (albeit this was not what happened [Herring, 2002]). While the hoped-for effect did not materialize in the case of Saddam Hussein's Iraq, the shadow of similar potential future actions can still work as a threat for other countries and a powerful tool in the hands of IGOs, such as the U.N. Security Council.

IGOs also communicate and enforce norms and policies through their power to generate international agreements, treaties, and protocols. By signing such documents, states announce their dedication to a given global norm or shared goal and their intention to adopt corresponding policy actions. International agreements are technically legally binding, although even here there are gray areas depending on whether states have signed, ratified, accepted, or approved them. By signing such agreements, states can expose themselves to coercive methods of enforcement of international law. A failure to uphold the agreement would bring with it the risk of lost credibility, weakened diplomatic ties, and even exposure to sanctions from other countries or the IGO itself.

Finally, IGOs can serve norm and policy dissemination by strengthening international and local NGOs and civil society organizations (Keck & Sikkink, 1999). The precedents created by IGO research bodies, position papers, projects, and agreements all provide tools for local NGOs and citizens to demand change at a country level (Asal, Murdie & Sommer, 2017; Sommer & Asal, 2018). In particular in regard to agreements and treaties, even if the IGO might lack power to enforce signee compliance (Parish, 2010), local activists and NGOs can use the treaty as grounds for demands (Doh & Guay, 2004; Cortell & Davis Jr, 1996). The research and guidelines generated by IGO research bodies can also provide valuable guidance for local organizations. For example, local NGOs have cited WHO guidelines as useful in implementing best practices and improving national health care systems (Hessini, Brookman-Amissah, & Crane, 2006). This is especially true if a country lacks the resources to conduct its own research.

IGOS, WOMEN'S RIGHTS, AND GENDER EQUALITY

Earlier, we offered three reasons why the World Society framework is such an appropriate context to explore abortion policy. First, abortion policy is considered highly susceptible to religious and cultural influences. Thus, states would look to culturally and religiously similar cultures for norm education and emulation. States may be located in religiously and culturally diverse regions. In such a case diffusion would be less likely in policy areas that are closely linked to morality issues. IGOs would serve as forums to find other states with common religious and cultural characteristics. Second, abortion policy is a morality policy, and thus less susceptible to market-driven influencers. Finally, the supply-driven explanation for World Society is particularly appropriate for abortion study, since international agreements and protocols both normalize a given policy position and provide grounds and support for local movements (Finnemore, 1993). In other words, IGOs supply material support and precedent to countries that might otherwise not initiate change, and to organizations that benefit from the support of a higher or more established authority. The WHO's 2003 guidelines are a prime example of such a document. We elaborate on such documents in Chapter 7.

As the discussion of SDG5 in this chapter, and in Chapter 1 demonstrate, rights to reproductive health are nested within a wider context of women's rights that include but are not limited to voting, education, vocational training, and the rights of women as workers. Within U.N. bodies, the shift toward a focus on reproductive rights was evident in the Plan of Action (PoA) from the 1994 ICPD in Cairo (Petchesky, 2003, pp. 34–35). In line with this effort, support for this women's rights agenda has increased over the years among a variety of U.N. agencies (Hessini, 2005). Reproductive rights, however, have been one of the most controversial aspects within the field of women's welfare.

There are several causal mechanisms by which international institutions influence policy concerning women's rights. Increased cooperation among countries and international groups gives support to nations and strengthens commitments to international agreements. Regional organizations can strengthen the resolve of national leaders and serve as a forum to discuss strategies. This in turn allows for the accumulation within a region of knowledge as well as practical experience (Hessini, Brookman-Amissah, & Crane, 2006). Agreements and diffusion of norms also create incentives and momentum for activists who apply them at the local level, which then boosts movements for women's rights (Htun & Weldon, 2012).

IGOs are also particularly important to look at specifically when examining the factors determining international norms of women's rights. Post World War

II, universalism and human rights became dominant themes within world culture. The United Nations was the main mobilizer of these themes and was given the task of developing models for use and introduction into sovereign nations. The socialization and education forums that exist within this IGO are not only a by-product of its actions, but a stated goal. Through this activity, the causes previously relegated to women's movements within civil society now found a new home within the U.N. framework (Berkovitch, 1999a).

Indeed, over the years IGOs have been influential in rewriting norms of women's rights and gender equality. Let us take the United Nations as a case of IGO efficacy regarding norms of women's rights. Unlike previous IGOs, it was vested with the power to set international standards for states on social issues (Berkovitch, 1999b). Women's rights and gender equality have been dominant principles in U.N. activity from its inception (Pietilä & Vickers, 1990), culminating in major initiatives such as SDG5. In fact, the U.N. Charter was the first international treaty to specify equality between the sexes. What is more, the Commission on the Status of Women was established within the first year of U.N. activity. The United Nations also adopted and standardized the principle of "women's rights as human rights" in 1979 with the adoption of CEDAW(Reanda, 1981). Writing 30 years after CEDAW's inception, Zwingel describes it as still "the most authoritative and steady piece of the international women's rights discourse" (2012, p. 115). Additionally, the United Nations has been dominant throughout the years in establishing new strategies and approaches to promoting gender equality, including gender mainstreaming and the HeForShe approach. In fact, the United Nations was the first body to adopt gender mainstreaming as a strategy to ensure full integration of women and gender equality values. The strategy first appeared at the U.N. Third World Conference on Women in Nairobi in 1985 and was adopted in a "platform for action" in 1995 at the U.N. Conference on Women in Beijing (Booth & Bennet, 2002). The even more recent HeForShe campaign actively promotes the re-evaluation of the advancement of gender equality not as an issue that needs to be promoted by women, but an issue that both concerns and requires the involvement of all genders. The campaign seeks to actively involve men in campaigns for gender equality (U.N. Women, 2018).

The European Union has also emerged as a dominant IGO in terms of (re)writing norms of gender equality for sovereign states. The European Union defines organizational norms and policies, and states are allowed or denied entry into the Union often based on their willingness to adopt these guidelines (Ellina, 2003). Active steps have been taken within the EU to alter the status of women in Europe and member states are called on to adopt new norms of gender equality (Plantenga, Remery,

Figueiredo, & Smith, 2009). Rather than limiting itself to a formal approach of equal treatment, the EU has gone so far as to adopt a gender equality agenda that includes positive action and gender main-streaming (Pollack & Hafner-Burton, 2000; Booth & Bennett, 2002).

Abortion in the International Sphere

There have been a few standout IGO efforts to address abortion rights, policy, and procedure. These efforts have taken the form of programs of action, treaties, and health care guidelines. They are diverse in terms of the organiza-tions that are parties to their drafting, the drafting process itself, their stance on abortion policy, and the level of obligation they entail for the sovereign states that choose to participate.

In the area of abortion rights and reproductive policy, the most prominent of these documents includes the 1999 U.N. ICPD PoA, the 2003 World Health Publication, Safe Abortion: Technical and Policy Guidance for Health Systems, and the African Union's 2003 Protocol to the African Charter on Human and Peoples' Rights on the Rights of Women in Africa. These three documents are generally cited as chief IGO efforts to address abortion issues. Let us examine each of those briefly.

The ICPD PoA was one of the first major international provisions to address family planning and abortion as an aspect of public health. A total of 179 states adopted the PoA directly following the 1994 conference. In the 1999 ICPD PoA, governments agreed that providers should be trained and equipped to provide abortion services where not illegal and that those services should be widely accessible. Since the ICPD, increased research, advocacy, and mobi-lization efforts have expanded the knowledge about unsafe abortions, raised awareness of women's experiences with unsafe abortions, examined the needs of women who pursue abortions, and linked abortion with other key health and women's rights issues (Hessini, 2005). The ICPD PoA has led to the involvement of new actors including policymakers, government officials, women's groups, legal advocates, human rights experts, and journalists (Hessini, Brookman-Amissah, & Crane, 2006).

The ICPD PoA also prompted the articulation of the 2003 WHO guidelines known as Safe Abortion: Technical and Policy Guidance for Health Systems. The guidelines aimed to provide clinical guidance for national health systems, while accounting for relevant ethics and policy considerations (Hessini, Brookman-Amissah, & Crane, 2006). Countries have cited the 2003 WHO Guidelines, along with the ICPD framework, as having been instrumental in helping their domestic healthcare systems develop treatment and access policy and as a significant piece of international abortion legislation protocol (Hessini, Brookman-Amissah, & Crane, 2006).

Among regional organization activity, the African Union's 2003 Protocol to the African Charter on Human and Peoples' Rights on the Rights of Women in Africa stands out. This was the first instance in international law where the right to safe elective abortion for a wide range of indicators was set forth (Hessini, Brookman-Amissah, & Crane, 2006; Gerson, 2005). Based on our survey of the literature and our survey of regional and international protocols on reproductive health, no other protocol has so decisively articulated abortion as a right for women.

Regional and Universal IGOs and the Protocols they Produce

One way to theoretically organize types of IGOs is to distinguish between regional and universal organizations. Universal organizations are bodies that include states from any part of the world. The United Nations is the ultimate example of such a body. Regional organizations require that a country belong to a specific region as a criterion for membership. By definition, such organizations primarily emphasize regional interests and activity (in addition, in some cases, to global concerns). Examples of such organizations include the African Union, the European Union, and the Gulf Cooperation Council.

As the brief discussion of the various provisions suggests, such bodies can generate explicit or general protocols. An explicit protocol would include concrete recommendations or mandates for public policy or action. It might demand that signing states adopt quantitative goals or specify policy measures that states are obligated to adopt as part of being partners to the protocol. An example of such a protocol might be the Treaty on the Non-Proliferation of Nuclear Weapons. This treaty specifies how nuclear arms may be handled, developed, obtained, and more. It articulates clear rules for how countries must approach non-proliferation, disarmament, and the development of nuclear power.

A general protocol, on the other hand, uses less-specific language and offers a more general framework for policy at the national level. For example, the U. N. SDGs, adopted in 2015, provide general goals but do not make concrete demands of states regarding policy, nor do they explicitly explain how the goals are to be reached. For example, in SDG1, "ending poverty," one of the targets is to "implement nationally appropriate social protection systems and measures for all, including floors, and by 2030 achieve substantial coverage of the poor and the vulnerable" (United Nations, 2015). It is up to individual states to decide how to implement this goal, and there are no specified obligations or sanctions for non-compliance. All U.N. member states to date have adopted the SDGs.

A survey of the literature and of IGO protocols in the area of reproductive rights indicates that explicit and detailed reproductive rights protocols emanate exclusively from regional, as opposed to universal international, bodies. Universal organizations seem to have difficulty generating more explicit protocols (Boyle, Kim, & Longhofer, 2015). Rather than taking a stance on a politically sensitive issue, many international organizations – including the United Nations – avoid taking positions on positive abortion rights, leaving it up to their member states (Gerson, 2005). This was apparent in the drafting process of the ICPD PoA, when numerous countries pushed for vague and non-binding language regarding abortion, which did little to promote access to abortion as a right (Boyle, Kim, & Longhofer, 2015). Thanks to this measure and the particular language used, the ICPD received universal approval. We go into the politics of the drafting process of the ICPD PoA and examine the implications for the PoA's impact on abortion rights around the world in detail in Chapter 7.

In comparison, the AU Protocol used distinctly more decisive language than the ICPD PoA, stating that "state parties shall take all appropriate measures to ... protect the reproductive rights of women by authorizing medical abortion in cases of sexual assault, rape, incest, and where the continued pregnancy endangers the mental and physical health of the mother or the life of the mother or the foetus" (African Union, 2003). Only some of the AU countries adopted this protocol and it was done in a staggered fashion. To date, of the 54 countries in the African Union, 36 countries have both signed and ratified the protocol; 15 have signed, but not ratified; and 3 have neither signed nor ratified. Yet, for those countries where it was ratified as well as for the continent as a whole, the AU Protocol demonstrates the effects of regional IGOs, whose directives use unequivocal verbiage. In the current chapter we focus on the influence of IGOs on reproductive policy, using large-N analyses. This allows us to uncover such systematic connections that may not be clear through case study methodology. Before we get to the empirical components, let us articulate what we expect to find.

HYPOTHESES

In order to test the influence of international organizations on domestic policy, we need to find a way to isolate the influence of international organizations from domestic sources of influence. Chapters 2–5 of this book highlight the various ways in which state actors and domestic players influence abortion policy. We need to separate and differentiate between activity to promote abortion rights at the international and national levels. Otherwise, how do we know that change is correlating with IGO activity and not with changes and influences on the domestic level we failed to account for?

In order to isolate IGO activity from state-level activity, we juxtapose the two. Alongside standout international treaties and protocols on abortion, we observe the correlation of the rate of female legislators and gender quotas with change in state abortion policy. Gender quotas aim to increase female legislator presence, which in turn has been proven to promote women's issues and agendas (Bratton, 2005; Campbell, 2004; Childs, 2001; Sapiro, 1998).

To elucidate the effects of international bodies and to distinguish between regional and universal IGOs and their different types of protocols, we focus on the policy changes following the ICPD PoA, WHO 2003 guidelines, and the AU Protocol. This – based on our review of the literature and international treaties – covers the important and consequential international law protocols on the subject of reproductive rights within the time frame studied. We expect protocol adoption to correlate with an increase in permissive abortion policy along the lines of the following hypotheses:

H6.1: Signing of global and regional IGO protocols positively correlates with increased permissiveness of state abortion policy.

H6.2: Explicit regional protocols have a stronger correlation with increased permissiveness than general universal IGO protocols.

In order to compare international players with the influence of domestic political players, we add women's legislative representation and gender quotas as two factors that are assumed to increase women's substantive representation, and concomitantly female-friendly policy. As we discuss in Chapter 4, the influence of women in the legislature on abortion policy has been thoroughly examined within the United States (O'Connor & Berkman, 1995). In U.S.-based literature, more female politicians lead to more permissive abortion policies. This holds true across party lines (Berkman & O'Connor, 1993; Norrander & Wilcox, 1999). This was found to be true in comparative cross-sectional analysis as well (Hildebrandt, 2015).

This connection was explored in-depth in Chapter 4. As we articulate there, the idea that more female legislators will lead to more permissive abortion policy is based on the hypothesized connection between descriptive and substantive representation (Pitkin, 1967; Schwindt-Bayer & Mishler, 2005; O'Regan, 2000). Female representatives will be most capable of offering substantive representation, as women share certain common experiences and concerns (Kittilson, 2005; Franceschet & Piscopo, 2008; Wangnerud, 2009; Grey, 2006; Celis & Childs, 2008). As the numerical representation of women increases, so too would the number of representatives capable of substantive representation of women's interests and rights. Therefore, the number of women legislators should increase the number of actors interested in promoting policy that benefits women. Accordingly, we put forth the following hypothesis:

H6.3: There will be a positive correlation between the percentage of women in the legislature and the permissiveness of state abortion policy.

A high rate of female representatives, along with permissive reproductive policy, may be more a reflection of a society that promotes gender equality than an indicator for the effects of female politicians. We therefore include a domestic institution aimed at advancing women's rights. Gender quotas test a national policy instrument aimed at increasing gender equality, as well as directly account for variance in institutional arrangement.

The purpose of gender quotas is to increase women's representation in the legislature, not only to redress past inequalities, but also in the hope that women's presence will raise distinctive issues and change priorities on the public agenda so as to serve the interests and values of female constituents (De Paola, Lombardo, & Scoppa, 2009). There is also the belief that correcting the imbalance in politics will help alleviate underrepresentation in other spheres. Indeed, gender quotas are the most visible and direct mechanism that political parties have used to increase women's parliamentary representation (Caul, 2001).

We discussed quotas earlier in the book, and indeed there is little research on whether quotas actually lead to changes in policy outcomes. There have been few findings regarding the theory that gender quotas lead to the advancement of gender issues (Forman-Rabinovici & Sommer, 2018a; Htun & Power, 2006). As discussed in Chapters 4 and 5, the election of women representatives may not reflect constituents who are particularly sympathetic to causes of women's rights. Rather, they may be a result of remedial policies. This renders the following hypothesis:

H6.4: There will be a negative interaction effect between female legislators and the presence of a quota system on permissive abortion law.

At this point, we reap the full benefit of using a comparative, multi-sphere framework. It is only within such a comprehensive perspective – and one that considers both domestic and international influences – that we can really articulate the effects on abortion policy. Thus, with those controls for domestic influence reflected in the specification of our models, let us move on to the empirical parts of this analysis.

METHOD

Data on state abortion policy was collected for 195 countries between 1992 and 2013. Multilevel linear models were estimated, utilizing original indexes for the dependent variables and both original and existing indexes for the independent variables. As the series of years are embedded in our data within countries, residuals are not uncorrelated and do not have a homogenous variance. The multilevel models account for issues arising from the repeated measures of our data set, which are not accounted for by standard fixed effects models (Quené & Van den Bergh, 2004; Hofmann, 1997; Gelman, 2006).

For the dependent variable, we use the Comparative Abortion Index, which is based on the U.N. Department of Social and Economic Affairs' global review of abortion policy. The report offers seven criteria under which state law may allow access to abortion services; saving a woman's life, preserving a woman's physical health, preserving a woman's mental health in cases of rape or incest, in cases of fetal impairment, for social or economic reasons, and on request. Each country-year is given a score based on the number of legal criteria accepted as grounds for abortion on a range from 0 to 7 (where a woman may access an abortion under all conditions including on request). For the purposes of robustness and to fix a potential measurement flaw in the first index, we also generated a weighted index (CAI2), where the weight of each criterion (Wi) is determined based on the percentage (Pi) of countries that allow that condition. On a scale of 0–1, 0 represents countries in which there are no conditions for legal abortion, and 1 represents a country that accepts all criteria for abortion. Please refer to Chapter 2 for a full description of the Index, comparisons to other attempts in the literature to quantify abortion policy, and the formula used for its weighted version.

Figure 6.1 shows the global bimodal distribution. For all years, on average 57% of states had either a score of 1 or 7. After 1 and 7, 3 was the most common score, on average accounting for 16% of states.

To test the robustness of our findings further, we employ the CIRI as an additional dependent variable, similar to how we use it in Chapter 2. This data set scores the extent of political rights for women based on several internationally recognized political rights (suffrage, right to run for office, and so forth [Cingranelli, Richards, & Clay 2014; Jan et al., 2015]). This indicator allowed an additional test for the correlation between a variable measuring a disparate, but still related, policy area. Significant effects of predictors in the CAI models

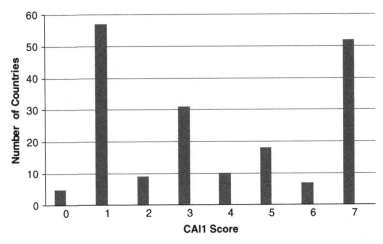

FIGURE 6.1: Distribution of CAI1 Scores Globally

that prove insignificant in the *CIRI* model provide us with a measure for distinctive validity.

To test the correlation between IGO activity and state abortion policy, we coded the ICPD PoA, published in 1995; the WHO 2003 document, Safe Abortion: Technical and Policy Guidance for Health Systems; and the AU Protocol, which added its first signatories in 2003. All three international provisions were coded using a binary coding system, with a value of 0 before their ratification or signing, depending on the document, and 1 after. Of the three, only the AU Protocol was not universally accepted by members of its founding union. Rather, it was ratified in a piecemeal fashion. Although these protocols are not completely comparable in nature (some requiring signing and ratification, and others serving as mere guidelines), all represent attempts by IGOs to discuss and promote abortion as part of a reproductive rights package. They, therefore, offer measures for the correlation between different types of IGO activity and state policy.

More specifically, the ICPD PoA had a binary coding in which a coding of one was given to a country for a year it signed and a zero was assigned if the country did not sign the protocol. The WHO guidelines had similar coding, with countries given a score of 1 for every year after the publication of the guidelines and a zero otherwise. In coding the AU Protocol, a country was given a score of 1 for the year it ratified, and every year thereafter. If a country did not ratify, it was given a score of zero for that state-year.

Like in other chapters in this book, female presence in government is measured by the percentage of seats of the lower house of parliament occupied by female legislators (Women in National Parliaments, 2015). Gender quotas were coded as dummy variables indicating whether a state has mandatory gender quotas in national elections or in the national government. A country was coded 1 for every year in which the elected body had been elected with a gender quota system in place, and 0 otherwise (Quota Project: Global Database of Quotas for Women [2017]). Additionally, we specified interaction terms for quotas and female representation.

Again, like in models estimated earlier in the book, control variables include the Polity score (Marshall, Gurr, & Jaggers, 2017), Muslim population size (Pew Research Center, 2009), Catholic population size (Maoz & Henderson, 2013), the Human Development Index (HDI [United Nations Development Programme, 2016]), and logged GDP (World Bank, 2017). Polity score allows us to control for political process as an interfering variable, as well as control for the potential for political representatives to wield influence, an important factor given our female legislator variable. To this end, we also specify a term for the interaction between Polity and quotas. This allows us to control for the influence the degree of democracy would have on the effect of quota- elected representatives on reproductive rights.

We delved into the questions related to religion and abortion in Chapters 2 and 3, where we discussed the effects of faith civil society on abortion and in particular looked at the effects of religion, religious denominations, and religious institutions on reproductive health policy. Muslim and Catholic population variables serve, thus, as controls (Minkenberg, 2002; Knill, Preidel, & Nebel, 2014). The HDI and logged GDP allow us to control for dependence on IGOs for financial support and programming, thus, neutralizing it and isolating it from the effects we are really interested in.

RESULTS

Figures 6.2 and 6.3 graph trends regarding abortion policy worldwide and reflect the correlation with international protocols. Figure 6.2 depicts the change over time in average CAI1 scores by world region. Figure 6.3 shows overall score distribution over time. In Figure 6.3, the percentage of countries with a score of 3 or less is approximately 60% in 1992. By 2014, this falls to approximately one in every two nations, with almost no countries having a score of 0. The percentage of countries with a score of 5 or higher in 1992 is approximately 35%; by 2014 it is just over 40%. The number of countries with a maximum score of 7 rises by approximately 5 percentage points during this entire period, being at approximately 20% in 1992 and at approximately 25% in 2014. Between 1995 and 1996 and 1998 and 1999, many countries seemed to

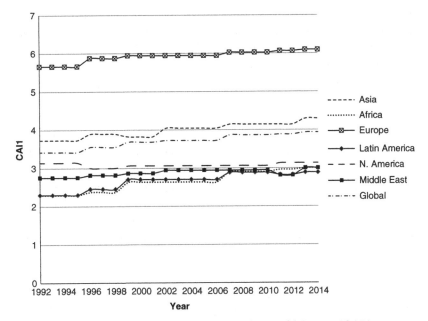

FIGURE 6.2: Average Abortion Score by World Region (CAI1)

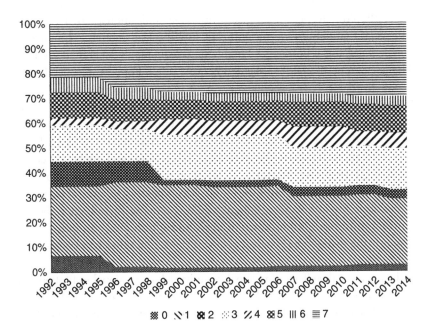

FIGURE 6.3: Distribution of CAI1 Scores Worldwide (1992–2013)

undergo changes in their abortion policy, with the general trend toward permissiveness. Between 1999 and 2007, though, there seemed to be almost no change, with only a few countries making any policy change. Though less dramatic than previous clusters of change, or change on average, there can be observed a cluster of countries that changed policy between 2007 and 2008, and general trends of movement between 2010 and 2013. The changes in averages and clusters of change correspond with our expectations regarding reaction to international protocol change. The clustered change in 1996 and 1999 could be a reaction to the ICPD PoA. The changes in 1999 may relate to countries that did not succeed in implementing change before the 1999 census was taken by the United Nations. The next significant cluster is observed in 2007–2008, which was the next abortion policy census taken following the WHO 2003 protocol and the AU Protocol. In this cluster, 14 countries adopted more permissive abortion policies. Six of these countries (43%) are AU members. Within the group of 14 countries, no continent has more representation than Africa.

To test whether those descriptive trends hold when alternative accounts are controlled for statistically, Table 6.1 presents a series of nested multivariate regression models. The coefficients for the ICPD PoA are positive and significant in all models. This coefficient was of substantial magnitude at 1.45. This number implies that with the introduction of an IGO protocol such as the ICPD PoA, average CAI_1 score worldwide could increase by 1.45 points. The WHO guidelines are insignificant in almost all models. The effect of female legislators is positive and highly significant for all dependent variables. The coefficient, though, is consistently quite small. For example, in Model 1, female legislators have a coefficient of .007. This means that for 1% increase in female legislators, the abortion score will rise by .007 in the model. A parliament that increases its female representation from 10% to 20% will be expected to have a .07-point increase in its CAI_1 score, which ranges from 1 to 7. The interaction terms between female legislators and quotas are consistently negative and significant in all abortion models. In sum, the models in Table 6.2 suggest that, controlling for the effects of other spheres, at least some protocols in the international sphere would systematically influence abortion policy. Furthermore, comparison of Models 1 and 2 in Table 6.1 with Model 3 supports the distinction between abortion rights and other types of women's rights.

To tease out the effects of regional vs. universal international institutions, the observations in Table 6.2 are limited to African nations, and include the AU Protocol predictor in addition to the independent variables for ICPD and WHO guidelines. We limited these models to only AU member states, as the Maputo

TABLE 6.1 *Predictors of Abortion Policy – The International Sphere*
Linear Mixed-Effects ML

	Model 1 (CAI1)	Model 2 (CAI2)	Model 3 (CIRI political rights)
ICPD PoA	1.45 (.750)*	.241 (.125)*	.406 (.114)***
WHO Protocol	−.006 (.034)	−.003 (.006)	.070 (.017)***
Females in Legislature (%)	.007 (.002)***	.001 (.000)***	.010 (.001)***
Electoral Quota	.251 (.073)***	.036 (.012)**	.225 (.049)***
Polity Score	.015 (.007)*	.002 (.001)*	.005 (.003)
Interaction (Quota and Females in Legislature)	−.006 (.003)*	−.001 (.000)*	−.002 (.002)
Interaction (Quota and Polity)	−.028 (.007)***	−.003 (.001)**	.016 (.005)***
GDP Logged	−.116 (.077)	−.022 (.013)	.010 (.016)
Muslims in Population (%)	−.008 (.005)*	−.002 (.001)*	−.004 (.001)***
Catholics in Population (%)	−.346 (.299)	−.070 (.048)	.028 (.087)
HDI	3.42 (.720)***	.539 (.117)***	.208 (.202)
Number of Countries	154	154	153
Total Number of Observations	2344	2344	1888
Constant	3.4 (1.7)*	.465 (.278)*	1.06 (.321)***

*p<.05 **p< 0.01 ***p<0.001

Protocol applies only to them. The AU Protocol had a significant effect in all models except for when CIRI was specified as the outcome variable. What is more, in the presence of the AU protocol, the ICPD is eclipsed and rendered statistically insignificant. The effects of the more explicit and tailored regional protocol eclipsed the effects of the broader universal measure. The regional IGO's platform was significantly more effective than that of the universal IGO. The interaction between female legislators and quotas maintained its negative direction and significant effect.

Figure 6.4 visually demonstrates the findings regarding the AU protocol in Table 6.2. This stacked column graph shows change in score distribution over time for African countries. While there is a general trend toward permissiveness, there are more dramatic changes after 2003. There is a large decrease in scores of 1, and a sizable increase in scores ranging from 4 to 7. While after the 2003 census 45% of African countries had a score of 1, and only 23% had a score ranging from

TABLE 6.2 *The Effect of Regional Institutions and Protocols Linear Mixed-Effects ML for Abortion Policy in African Nations Only*

	Model 1 (CAI1)	Model 2 (CAI2)	Model 3 (CIRI political rights)
Females in Legislature (%)	−.007 (.005)	−.001 (.001)	.024 (.003)***
Polity score	.001 (.012)	−.001 (.002)	.008 (.005)
Quotas	.587 (.123)***	.08 (.017)***	.102 (.09)
Interaction (Quotas and Females in Legislature)	−.009 (.006)*	−.001 (.001)	.002 (.004)
Interaction (Quotas-polity)	−.073 (.012)***	.009 (.002)***	−.004 (.009)
ICPD PoA	.995 (1.06)	.141 (.167)	.285 (.144)
WHO Protocol	.026 (.062)	.001 (.009)	.000 (.037)
AU Protocol	.302 (.061)***	.044 (.009)***	.024 (.041)
GDP Logged	.141 (.131)	.024 (.019)	.023 (.023)
Muslims in Population (%)	−.010 (.007)	−.002 (.001)*	−.002 (.001)*
Catholics in Population (%)	.185 (.694)	.001 (.100)	−.061 (.169)
HDI	−.042 (1.1)	−.092 (.159)	.015 (.276)
Number of Countries	49	49	48
Total Number of Observations	694	694	552
Constant	−1.05 (2.99)	.312 (.446)	.901 (.513)*

*p<.05 **p< 0.01 ***p<0.001

4 to 7, by 2011, 7 countries had changed their policy. After 2011, 36% had a score of 1, and 32% had scores from 4 to 7. The change over time reflects the gradual adoption of the Protocol, and the adoption of a new regional norm over time.

Figure 6.5 further elucidates the phenomenon of the quota interaction. The dashed line indicates the significance of female legislators on the CAI within a quota system. As we move from 0% women legislators on the left to the right, where their share is more than half, the increase in permissive reproductive policy is limited to less than 2 points on the scale. In contrast, if we follow the dashed-dotted line from left to right, we observe the correlation with an increase in the number of women legislators when no quotas are in place. When quotas are absent, the effect on CAI of an increase from 0 to 50% in the share of women legislators is approximately three times the limited effect when the same

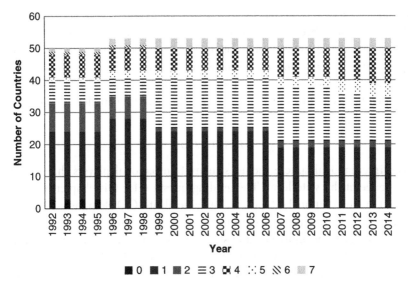

FIGURE 6.4: Distribution of CAI1 Scores Africa (1992–2013)

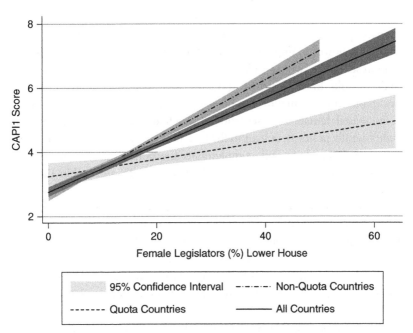

FIGURE 6.5: Interaction between Female Legislators and Quota on CAI1 (2013)

number of legislators was elected in a system where quotas were present. While this graph only reflects a single-year snapshot of the effects of quotas, a look at the data over time reveals similar patterns. Of the 67 countries in the study with quotas, only 8 (12%) underwent liberalizing changes in their abortion policy after the institution of a quota. Indeed, 2 of the 67 countries (3%) actually diverted to less- permissive abortion policy after enacting an electoral quota.

DISCUSSION

The international sphere includes many transnational players that bid for influence at the state level. The guiding question for this chapter was how might the international sphere – and specifically its IGO elements – influence state policy? Within the field of women's rights and reproductive policy, IGOs in particular try to influence and strive to set common universal standards. They have the potential to be norm setters and educators by creating forums for communication as well as by generating legal documents to try to bind state action.

When we tested the relationship between international protocol and changes in abortion policy, they were highly correlative. That said, the extent of policy change depends on the nature of the protocol. Female legislators, while significantly and positively correlating with permissiveness of reproductive health policy, had a substantively small effect. Their negative interaction with quotas, however, implies a relationship between descriptive and substantive representation, whose link is not automatic. Based on the significant negative results found for quota policies, as well as the small number of times quota implementation has been followed by policy change, the hope that increased female representation through quotas will also yield more female friendly policy is, at least in the area of sexual and reproductive health policy, not a sure bet. This complements the conclusions we reached in Chapters 4 and 5 regarding quota influence and efficacy within the state sphere.

As predicted in Hypothesis 6.1, international protocol variables were consistently correlated with increasingly permissive reproductive health policy with a significant effect. Of all the variables tested, IGO protocols also had the most pronounced effects. Extent of the effect seemed to be determined by the nature of the protocol. The ICPD coefficients were significant when specified with the variable for WHO guidelines. The latter document, which was mere guidelines, was statistically insignificant. When specified in the same models with the AU Protocol, however, the ICPD PoA lost its significance. As predicted by Hypothesis 6.2, protocols that take a direct position on abortion, such as the 2003 AU Protocol, are more likely to correlate with change. The ICPD, which takes a mildly supportive but mostly ambivalent stance on abortion and is conspicuously universal in nature and vague in verbiage, loses significance when specified in the same model with a protocol such as the AU Protocol. Overall, the significance of the IGO protocol provides support for the World Society theoretical framework.

Correlating with our findings in earlier chapters, female leadership is a strong predictor of state policy on sexual and reproductive health. As hypothesized (H6.3), a higher number of female legislators in national government corresponds with more permissive abortion policy in general models. Yet, these effects might be context dependent. The negative interaction between female legislators and quotas sheds light on the likelihood of female legislators having the causal effect of leading to more permissive abortion policy.

Our findings on quotas relate to our findings in Chapter 5. As predicted in H6.4, when women achieve their legislative positions through quotas, their correlative effect is attenuated. This implies that the correlation between female legislators and permissive reproductive rights policy is not entirely one of causation, but rather there are mitigating factors. Both may be caused by a general cultural tendency toward gender equality, as women elected through quotas do not correspond with more permissive abortion policy. The statistical significance of these findings concerning women's leadership and quotas is maintained when controlling for a host of international effects. This is particularly interesting in light of our Rwandan case study in Chapter 5. There too, we saw that the efficacy of female legislators could be contingent on cultural context and political circumstances.

The findings regarding quotas raise questions about the extent to which domestic institutions might promote norm change through institutional electoral means. Although one of the purposes of quota policy is to promote women's welfare policy, very few quotas correlated with a positive change over time in abortion policy. What is more, quotas interacted negatively with number of female legislators. These findings call into question the efficacy of quotas regarding the goal of advancing women's interests in political agendas. Further attention should be paid to different types of quotas and their unique effects.

What are the key lessons from our findings concerning the importance of the international sphere and specifically concerning the influence of IGOs? The protocols that we tested are essentially an expression of the norms that are being processed in IGO forums and that turn into global norms. As discussed earlier, when a certain value or principle is shared among enough states, it becomes a global norm. These norms can then be codified in treaties and protocols. Thus, they are translated into standard practice even for states that have yet to adopt the norm.

In this case, the ICPD PoA communicated that abortion was an acceptable form of family planning and practice in women's health. Its mentioning of abortion and endorsement of safe abortion procedures took steps to normalize the medical procedure. Simultaneously, its indecisive, and at times discouraging, language served to undermine some of this message. We elaborate on the significance of this language in the next chapter. In the AU charter, the language was significantly more decisive. This kind of language sends a considerably stronger message about norms of abortion. The results reflected the discrepancy in effects in our multivariate models.

These protocols can have powerful norm-communicating functions beyond their power as legally binding documents. These functions relate to the other mechanisms by which IGOs transfer norms among states. First, in the formation of these treaties and protocols, they open up a range of forums for debate and education. These forums represent areas where countries and their leaders undergo socialization, as they are exposed to new ideas and new arguments for and against policy change.

The discussions surrounding protocol creation also facilitate education. States can see what other states have chosen, what policy structures have been tried, and what research is out there. Access to this information allows countries to choose best practices for their own political, cultural, and institutional contexts. As discussed earlier, the fact that they are more likely to find states similar to themselves in such a large forum, further enhances the IGO capacity to teach about policy. If countries are only exposed to their neighboring countries, they are exposed to limited policy models and not necessarily to options that truly suit their needs. In large IGO forums, countries with similar profiles connect. The forums that are created to discuss and draft treaties and protocols become ideal places to exercise this type of "policy shopping." Finally, even if these treaties themselves are at times difficult to enforce for IGOs, they provide important tools for NGOs and local civil society groups. If a country has signed a given treaty, local groups can use this signature as a precedent and an incentive for policy change.

All of this shows again why the ICPD PoA and the AU Charter had different levels of influence. As we discuss further in Chapter 7, in the ICPD discussions, countries were exposed simultaneously to pro- and anti-abortion positions. This meant that the socialization and education process presented

conflicting views, neither strongly socializing nor educating on any one position. In the ICPD discussions, perhaps ability to change came more from the
fact that interest groups with mutual agendas had the opportunity to connect
and strengthen one another. Those who already had a certain view found
existing allies. This was in contrast to the AU Charter, where there was less
forceful resistance to abortion as a right and norm, allowing for a stronger and
clearer message, and for more effective socialization and education to take
place.

CONCLUSIONS

The international sphere has a range of potential means to influence domestic
policy. Within the realm of transnational activity, IGOs in particular have
tools to influence reproductive rights. The treaties and protocols generated by
these organizations correlate strongly with policy change, and we can hypothesize many mechanisms through which this influence unfolds.

IGO activity found its way into Chapter 4 as a potential confounding factor
in identifying women's substantive representation. As discussed there, countries may be motivated to follow IGO prompts as a means of gaining access to
international resources. We concluded that women representatives indeed
exercise influence in a variety of regimes. In the current chapter, though, we
went a step further and tried to look at how IGOs function as an additional,
complementary layer of influence. It is not just a discussion of how either
IGOs or state representatives use their influence, but how the two function
side by side. While based on previous chapters we conclude that female
representatives exercise influence, the findings of this chapter show that
IGOs should also be considered. Their influence is significant, even when
controlling for domestic influences such as women's leadership and gender
quotas.

As for the U.N.'s SDGs – and in particular the 5th Goal, Gender Equality –
the findings in this chapter can be instructive. To the question of whether the
international sphere in general, and its IGO elements in particular, have the
ability to influence reproductive health policy, the answer is yes. However, for
reasons pertaining to the range of functions of intergovernmental organizations, measures and protocols that use precise language produce distinctly
superior results to measures that strive for consensus at the expense of clarity.
Let us now delve deeper into the intricacies of the effects of the international
sphere as we focus on particular case studies in Chapter 7.

7

Case Studies in the International Sphere: The ICPD PoA and the Maputo Protocol

As we saw elsewhere in this book, and in particular in Chapter 6, IGOs can be powerful influencers over public policy. They are not just a reflection of their parts – the sovereign states – but can take on a life of their own as autonomous actors in global politics (Barnett & Finnemore, 1999). Based on shared interests and values, they aim to create international standards in various areas including war and peace, law, labor, human rights, and health, to name a few. Often, the products of their efforts at norm setting and their preferred toolbox involve international treaties and protocols. That is why it is important to include standout international agreements when analyzing how the international sphere affects abortion policy around the world. These international treaties and protocols can be drivers of global change and can facilitate the education, socialization, and NGO strengthening mechanisms exercised by IGOs.

In this chapter we will first look at international agreements in general: What are the different kinds of agreements? What type of bodies and what sorts of political entities enter into them? What does being a signatory entail? We then pick two of the most prominent international agreements in the area of reproductive policy as our case studies to see how such international arrangements influence abortion policy and law. For each of the two agreements, we examine the drafting and ratifying processes. We then examine how the nature of the writing process and the type of obligation it entailed correlated with policy outcomes in each case.

The discussion in this chapter complements the analysis in Chapter 6 in two major ways. First, by delving into the details of the two case studies, we are able to illustrate much of the theoretical and empirical work presented in the previous chapter. Furthermore, those case studies allow us to more fully analyze the causal mechanisms underlying international influence on abortion policy at the national level.

We aim to observe aspects of the case studies that shed new light on the discussion of the effects of IGOs on abortion policy. This, therefore, does not include a comprehensive review of international law in general or of the ICPD PoA and the Maputo Protocol in particular. We hope, however, that the wealth of information provided in the case studies and the insights derived from them prove to be sufficiently insightful.

WHAT ARE INTERNATIONAL AGREEMENTS?

International agreements are made between two or more sovereign states. They can be made directly between countries, or under the auspices of a third party. IGOs such as the United Nations, the European Union, and the African Union are often such third-party facilitators. As the international system has developed and grown since World War II, the number of such agreements has skyrocketed. These agreements have yielded rules and regulations in areas spanning economic, social, communications, environmental, and human rights activity (Simmons, 1998).

Agreements between states and agreements facilitated by international bodies can take many forms. The U.N. Treaty Reference Guide defines 10 different instruments used in international law to formalize agreements or understandings between countries. Yet, the Guide states that this is not an exhaustive list. International agreements can be codified as treaties, agreements, conventions, protocols, charters, declarations, and more. Each term implies a different form, function, number of players, level of commitment, severity of subject, degree of detail, and so forth (United Nations, 1999; Raustiala, 2005). Agreements also differ in their aims, ranging from policy change to ratification of the status quo and from specifying monitoring to sanctions for non-compliance (Raustiala, 2005).

Unless expressly drafted otherwise, international agreements are often legally binding. They can be contracts or pledges (Raustiala, 2005). Contracts imply a legally binding treaty. Pledges are statements of intention, with no legal obligation, often setting a norm or making an effort to motivate nations to abide by existing norms.

Even within the realm of legally binding agreements, there are grey areas depending on whether states have signed, ratified, accepted, or approved the agreement. When a state signs a treaty, it indicates interest in proceeding with the treaty-making process. It qualifies the state to ratify, accept, or approve. Ratification is the act that legally binds the state to uphold the terms of the agreement. Acceptance and approval have similar meanings but imply no requirement that the treaty be ratified by the head of state (United Nations, 1999).

How binding are international agreements in reality? First, even within the legal bounds of agreement making, a state may submit reservations. This means it may formally reject certain provisions of the treaty. There are also elements of formality of the agreement that influence how binding it may be. First, it depends on the level of government at which the treaty is signed. If the head of government signs, it represents a considerably more visible and credible sign of commitment than if a low-level bureaucrat does. The higher up in the state's chain of command, the more visible the pledge and the more likely it is to be respected by other government office holders and state organs. Second, binding formality depends on the level of detail in the agreement itself. There can be deliberate ambiguity or avoidance of contro-versial matters on the one hand and on the other there may be highly detailed, precise writing that carries greater obligation (Lipson, 1991). Often, the greater the desire for compliance and broad participation, the more ambiguous the text, so as to enable cooperation (Raustiala, 2005). Indeed, obscure language might increase the number of states willing to join as signatories. This would be more typical of universal treaties. Regional treaties, treaties with limited signatories, or treaties on a very limited topic are more likely to have a well-defined set of goals.

With that in mind, international agreements are notoriously hard to enforce. Studies have found significant gaps between formal ratification of treaties and ratifying states' actual application of treaty standards. For example, Avdeyeva (2007) observed the activity of 25 post-communist countries who signed CEDAW and the U.N. Beijing Platform of Action, committing to greater state action to combat violence against women. Of these, only 4 took action to implement greater institutional supervision, 17 did not implement the recommended police training, only 11 ran the recommended public awareness campaigns, and 14 gave no or minimal support for recommended NGOs. Overall, she found a high rate of state non-compliance when it came to adopting the recommendations stipulated by CEDAW and the U.N. Beijing Platform of Action.

In fact, some research even implies that ratification of treaties relieves pressure on states to implement any real change. This logic would suggest that even if there were pressure for change, with the signing of a treaty, the inclination to monitor state action could be diminished (Hathaway, 2002). It is clearly not enough that a state signs an international agreement. For genuine implementation, the administration also needs to enact corresponding legisla-tion (Goodman & Jinks, 2003).

Countries may sign agreements because of social pressure, as a means of appeasing other states, or to gain entry into other valuable relationships. International organizations and other member states can try to enforce an agreement through different forms of material coercion, but this only works if they have effective and significant enough means of pressure. If they have little to offer or take away from a non-complying state, their coercion capabilities are seriously limited.

Koh (1999) describes two ways that international law might be enforced. First, within the "horizontal" method, sovereign states and IGOs may pressure and attempt to coerce compliance. IGOs can be platforms for "shaming and blaming" nation-states for violating international norms (Murdie & Davis, 2012; Murdie & Peksen, 2015). These platforms can be particularly important when countries that provide foreign aid decide who will be an aid recipient based on IGO and International Nongovernment Organization recommendations (Dietrich & Murdie, 2017). Second is the "vertical" method, in which a variety of actors, including state actors, International Nongovernmental Organizations, and local civil society movements use international agreements as a basis to demand certain policies. The European Union, for example, has a built-in fire alarm system, in which citizens, local organizations, businesses, and interest groups can alert the Union of cases of state non-compliance (Martin, 2000).

Both the "horizontal" and "vertical" methods depend on certain conditions that are in no way guaranteed. In the horizontal scheme, the countries interested in enforcing behavior must have a strong enough means of coercion, one that trumps whatever reason the non-compliant country may have for ignoring the protocol in the first place. When the non-compliant country claims a lack of resources or democratic support, means of coercion do not only lose their effectiveness but also their legitimacy. In the vertical scheme, specific actors have to pick the cause, a civil society has to be relatively established, and the regime has to be responsive to its citizens. These conditions are also far from guaranteed in the case of many countries.

Regardless of how enforceable these laws are, they are often followed (Koh, 1996). Additionally, sometimes both the horizontal and vertical methods of enforcement – or at least one of them – are effective. In particular in the area of women's reproductive rights, the vertical method has proven significant, with civil society and NGO groups often emerging as significant agents of change in national policy (Hessini, 2005; Brookman-Amissah & Bando Mayo, 2004; Adams & Kang, 2007). Given their potential for impact, their ability to create norms, and the possibility of their enforcement, we set out to look at how recent international treaties and protocols have impacted abortion policy around the world.

As mentioned in Chapter 6, these treaties also have value beyond their mere legal consequences. Those treaties serve as sites of socialization and education and create and strengthen epistemic communities. Haas describes an epistemic community as "a network of professionals with recognized expertise and competence in a particular domain and an authoritative claim to policy-relevant knowledge within that domain or issue-area" (1992, p. 3). These communities are made up of professionals from a variety of disciplines and backgrounds. The experts are character-ized by shared normative beliefs, shared causal beliefs, shared notions of validity, and a shared belief in a set of policy practices. In other words, they are coordinated in how they identify difficulties and challenges and the types of goals they set. Likewise, they have a common understanding of causes and proposed solutions (Haas, 1992; March & Olsen, 1998). These are communities of knowledge validation, combining norm crea-tion with policy practice. They define social phenomena and socially construct knowledge (Adler, 2005). These communities – often function-ing within or organized by IGOs – can set agendas and reframe issues to direct the international community (Risse, 2000).

IGOs as sites of treaty and agreement creation have a strong role in creating epistemic communities. When treaties are negotiated, a group of national, IGO, and NGO experts, all of which have interest and share knowledge in the topic at hand, take part. The treaties themselves are a result of these experts finding common ground on normative beliefs and best practices in order to generate an agreement. Both the debates and the treaty that results construct knowledge, frame the issue, and direct the international community. Let us now examine how this plays out in the context of women reproductive rights and abortion policy.

LANDMARK IGO AGREEMENTS ON REPRODUCTIVE RIGHTS: THE ICPD POA AND THE PROTOCOL TO THE AFRICAN CHARTER ON HUMAN AND PEOPLES' RIGHTS ON THE RIGHTS OF WOMEN IN AFRICA

When looking at how international agreements can affect policy and repro-ductive rights, IGO-based agreements are a good place to start. They are typically not limited to just two or a handful of countries. Indeed, IGOs have in recent years been the leaders in framing women's rights and repro-ductive rights as integral parts of international development. The U.N.'s SDGs discussed in Chapters 1 and 6 are a good example, and SDG5 pertaining to gender equality is particularly pertinent.

We chose the ICPD PoA and the AU Protocol as they are both widely cited as standout documents in their effort to address reproductive and abortion rights. Both were innovative for their time in how to address reproductive health and how to create international frameworks for abortion rights.

These agreements are part of a legacy of international and regional IGO agreements for advancing women's rights. This legacy includes agreements such as CEDAW (1979), the U.N. Declaration on the Elimination of Violence Against Women (United Nations General Assembly, 1979), the WHO "Safe Abortion: Technical and Policy Guidance for Health Systems" (World Health Organization, 2003), the U.N. Security Council Resolution 1325 (Office of the Special Adviser on Gender Issues and Advancement of Women, 2000), the U. N. SDGs (United Nations, 2015a), the Inter-American Convention on the Prevention, Punishment, and Eradication of Violence against Women (Organization of American States (OAS, 1994), and the Istanbul Convention (Council of Europe, 2011). None of these other conventions, however, aimed to address women's reproductive or abortion rights in the comprehensive or ground-breaking ways found in either the ICPD PoA or the AU Protocol.

Countries have cited the ICPD framework as having been instrumental in helping their domestic health care systems develop treatment and access policy. The framework was also described as a significant piece of international abortion legislation protocol (Hessini, Brookman-Amissah, & Crane, 2006). It is seen as the first time a major international agreement addressed women's rights and reproductive rights as an integral part of development, as well as having importance in their own right. The ICPD PoA represented a new era of development policy, where human rights, rather than demographic data, became the focus for policymakers. The AU Protocol is groundbreaking in how it decisively and clearly states abortion as a woman's right (under certain conditions). Before the AU Protocol, no international agreement ever dared to so boldly promote a woman's right to abortion. Let us now look more closely at the two cases at hand.

Abortion in the ICDP PoA

The ICPD was held in Cairo from September 5 to 13, 1994 (United Nations Population Fund, n.d.; Fincher, 1994). It was part of a series of U.N. conferences that focused on population and development. The ICPD was remarkable in its diversity of participants (DeJong, 2001). Close to 200 countries sent delegations and over 4,000 individuals from

1,700 organizations participated in the ICPD and the NGO activities that ran parallel to government negotiations. NGOs participated as outside lobby groups, as official representatives within government delegations, and as technical and research advisors for intergovernmental discussions (Hempel, 1996; Fincher, 1994).

The goal of the ICPD was to address development issues including human rights, population growth, sexual and reproductive health, gender equality, and sustainable development (United Nations Population Fund, n.d.). It resulted in the writing of the ICPD PoA, which was adopted unanimously by the U.N. member states in attendance and overall by 179 member states (Fincher, 1994). The ICPD PoA laid out a long-term vision for reaching development goals. Unlike previous attempts to formulate such goals, the ICPD PoA placed emphasis on individual and human rights, rather than setting quantitative population targets (United Nations Population Fund, n.d.).

The ICPD PoA resulted in a whole new way of addressing development. Individual dignity, human rights, and the right to family planning were reframed as the heart of development. Many see this conference as one of the first instances in which fulfilling the rights of women was articulated as a crucial part of development (United Nations Population Fund, n.d.). Glasier and Gülmezoglu even go as far as saying that "the notion of reproductive health was born in Cairo in 1994" (2006, p. 1550). Conference goers agreed that reproductive rights were human rights. Issues such as poverty, hunger, environmental degradation, and political instability could not be fully solved without securing women's sexual and reproductive health as well as their rights under law (Germain & Kidwell, 2005; Gerntholtz, Gibbs, & Willan, 2011).

Women needed autonomy over their reproductive lives in order to address population goals (Glasier & Gülmezoglu, 2006). Reproductive and sexual health were necessary to improve the quality of life for women, their families, and their communities. This new outlook represented a critical shift within the population field (Pollack Petchesky, 1995). It was a move away within the development field from setting demographic targets and toward putting emphasis on improving individuals' quality of life (Hempel, 1996; DeJong, 2001; Jacobson, 2000). The ICPD is credited with establishing this new paradigm in population and demographic policy (DeJong, 2001).

As a result, the idea of the "interrelationship" between issues was a dominant concept throughout the ICPD PoA. Section 1.5 of the preamble states:

The 1994 Conference was explicitly given a broader mandate on development issues than previous population conferences, reflecting the growing awareness that population, poverty, patterns of production and consumption and the environment are so closely interconnected that none of them can be considered in isolation.

Of the guiding principles outlined in Chapter 2, the interconnectedness of all issues again is given emphasis. Principle 6 states that:

Sustainable development as a means to ensure human well-being, equitably shared by all people today and in the future, requires that the interrelationships between population, resources, the environment and development should be fully recognized, properly managed and brought into harmonious, dynamic balance.

All of Chapter 3 is dedicated to the "Interrelationships Between Population, Sustained Economic Growth, and Sustainable Development," and the word "interrelationship" appears in the ICPD PoA no less than 37 times.

The ICPD PoA emphasized the value of investing in women and girls both as an end unto itself and as a way to achieve society-wide development goals. The PoA addresses reproductive health, women's empowerment, family planning, gender-based violence, and female genital mutilation. It also addresses the connection between these topics and topics such as poverty, urbanization, migration, and aging (United Nations Population Fund, n.d.). For example, Chapter 4 of the ICPD PoA, which focuses on gender equality, equity, and the empowerment of women, begins by stating that gender equality is both a goal unto itself, as well as a necessity for achieving any other development goal. "The empowerment and autonomy of women and the improvement of their political, social, economic and health status is a highly important end in itself. In addition, it is essential for the achievement of sustainable development." The chapter's introduction concludes by stressing that the "experience shows that population and development programmes are most effective when steps have simultaneously been taken to improve the status of women." While addressing poverty, and methods for its eradication, Section 3.16 states:

Eliminating social, cultural, political and economic discrimination against women is a prerequisite of eradicating poverty, promoting sustained economic growth in the context of sustainable development, ensuring quality family planning and reproductive health services, and achieving balance between population and available resources and sustainable patterns of consumption and production.

The ICPD PoA was the first major international agreement to make recommendations on unsafe abortions. It principally addressed abortion under the topic of "health, morbidity, and mortality" and discussed the public health impact of unsafe abortions and the need to reduce recourse to abortion as a means of family planning. It also stated that where abortion was not illegal, countries should ensure that women had access to safe abortion procedures (Hessini, 2005). One of the ICPD PoA's great contributions to reproductive rights advocacy was that it moved the debate on contraception from the moral arena to that of public health (Fincher, 1994).

Attendees were careful to moderate rhetoric so as to maintain the inclusive nature of the process and of the agreement itself. The language used showed great reverence toward the sovereign rights of each country, as well as various ethical norms and values of different religious and cultural traditions (Fincher, 1994). The ICPD PoA writers were hesitant to make any statement that would alienate a country or a religious group. For example, when discussing the topic of abortion, great consideration was given to the desires and sensitivities of the Catholic Church and of states with large Catholic populations. In general, the Holy See was granted significant influence over the process, especially in addressing topics of reproductive health (we will further elaborate on this issue later on in this chapter). In the end, the ICPD only went as far as to recognize unsafe abortions as a major public health concern. It encouraged accessible, high-quality family planning services as the solution (Germain & Kidwell, 2005).

The ICPD PoA addressed abortion in a few sections. It appears a few times in Section 7, Reproductive Rights and Reproductive Health. In Paragraph 7.24, it states that "Governments should take appropriate steps to help women avoid abortion, which in no case should be promoted as a method of family planning, and in all cases provide for the humane treatment and counselling of women who have had recourse to abortion" (UNFPA, 1995). In Paragraph 7.6, it states that "Reproductive health care in the context of primary health care should, inter alia, include ... abortion as specified in paragraph 8.25, including prevention of abortion and the management of the consequences of abortion ... " (UNFPA, 1995). Paragraph 7.63 states that any measures or changes related to abortion within the health system can be determined only at the national or local level according to the national legislative process. In circumstances where abortion is not against the law, such abortion should be safe. In all cases, women should have access to quality services for the management of complications arising from abortion (UNFPA, 1995).

Section 8, "Health, Morbidity, and Mortality," contains Paragraph 8.25, which is cited as summarizing and embodying the ICPD PoA statement on abortion:

In no case should abortion be promoted as a method of family planning. All Governments and relevant intergovernmental and non-governmental organizations are urged to strengthen their commitment to women's health, to deal with the health impact of unsafe abortion as a major public health concern and to reduce the recourse to abortion through expanded and improved family-planning services. Prevention of unwanted pregnancies must always be given the highest priority and every attempt should be made to eliminate the need for abortion. Women who have unwanted pregnancies should have ready access to reliable information and compassionate counselling. Any measures or changes related to abortion within the health system can only be determined at the national or local level according to the national legislative process. In circumstances where abortion is not against the law, such abortion should be safe. In all cases, women should have access to quality services for the management of complications arising from abortion. Post-abortion counselling, education and family-planning services should be offered promptly, which will also help to avoid repeat abortions.

(UNFPA, 1995)

The ICPD's position on abortion is considered one of its glaring weaknesses (Ngwena, 2010). The language is indecisive and the statements inconsistent not only in terms of the minimum standards of abortion services each woman should enjoy but also in terms of its expectations from states in terms of policy. This lukewarm wording and these internal inconsistencies (if not real contradictions) reflect the writers' efforts to placate both those who called for expanded women's reproductive rights and autonomy on the one hand and forces that opposed abortion on the other.

The language used is an attempt to both recognize the proven connection between improved women's reproductive health and access to safe abortion, and cultural and religious opposition to this medical procedure. In fact, a more critical reading of the document would point to the fact that the meek position that the PoA takes does not ensure abortion as a reproductive right, marginally recognizes it as a universally used method of family planning, and then delegitimizes it. Care for women is limited to the care they receive after an abortion, when many of them are inevitably coping with the ramifications of an unsafe, illegal procedure. As mentioned in Chapter 1 of this book, the number of illegal abortions are in the tens of millions a year worldwide.

The PoA recognizes unsafe abortion as a problem, without acknowledging that the best method to prevent unsafe abortions is to grant legal access to safe ones. It also recognizes that abortions and unsafe abortions happen all over the world, while simultaneously denying it as a part of family planning. These internal contradictions and weak language in the abortion provisions failed to provide governments with a clear directive for action (Hessini, 2005). We might note that this indecision was not limited just to abortion. In general, attendees wanted to avoid any controversy, avoid quantifying problems, and avoid offering concrete solutions or direct recommendations (Fincher, 1994).

Women's access to safe abortion was one of the prickliest issues at the ICPD. Negotiations over this topic proved particularly tricky. The conference organizers and attendees were wary of the topic, while religious organizations, states, and the media all attempted to promote their own framing of the issue. The framing of faith organizations in particular was, more often than not, toward restrictive abortion policy. One of the most vocal opponents of abortion as a right or valuable service was the Holy See. In a written reservation submitted to the PoA, the representative of the Holy See intimated:

> The intense negotiations of these days have resulted in the presentation of a text which all recognize as improved, but about which the Holy See still has grave concerns. At the moment of their adoption by consensus by the Main Committee, my delegation already noted its concerns about the question of abortion. The chapters also contain references which could be seen as accepting extramarital sexual activity, especially among adolescents. They would seem to assert that abortion.
>
> (UNFPA, 1995, p. 200)

Drafting of the ICPD PoA

To understand the difficulties and need for compromises during the ICPD PoA writing process, one need look no further than the struggles and debates between pro-choice interest groups and the Catholic Church. Women's rights and pro-choice groups participated in lobbying efforts throughout the process. While women's rights NGOs and IGOs are often partners, the ICPD PoA writing process had some extremely powerful bodies providing pushback to such effort by interest groups. The Roman Catholic Church was unique among religions, as the Holy See had the status of an observer state. During the ICPD, the Holy See took a stand specifically on abortion and more so than on associated topics such as contraception, sterilization, the use of condoms, or AIDS/HIV prevention.

It is believed that the delegation of the Holy See chose to address abortion, rather than these other issues, because there was a general world consensus concerning the other topics, while abortion was then – and still is – a contentious topic generating debates internationally as well as within many countries (Fincher, 1994). The pull from both sides of the normative spectrum – and the desire to satisfy both sides – account for the watered-down and indecisive final document.

The Holy See was not alone, though, in submitting reservations specifically on abortion. Many countries submitted oral and written reservations on even the meek statements on abortion provided in the PoA. The Honduran statement, for example, read:

> ... one accepts the concepts of "family planning", "sexual health", "reproductive health", "maternity without risk", "regulation of fertility", "reproductive rights" and "sexual rights" so long as these terms do not include "abortion" or "termination of pregnancy", because Honduras does not accept these as arbitrary actions; nor do we accept them as a way of controlling fertility or regulating the population.
>
> (UNFPA, 1995, p. 188)

The Nicaragua reservation stated that:

> ... we accept the concepts of "family planning", "sexual health", "reproductive health", "reproductive rights" and "sexual rights" expressing an explicit reservation on these terms and any others when they include "abortion" or "termination of pregnancy" as a component. Abortion and termination of pregnancy can under no circumstances be regarded as a method of regulating fertility or a means of population control.
>
> (UNFPA, 1995, p. 191)

Some of the other countries with reservations on the abortion provisions included the United Arab Emirates, Yemen, the Dominican Republic, Guatemala, Malta, and Peru (UNFPA, 1995).

Let us now move on to examine another, and very different, international agreement, considered by many to be pivotal in the history of international influences on abortion policy around the world. Throughout this chapter we use Maputo Protocol interchangeably with the AU Protocol or with the Protocol to the African Charter on Human and Peoples' Rights on the Rights of Women in Africa. All three pertain to the same document.

Abortion in the Protocol to the African Charter on Human and Peoples'
Rights on the Rights of Women in Africa

The rate of unsafe abortions in Africa is the highest in the world. While 16% of the women in the world reside there, 25% of the world's unsafe abortions happen on this continent. Globally the ratio of unsafe abortion-related deaths is 330 to 100,000 abortions; in Africa it is more than double at 680 to 100,000. As much as 99% of abortions carried out in Africa are estimated to be unsafe, and Africa constitutes about 40% of deaths related to unsafe abortion world-wide. In some countries on the continent, unsafe abortions are responsible for more than half of maternal mortality (Ngwena, 2010). Of course, death is the most extreme outcome, but unsafe abortions can also result in chronic pain, secondary infertility, uterine perforation, and many other medical complications (Brookman-Amissah & Bando Mayo, 2004; Ngwena, 2010). The extreme nature of the African unsafe abortion epidemic was met head-on in the AU's 2003 Protocol to the African Charter on Human and Peoples' Rights on the Rights of Women in Africa.

The Protocol to the African Charter on Human and Peoples' Rights on the Rights of Women is a legally binding supplement to the African Charter on Human and People's Rights of the African Union. It was adopted in Maputo, Mozambique in July 2003, and entered into effect in November 2005. Its legal authority is derived from the AU Constitutive Act (Viljeon, 2009).

The document aimed to correct weaknesses in the African Charter on Human and Peoples' Rights regarding women's rights (Gerntholtz, Gibbs, & Willan, 2011). It strove to reinforce and push implementation of international human rights norms and laws regarding women's rights. These norms had been stated in documents and protocols, but until then had not been successfully implemented in many African countries. The document specified rights that had been alluded to in the Charter, but this time concretely stated women's equality and a commitment to women's rights (Viljeon, 2009).

While it addressed a range of women's rights, it was particularly strong on issues of reproductive health. The protocol functions as a tool to ensure universal access to reproductive health and the forging of enabling environments (Gerntholtz, Gibbs, & Willan, 2011). Like the ICPD PoA, a range of states, NGOs, and regional activist groups drafted the Protocol. Unlike the ICPD PoA, however, it was written over a number of years, with drafts passing through the hands of these states and non-state actors multiple times (Adams & Kang, 2007). In fact, the drafting was primarily the initiative of civil society (Ngwena, 2010).

The Protocol requires not just signing, but also ratification. For states that ratify the Protocol, it is a legally binding treaty, although as with many international protocols, enforcement is a challenge. Ratification, however, may have distinct implications. For instance, the ratification of the protocol may give activists grounds on which to hold states accountable (Adams & Kang, 2007).

As this book goes into print, 36 African states have signed and ratified the protocol, 15 have signed but not ratified, and 3 states on the continent have neither signed nor ratified. The trend of signing and ratification had a regional component; Southern and West African countries have largely ratified. Most countries that have not ratified are in Northern Africa, and the Northern areas of East, West, and Central Africa. The first country to ratify was Comoros (March 2004) and the most recent was Swaziland (October 2012). States that have signed but not ratified include Algeria, Sudan, Niger, and Ethiopia. South Sudan was the newest country to sign, in 2013, but never ratified. States that have neither signed nor ratified include Botswana, Egypt, and Tunisia.

The AU Protocol is considered one of the world's most progressive treaties on women's rights. It goes beyond measures taken in any of the previous leading international treaties on women's rights including the ICPD PoA, the Beijing Platform for Action, and the CEDAW (Adams & Kang, 2007). Since 2003, any other IGO-based document (the SDGs included) has yet to use this level of decisive language regarding reproductive rights. The Protocol includes specific forms of women's rights' violations found in parts of Africa, in addition to addressing issues found in these older treaties (Adams & Kang, 2007). The AU Protocol uses a definition of discrimination closely modeled after the definition found in CEDAW (Banda, 2006).

The Protocol covers a broad range of issues. It addresses both women's issues and applies a gendered perspective to general human rights and development issues (African Union, 2003). Women's issues addressed include discrimination against women, elimination of harmful practices, marriage and divorce, reproductive rights, widows' rights, and rights of inheritance inter alia. General issues treated with a gendered perspective include the right to life, integrity and security of the person, access to justice and protection under law, right to peace, protection in armed conflict, education, economic and social welfare rights, food security, and adequate housing.

The Protocol's treatment of abortion is considered ground-breaking. It contributes to transforming African abortion law from a crime and punishment model into a reproductive and public health paradigm. While this built on and continued the ICPD theme of seeing reproductive health as a human right, it went much farther than the ICPD PoA ever had (Ngwena, 2010; Ebeku, 2004). Article 14.2, Section C states that:

> ... state parties should take all appropriate measures to ... protect the reproductive rights of women by authorising medical abortion in cases of sexual assault, rape, incest, and where the continued pregnancy endangers the mental and physical health of the mother or the life of the mother or the foetus. (African Union, 2003)

While it does not require states to legalize abortion on demand, the Protocol lays out a number of scenarios under which abortion must be legalized. This is the first time in international human rights law that a right to abortion has been enshrined in legal code. It is also the first time abortion is specified as a human right, and as an enforceable obligation (Davis, 2009; Ebeku, 2004; Wing, 2012). Unlike other international agreements that address abortion, this clause also provides a practical template for state abortion law (Ngwena, 2010).

The Protocol challenges the consensus reached at the ICPD (Ngwena, 2010). It clearly states abortion as a woman's right under certain conditions (Chirwa, 2006). Rather than addressing it as an undesirable practice that should be avoided, it neutrally recognizes abortion's universal role in family planning. But how was the African Union able to reach such an achievement in drafting and ratifying a consistent, detailed, and coherent protocol? In what ways was the drafting process here different than other cases of IGO agreements pertaining to abortion in general and the ICPD PoA in particular?

Drafting of the AU Protocol

In general, during the drafting process, some state parties were resistant to the Protocol's content, arguing that men and women could not be considered equal; they are different and have different roles requiring a differential treatment (Banda, 2006). Article 14.2.C specifically was the object of certain strong objections. Libya, Rwanda, and Senegal in particular objected (Banda, 2006; Adams & Kang, 2007). That said, accounts suggest that the levels of acrimony, controversy, and contention surrounding abortion did not reach those seen in the drafting process of the ICPD PoA.

Perhaps one of the reasons why abortion did not attract as much attention in the drafting process of the AU Protocol was that certain regional issues were by comparison more controversial. Any opposition to a move toward a mandate on abortion was dwarfed in comparison with the resistance generated against the effort to ban polygamy (Davis, 2009). Compared to other areas of the world, polygamy, early-age marriage, and traditional marriage are particularly contentious topics in Africa (Walker, 2012; Ebeku, 2004). Activists for the rights of African women have found these issues especially thorny and difficult to change. In Article 6 of the Protocol, the final text regarding polygamy represents a compromise on the issue. Monogamy is encouraged, but polygamy supporters clearly held their grounds:

> Monogamy is encouraged as the preferred form of marriage and that the rights of women in marriage and family, including in polygamous marital relationships are promoted and protected . . .

Opposition to polygamy, traditional marriage practices, and female genital mutilation are often met with accusations of Westernization and lack of respect for traditional local and Muslim cultures (Adams & Kang, 2007). Polygamy especially is considered to be so deeply entrenched in many African cultures that it had to be recognized in the Protocol, despite its rejection by the proverbial frameworks of international human rights (Ssenyonjo, 2007; Jonas, 2012). This made it difficult to address these specific issues. Eight different countries have registered a reservation on one or more clauses related to marriage (Viljeon, 2009; Mujuzi, 2008), in comparison to three reservations on the abortion clause. We can see how other and more contentious topics left abortion debates easier to resolve.

In sum, the AU Protocol is significantly more successful in producing an impactful document on reproductive rights. Certain elements in the drafting process help us explain why that is. First, the groundwork done by activists and NGOs as they worked toward a regional agreement formed some basic understandings and created the necessary common ground to build upon. In addition, the agenda setting and prioritization in the discussions themselves, and the fact that abortion did not take center stage – particularly in comparison to other topics – all contributed to the successful conclusion of the process in the form of the Maputo Protocol.

DISCUSSION

Looking at both the ICPD PoA and the AU Protocol, we can see that when IGOs choose to address abortion, they have the power to legitimize the discussion of this topic, break down taboos surrounding it, and generate a discourse that encourages more permissive abortion policy worldwide.

The ICPD PoA provided a platform for states, NGOs, and civil society actors to revisit abortion policy, understand the impact of unsafe abortions, hear actors who support legalizing abortion, and find partners and structures to help advance safe abortion procedures at the state level. Even without a strong stance, or even a clear stance, the ICPD marked several significant accomplishments. First, it took abortion out of the realm of morality policy and into the realm of public health and international development. Second, it pushed countries to address the critical issue of unsafe abortions and frame it as an unacceptable and avoidable problem. Third, where abortions were legal, it encouraged national health care systems to provide services in a safe and affordable manner and, where the procedure was illegal, to give women a method of coping with post-abortion needs. Fourth, it gave a platform to pro-choice groups to push an agenda and find allies. Given that one of the benefits of international agreements is their empowering effect for civil society, this latter upshot was crucial.

The AU Protocol canonized abortion as a right. It stated that under designated conditions abortion was a right, meaning that denying a woman an abortion amounted to a human rights violation. This had a few effects. First, it forced the hand of any country who ratified the Protocol to codify this position in law. Second, if countries signed without ratifying, it still gave civil society groups and citizens grounds on which to push for change. Third, its absolute language signaled to other IGOs that it could be done; abortion could be defined as a right. This set a new standard for how abortion could be addressed if an organization were serious enough about advancing reproductive rights. Within a world society framework, a strong regional IGO taking a clear stance on a universal issue would potentially influence not just member states, but also other IGOs and international NGOs. That said, while the two agreements may be similar in the level of innovation, certain vital disparities meant that their ramifications would be fundamentally different.

Drafting Procedure and Level of Commitment

Comparing the drafting procedures of these two protocols demonstrates how the final product is affected by the nature of the writing process and the goals of the drafters. The interest of drafters to achieve consensus, or embrace conflict, had a big influence on the final results. In the ICPD PoA, the effort to achieve consensus, and the fear of conflict and alienation, resulted in an unclear and weak position. As a result, policymakers often find it hard to use the ICPD PoA as an outline for policymaking, as it takes indistinct positions and refrains from defining quantifiable – or clearly designated – goals and policies. When policymakers returned to their home countries, the implications of the ICPD PoA remained unclear. The ways in which the new agreement was to be applied, and what obligations it conferred, were all shrouded in uncertainty largely stemming from the document itself and its ambiguity and inconsistency on key issues (European Parliament, 2003).

This stands in stark contrast to the AU Protocol. Drafters of the African agreement did not shy away from concrete statements that were consistent and far-reaching in their policymaking implications. As a result, they generated a new framework and a new set of standards in supporting reproductive rights in international treaties. The African Union offered countries a clear legal skeleton on which to build their national abortion policies.

The need for signing vs. ratifying also distinguishes between levels of commitment each document demands. The ICPD only requires signing and allows for ample reservations. It does not legally obligate countries to take any action pursuant to this signature. Their signature amounts to a good faith gesture, signaling intentions to uphold the principles of the PoA. While its publication was followed by change in international policy, the impact of the ICPD PoA was not nearly as strong as that of the AU Protocol. The AU Protocol required countries not only to sign, but also to ratify, and was followed by a considerably larger movement toward change.

Reservations

Written and oral reservations were more conventional and lengthy in regard to the ICPD PoA than they were in the AU Protocol. Twenty-one countries submitted either oral or written reservations (although two later withdrew those reservations). This constitutes 12% of the 179 states that signed the ICPD PoA. Reservations covered 19 pages of the ICPD PoA. In comparison, 6 ratifying countries have submitted reservations to the AU Protocol, constituting 10% of AU members and potential signers and ratifiers. The reservations were significantly shorter, with some of them being only a few lines long (Asuagbor, 2016).

These features of both documents – their degree of tolerance for reservations and the need to only sign versus sign plus ratify – perhaps are responsible for some of the difference in their impact. After the publication of the ICPD PoA, there was change in the degree of permissiveness of world abortion policy. Yet, the weak, unclear language and the absence of a mechanism for commitment might have mitigated its impact.

Education and socialization impact

As sites of epistemic communities with the power to educate and socialize, the degree of consensus takes on even greater meaning for these two protocols.

The strength of an epistemic community to socialize and educate is based at least partly on the homogeneity of opinion within it. If community members diverge very little in their beliefs on norms and best practices, the community can deliver stronger messages. Indeed, as the burgeoning literature on epistemic communities suggests, such homogeneity is by definition a characteristic of the community. Epistemic communities share common normative frameworks through which they analyze the world. Subsequently, epistemic communities are better capable of directing and dictating international norms in a cohesive manner.

The group of nations drafting the ICPD PoA was heterogeneous in its beliefs on norms and best practices. Consequently, the document presented a watered-down and insubstantial interpretation of reproductive rights, as the group of nations drafting the agreement could only find common ground through mitigated clauses. While they provided forums for education and socialization, the messages were neither clear nor consistent. Hence, they fell short of achieving their goals.

The AU Charter forum on reproductive rights represented a more cohesive and homogenous group. This homogeneity was achieved at least partly due to the work done by NGOs in advance. Such homogeneity allowed an epistemic community to form consisting of leaders and office holders in most of the African countries that were signatories to the Charter. While some disagreement persisted, those involved were much more unified as to how to address abortion policy.

This may also be partly due to both the urgency of the matter in Africa and the fact that the level of contentiousness around abortion paled in comparison to some of the other topics under debate. Compared to other questions on the agenda, the participants were much closer to each other in their positions on that question and were accordingly able to agree on the abortion policy question. The discussion and text generated by the leaders, representatives, and experts of this community of African nations had much more potential as a forum of education and socialization. Indeed, as we saw in Chapter 6, there was dramatic change in average type of abortion policy among African nations. Countries introduced into their legal codes many more conditions under which a woman could access abortion. Only between 2003 and 2011, seven countries changed their policy. In 2003, 45% of AU states only allowed abortion in case of danger to the mother's life. By 2011, this figure was down by 9%, as an increasing number of countries put more permissive policies on their books.

The cohesion and homogeneity of the epistemic community also allowed specifically for abortion to be addressed. By discussing abortion in a more homogenous forum and with a smaller number of participants (largely limited to AU members and African civil society organizations), the issue could be more strongly addressed. This is particularly notable in comparison to the much larger ICPD PoA forum. In the United Nations, the range of actors is considerably more diverse and its number is much larger. As we discuss extensively above, countries and cultures diverge significantly, surely making it harder to articulate a stronger, more coherent voice as a part of an international treaty.

CONCLUSIONS

Both the ICPD PoA and the AU Protocol stand as case studies for the significance of international protocols in shaping reproductive rights. We find that international protocols had a positive influence on liberalization of worldwide abortion policy, but the magnitude of their effects correlated with the strength of the position they took, the decisiveness of their language, the cohesiveness and consistency of their framing, the extent to which they were able to forge a homogenous epistemic community, their ability to capitalize on agenda setting and prioritization, the work NGOs contributed, and their willingness to define abortion as a right in the face of conflict and at the expense of consensus. These two international agreements were chosen as case studies because each in its own way represented a groundbreaking change in how international organizations addressed the issue of reproductive rights.

Features of protocols observed in the discussion also define how international advocates of abortion rights, civil society players, or even the IGOs themselves can use these protocols as grounds to demand action, to "shame and blame," or to use them as a basis for aid distribution. For example, if countries are not required to ratify the protocol, and only sign it, there is no legal basis on which to offer or deny aid if a country fails to adopt specified measures. If the language is indecisive or unclear, the protocol's binding power as a contract is diminished. International forums, civil society players, and other states cannot accuse a country of non-compliance if it is not clear what constitutes compliance.

Along the lines of findings in Chapters 2 and 3 of this book, the power of the civil society sphere, and specifically of organized religion, is evident in the international sphere as well. The evidence suggests that the Church demonstrated similar tendencies in the drafting process of the ICPD PoA as seen in previous chapters. As a result, it was able to seriously limit and constrain the scope of abortion provisions in the international framework that emanated from Cairo. The Church is one example of a type of player that has a sway in several of the spheres examined in this book, but others can also play a crucial role. In the drafting of the AU Protocol, it was local and regional NGOs.

This underscores the importance of a multi-sphered, comparative framework; abortion rights are influenced at a number of levels, and there is interplay among those spheres of influence. These include the international level, as well as the levels of national politics and civil society. Indeed, as both cases demonstrate, it would be impossible to fully grasp processes at the international level without considering interrelations with civil society and national politics. We continue to elaborate on this point, in the next and final chapter of this book.

8

Conclusions

Final Thoughts and Avenues for Future Research on Abortion Policy

On September 28, 2018, in a statement to mark International Safe Abortion Day, the Special Procedures of the U.N. Human Rights Council tweeted "unsafe abortions cause the deaths of some 47,000 women each year and a further five million suffer some form of temporary or permanent disability." According to the experts at the Special Procedures office, in the context of the SDGs, abortions are seen as not only important in their own right, but also inextricably linked to a host of other goals. According to the independent U.N. experts in 2018, access to safe abortion is a precondition to allow women to enjoy other types of rights including "life, health, equality and freedom from discrimination." This builds directly on the legacy of those who convened in Cairo in 1994, who had agreed that poverty, hunger, environmental degradation, and political instability could not be fully solved without securing women's sexual and reproductive health.

The policy question about abortion rights continues to this day to be at the core of political debates in various countries, through referenda, legislative, executive, and judicial action. This is part of the reason why some international organizations have been unable to form a coherent conclusion on the question of abortion rights. Yet, WHO (2003) data indicate that rather than reducing the number of women seeking abortion, outlawing abortion only leads to more clandestine and unsafe procedures. The conclusion of the statement by the U.N. experts in 2018 asked countries to "demonstrate their commitment to eliminating discrimination against women in their legislation and to advancing women's and adolescents' sexual and reproductive rights, in accordance with international human rights standards."

In the three parts of this book, we analyzed the multifaceted ways in which international bodies, national governments, and civil society organizations influence abortion policy. Whether through gender quotas, international treaties, or norm creation, we have shown how abortion policymaking around the world is systematically influenced by those three spheres. Now, it is time to draw conclusions about each of the spheres, think some more about their interconnected natures, and consider the ways in which research could develop from here.

Accordingly, this chapter summarizes and ties together findings, cases, and theories from the book's three different parts. By bringing conclusions pertaining to all three spheres of influence – civil society, national, and international – we look at how actors in different arenas interact with and complement each other. On top of concluding this project, we also hope to leave readers with a stronger sense of what remains to be done. What we uncover in this book is valuable, but much still remains to be discovered to fully understand the determinants of women's welfare policy around the world. Let us begin with an examination of what we understand about each of the spheres separately.

FAITH CIVIL SOCIETY

Players in the sphere of civil society, even outside of democracies, are significant in shaping state public policy. Religious institutions are a classic example of players within this sphere, but religion's relationship with the state and the people is so multidimensional that it cannot be analyzed without taking into account numerous ways in which religion may influence the state.

We attempted to isolate a few aspects of the state-religion relationship. The large-scale quantitative analyses in Chapter 2 shed new light on scholarly understandings, public discourse, and feminist discourse, which often entertain the notion that religion is at odds with women's welfare and gender equality. Our findings suggested that when it came to state abortion policy, Muslim, Catholic, and Buddhist population size – as well as religiosity – negativity correlated with degree of permissiveness of abortion policy. Furthermore, abortion policy was unique in how it interacted with religion. Our various measures of abortion rights were affected differently by faith civil society than other types of women's rights, such as political rights for women.

The presence or absence of laws regulating religion was insignificant in predicting abortion policy. We were surprised to find that degrees of religious freedom did not correlate with permissive abortion policy. Likewise, we could find no effect for the separation of religion and state. The effect of religiosity was contingent on religious denomination, with a heightened effect when the dominant religion in the country was Islam.

This aspect of faith civil society was further elaborated, along with other facets, in the case study investigations of Chile and Bahrain. These case studies further elucidated the power of religious institutional structure, and its policy ramifications. By operating as a unified and cohesive organization, the Catholic Church, so it seemed, is able to achieve results even in the absence of a devoutly religious population. Islam does not have the same unified hierarchical structure as the Catholic Church. It is, therefore, less influential unless it can rely on a religious constituency.

The case studies of Chile and Bahrain allowed us to examine more closely the causal pathways and mechanisms that underlie the effects of faith civil society on reproductive policy. Those case studies demonstrate what the numbers and regressions in Chapter 2 actually look like in the day-to-day lives of real people. The analysis of the role of faith civil society in Bahrain explains how despite the religious nature of this Persian Gulf country, a relatively permissive abortion policy lasted for over five decades. What is more, the analyses of Chile and Bahrain also brought into the picture additional variables, largely overlooked in the quantitative analyses, allowing us a more in-depth understanding of the political processes and institutional influences involved.

The Republic of Chile and the Kingdom of Bahrain have disparate policies on abortion, and very different relationships with the religious sects and institutions in their societies. These differences demonstrate how nuanced the relationship between religion and the state is, and how unexpected the influence of civil society players may be. Chile has no official state religion, and its population is not religious. That said, the role the Catholic Church played as a social service and lobbying agent in civil society has granted it meaningful political sway in a number of Chilean regimes. The Church has had a critical role as an arbiter between the state and the people during some of the most contentious periods of modern Chilean history. The Vatican has brokered international agreements and treaties for the country, helping it avoid war. During the harshest years of the Pinochet regime, Church representatives spoke out against oppression and in support of human rights. The Church provided services, support, and counseling for those affected. Its institutions and representatives in Chile have helped the state transition to democracy after it experienced one of the darkest periods in its history. All of this activity was made possible by its united hierarchal structure and strong Vatican-supported institutions. A standout example of this would be the Vicariate of Solidarity, a humanitarian organization founded by Cardinal Silva. The organization provided social services and legal aid for victims of regime violence. It also disseminated information internationally and, with the backing of the Vatican, publicly criticized and lobbied the Pinochet regime on issues of human rights violations.

The interaction between institutionalized faith civil society on the one hand and the public on the other is particularly interesting, as the case of Chile demonstrates. The case study of Chile suggests that the Catholic Church does not require its followers to be particularly observant, nor does it need any official recognition in order to sway state abortion policy, or state policy in general. As long as the Catholic population is sufficiently large, the Church has the footing necessary to carry influence. From there, its highly organized political machine, solid hierarchies, and role as provider of social services allow it to dictate policy and negotiate in politics in a way rarely seen in other religious sects.

Future research may examine the complementary role a Catholic constituency has and its influence on the ability of the Church to affect policy. More specifically, while we find that size of the Catholic constituency in Chile was sufficient to lend the Church political sway to wield power and influence, the story we tell does not delve into the specifics. How does religious constituency size relate to critical mass theory? What is the size necessary for different religions to influence policy, and specifically reproductive rights policy? How big is big enough when it comes to enabling religious civil society to influence abortion rights? In what ways is the effect of constituency size contingent on the institutional robustness of the particular denomination? Future research might take these up as important questions.

While its official state religion is Islam and Sharia is protected in the Constitution as the primary source of law, Bahrain is starkly different, not just in the denominational realm but also in the types of institutions of faith civil society. Divided between Sunni and Shia factions, neither of which have a centralized institutional presence in civil society, faith civil society influences politics differently. The state has even taken steps to minimize religious leadership's participation in politics in order to prevent further Shia influence in state affairs. This complicated relationship between the state and religious factions and the degree of religiosity among the population leave room for a permissive abortion policy. Indeed, organizations such as the Bahrain Reproductive Health Association, a local affiliate of the International Planned Parenthood Federation, has operated in this political landscape for years.

Another interesting aspect of the relationship between women's rights and religion demonstrated in the case of Bahrain, and in the analysis in Chapter 2, is how reproductive policy is determined differently from other types of women's welfare policy. Though Bahraini women have had the right to an abortion for over 40 years, they were only given the right to vote and run for political office in 2002. This discrepancy between different types of women's rights policy repeated itself in the case studies of Rwanda and New Zealand in Chapter 5. Throughout the book, we attempt to theorize on such disparities. This book is a good starting point for a much more in-depth investigation. First, we are able to show empirically how abortion rights are systematically different from other types of women's rights. Second, we explain disparities of that sort, for instance, based on international influences and priorities of nondemocratic regimes. It would be important to further develop these observations into an independent research agenda. Such an agenda would include a comprehensive analysis of how the production of abortion rights is different politically, institutionally, and otherwise, from how other types of women's rights are generated and protected. Naturally, the distinction between doctrinal and nondoctrinal issues is pertinent here as well.

The comparative approach we use would benefit this new agenda. We examine questions while considering regime types and political realities worldwide. In order to understand the systematic influences on abortion rights, and women's rights in general, research would benefit from drawing conclusions based on broad databases such as the one compiled for the purposes of this book.

DIMENSIONS OF REPRESENTATION

The connections between women's representation and abortion policy in democracies have been proven in numerous studies. Our work in this book expanded that discussion to a wider variety of regimes, so as to understand how abortion policy is made at the state level worldwide. A better understanding of the connection between women's descriptive and substantive representation, beyond the context of democracy, is important to understanding the type of political influence women may wield in many parts of the world and how reproductive rights are determined within the state sphere. We hypothesized that in a range of political contexts there were a number of reasons that the link might be maintained between women's representation and abortion rights, and a number of reasons why at times it might merely appear to exist.

We developed and juxtaposed three theoretical frameworks aiming to explain why women's political presence might correlate with policy agendas generally associated with female representation, even in nondemocratic contexts. In two of the scenarios, there was only the appearance of substantive representation. In the first of these scenarios, women's representation and women's welfare policy were both encouraged by the state as a means of appeasing IGOs and other powerful states. In the second scenario, the regime had a liberal attitude toward gender equality, resulting in higher rates of women's representation and more permissive women's welfare policy, unrelated to the powers of the representatives. Because of a correlation between women's representation and women's welfare policy, both of those may appear to be cases of substantive representation. This effect, however, would really stem from a third confounding variable. In the third theoretical account we developed, however, there was a real connection between descriptive and substantive representation. Less-than democratic regimes might allow female representatives to exercise political power and shape policy in certain areas.

Within the state-level sphere, our theoretical framework focused on representation as a critical concept in examining how state characteristics define public policy. We argued that representation could be a significant determinant of public policy and not just in democratic states. The type of regime might define the extent to which state institutions are built to translate public will into public policy, but even beyond democracy, representatives might, to some extent, exercise influence and represent constituents. In the context of abortion policy, the rate of women's representation was examined not only as a factor unto itself, but also in the context of regime type and electoral gender quotas. In addition, the case studies of New Zealand and Rwanda introduced the importance of top-down versus bottom-up change and the question of the consequences of belonging to the ruling political party as it influences the efficacy of women leaders.

As far as regime types are concerned, New Zealand represents almost the exact opposite of Rwanda in that it has been a stable democracy for close to 200 years. New Zealand has historically been a leader in female political participation (yet, with incremental change in this respect). Both, though, boast a rate of female leadership far exceeding the world average. Gaps between abortion policies on the books and what exists in reality are true for both countries. In 2012, Rwanda passed a considerably more permissive abortion policy than what previously existed. That said, legal and bureaucratic requirements limit the true permissiveness of the law as it is implemented on the ground. Given the country's political, social, and economic profile, New Zealand has a surprisingly restrictive abortion policy. In reality, however, free and safe abortion services are widely available, and a relatively small number of women resort to the procedure. As highlighted in Chapter 5, this might also have to do with the wide extent of contraceptive use. The case studies for both countries highlight the significance of women in politics and female political leadership.

Both case studies individually have highlighted issues concerning the efficacy of female leadership and the importance of how they are situated politically, whether in the ruling authoritarian party, outside of it, or in a democratic regime. As far as electoral quotas and their efficacy are concerned, societal acceptance of gender equality seems to be of defining significance in the extent to which women officials can exercise substantive representation and translate their presence into policies favorable to their organic constituencies. This means that the efficacy of women, especially those elected through quotas, is contingent on additional cultural and social factors. Finally, these cases demonstrated the importance of analyzing policy implementation side by side with and even unrelated to analysis of law on the books. While that is beyond the scope (and goals) of this book, it is certainly a worthy task for scholars studying women's rights in general and reproductive policy in particular.

INTERGOVERNMENTAL ORGANIZATIONS

Our findings for IGOs can inspire and be a source of motivation for international and local actors who hope to influence women's rights and reproductive health. Primarily, we would point to the critical role of international organizations in establishing norms of reproductive health and women's welfare. To yield results, decisive language should be favored over pacifying phrasing when crafting treaties and protocols. The findings from our case studies and quantitative analyses suggest that clear verbiage is more important than consensus if trying to make a meaningful change. Side by side with international organizations, local political actors have an important role in promoting and shaping women's rights policy.

Returning to the SDGs of the United Nations, and in particular to SDG5, the findings concerning effects of the international sphere are instructive at various levels. To those who ask if the international sphere in general – and IGOs in particular – have the ability to influence reproductive health policy, the answer is yes. Yet, questions of best practice in this realm remain unanswered. It is now a question of how to produce the most significant result. The importance of precise language in protocols was further clarified and elaborated as we studied the ratification processes in detail in the case studies of the ICPD PoA and the Maputo Protocol.

The ICPD PoA was published following the U.N.'s International Conference on Population and Development in Cairo in September 1994. It was part of a series of conferences that focused on population and development and that was attended by close to 200 country delegations, as well as over 4,000 individuals from approximately 1,700 NGO and lobbying organizations. The issues addressed ran the gamut from human rights, population, and reproductive health to gender equality and sustainable development. The

Conference resulted in a new way of addressing development. Individual dignity, human rights, and the right to family planning were reframed as the heart of international development. This represented a critical shift within the population field.

Women's access to safe abortion was one of the knottiest issues discussed at the ICPD. The Conference organizers and attendees were wary of the topic, with religious organizations, states, and the media all trying to frame the topic and influence the decision-making processes. The Conference avoided defining abortion as a "right," although it recognized that abortion did exist and encouraged measures to reduce the health implications associated with unsafe abortions (Fincher, 1994). While at the time the ICPD PoA represented a breakthrough in addressing abortion, internal contradictions and weak language in abortion provisions failed to provide governments with a clear directive for action (Hessini, 2005).

We compared the ICPD PoA, a universal agreement, to a regional agreement of a different IGO, the African Union. The Protocol to the African Charter on Human and People's Rights on the Rights of Women in Africa is a supplement to the African Charter on Human and People's Rights of the African Union. It was finalized and published in Maputo in 2003. It derived its legal authority from the AU Constitutive Act (Viljeon, 2009). The aim of the document was to reinforce and push implementation of international human rights norms and laws regarding women's rights that had been stated in other documents and protocols, but until then had not been successfully implemented in several African countries. It specified rights that had been alluded to in the Charter, concretely stating women's equality and a commitment to women's rights (Viljeon, 2009).

The Protocol's treatment of abortion was ground-breaking. It converted African abortion law from a crime and punishment model into a paradigm of reproductive and public health. It was the first time abortion was specified as a human right and as an enforceable obligation in an IGO agreement, challenging the consensus reached at the ICPD (Ngwena, 2010). Also, unlike the ICPD PoA, the AU Protocol provided a template for state abortion law (Ngwena, 2010).

Changes that followed each document point to the power that a united group of nations can have in the international arena. Such a group may produce a transnational epistemic community that further supports and sustains the international agreement. Such group of experts with common normative and analytic frameworks may be essential to move forward in translating common understandings at the level of the IGO into policymaking at the level of the nation-state.

CONNECTING THE SPHERES: WOMEN LEADERSHIP AND BEYOND

The findings in this book suggest that connecting the spheres is invaluable, as agents and institutions in each affect each other and as norms travel between them. The Catholic Church made an appearance in both Parts I and III as a powerful player in both civil society and the forums of international organizations. It demonstrated the same tendencies in both influencing Chilean abortion law and the drafting of the U.N. ICPD PoA. The Church is one example of a player that has sway in several of the spheres examined in this book. When such players have a meaningful influence on producing reproductive rights in one sphere, it would be wise to observe how their power is wielded in other spheres as well. Likewise, in the case of the African Union and the Maputo Protocol, at least the initial drafting was primarily the initiative of civil society (Ngwena, 2010). As such, activities of civil society were then translated into influence at the international level.

The interrelations among the three spheres this book is focused on and the consequences of those connections are embodied not only by players analyzed throughout this chapter, but indeed by the women leaders themselves. Their careers symbolize the interconnected nature of civil society, the state, and the international sphere in the area of reproductive health.

Take, for example, President Michelle Bachelet, the first woman president of Chile. Not only a domestic leader, she has served extensively as a leader in international organizations concerned with women's rights. After leaving office following her first term as president from 2006 to 2010, Ms. Bachelet was appointed the first executive director of U.N. Entity for Gender Equality and the Empowerment of Women. Under her guidance, this office was transformed into the entity known as U.N. Women. Ms. Bachelet assumed the international position, only to return to Chile and reassume the position of president of the republic a few years later in 2014.

As leader of U.N. Women, Ms. Bachelet worked to enhance "efforts by other parts of the UN system (...) to work for gender equality and women's empowerment" (U.N. Women website). When Ms. Bachelet reassumed the office of president of Chile in 2014, she continued pursuing these goals at the national level. For example, she established the Ministry of Women and Gender Equality and appointed Claudia Pascual as its first leader. President Bachelet then went on to legalize abortion in some circumstances (rape, danger to mother's life, and fetus inviability), despite much opposition. With this bill, Chile no longer claimed one of the world's most restrictive abortion laws.

Another example would be Margot Wallström of Sweden. Ms. Wallström served extensively in her national government including as Deputy Prime Minister of Sweden and Minister for Foreign Affairs. From 2010 to 2012, Ms. Wallström served in the United Nations as the Special Representative of the Secretary General on Sexual Violence in Conflict. She was in charge of increasing visibility, developing legislation, and enhancing national accountability and prevention strategies in protecting women's rights under extremely complicated circumstances of conflict.

In her first assignment as Special Representative in the Democratic Republic of Congo, she helped investigate allegations of mass rape by the military. A month later, Wallström addressed the U.N. Security Council on this topic, stating that the rapes in the North and South Kivu provinces "were not an isolated incident but part of a broader pattern of widespread systematic rape and pillage" (MacFarquhar, 2010). When called in 2012 to serve as foreign minister in Stefan Löfven's government, Wallström left the U.N. agency only to pursue similar goals and a feminist foreign policy in her new position. As Minister of Foreign Affairs she launched the world's first "feminist foreign policy" (Government Offices of Sweden, 2018; Vogelstein and Bro, 2019).

These women not only symbolize the connection among the spheres but are themselves agents connecting them. They demonstrate the importance of not only looking at each sphere individually, but also of understanding the exchange of ideas, norms, players, influence, and activity among them. For a human rights and morality and health issue such as abortion, understanding this web of influences is indispensable.

AVENUES FOR FUTURE RESEARCH

Before we conclude, the research presented in this book has several key implications for future work. First, the findings here call for further clarification of the nuanced effects of religiosity on development in general. We would also emphasize the need to look within religious denominations and their structures and hierarchies to understand how this dictates denomination behavior and influence.

Second, research should be done into different families of women's welfare policy. Such a typology may be crucial in a field where dissimilar types of policy are often lumped together into one broad category. Such a broad category of policies appears to be theoretically unsound and may be misleading for scientists and practitioners alike.

Finally, our research does not examine causal mechanisms, at least not in the sense that we provide conclusive evidence for their existence. Variables examined represent a complex and potentially multi-directional networks of causal connections. Therefore, the conclusions that we can reach given our methods and data have their limits and are intrinsically qualified. Future research could contribute greatly to untangling those causal effects. To what extent are women leaders the cause for the types of abortion liberalization and criminalization we described? How do religion and state-religion features affect the type of abortion policy in place? What are the ways to ascertain the causal pathways leading from international organizations of different sorts – intergovernmental bodies and otherwise – to changes in abortion policy?

Once those causal questions are examined and resolved, the next step would be to broaden the scope of examination to other bodies beyond those that we focus on here, such as international nongovernmental organizations in the international sphere, other state actors beyond women representatives, and other elements within the sphere of civil society, beyond faith civil society.

The questions we leave unanswered are both fascinating and critically important for the future of women's health and well-being around the world. We hope future research can build on the theoretical, conceptual, and empirical foundations laid out in this book to successfully come to grips with those challenges and further advance our understanding of the production of reproductive rights.

References

Abbas, J. A., & Weir, D. (2005). Islamic perspectives on management and organization. *Journal of Management, Spirituality and Religion*, 2(3), 410–415.

Abbott, K. W., & Snidal, D. (1998). Why states act through formal international organizations. *Journal of Conflict Resolution*, 42(1), 3–32.

Adams, M., & Kang, A. (2007). Regional advocacy networks and the protocol on the rights of women in Africa. *Politics and Gender*, 3, 451–474.

Adler, E. (2005). *Communitarian international relations: The epistemic foundations of international relations*. New York: Routledge.

African Charter on Human and Peoples' Rights. (2014). *General Comment No. 2 on Article 14.1 (a), (b), (c) and (f) and Article 14. 2 (a) and (c) of the Protocol to the African Charter on Human and Peoples' Rights on the Rights of Women in Africa*. Luanda, Angola: Author.

African Commission on Human and Peoples' Rights. (2016). *Ratification Table: Protocol to the African Charter on Human and Peoples' Rights on the Rights of Women in Africa*. Retrieved from www.achpr.org/instruments/women-protocol /ratification//

African Union. (2003). *Protocol to the African Charter on Human and People's Rights on the Rights of Women in Africa*. Maputo, Mozambique: Author.

Akwei, I. (2017, July 10). *Rwanda has been ranked highest country in the world with most women in parliament as of January 2017*. Retrieved July 5, 2018, from www .africanews.com/2017/07/10/rwanda-tops-un-list-of-countries-with-most-women-in-parliament//

Alesina, A., Devleeschauwer, A., Easterly, W., Kurlat, S., & Wacziarg, R. (2003). Fractionalization. *Journal of Economic Growth*, 8, 155–194.

Alger, C. F. (2002). Religion as a peace tool. *The Global Review of Ethnopolitics*, 1(4), 94–109.

Al Gharaibeh, F. (2011). Women's empowerment in Bahrain. *Journal of International Women's Studies*, 12(3), 96–113.

Allahbadia, G. M., Allahbadia, S. G., & Arora, S. (2009). Hinduism and reproduction in contemporary India: Vedic learnings. In *Faith and fertility: Attitudes towards reproductive practices in different religions from ancient to modern time*, edited by E. Blyth and R. Landau (pp. 111–136). London: Jessica Kingsley Publishers.

Al-Rasheed, M. (2011). Sectarianism as counter-revolution: Saudi responses to the Arab Spring. *Studies in Ethnicity and Nationalism*, 11(3), 513–526.

Altemeyer, B., & Hunsberger, B. (2004). A revised religious fundamentalism scale: The short and sweet of it. *The International Journal for the Psychology of Religion*, 14(1), 45–54.

Alvarez, R., & Brehm, J. (1995). American ambivalence towards abortion policy: Development of a heteroskedastic probit model of competing values. *American Journal of Political Science*, 39(4), 1055–1082.

Asal, V., Brown, M., & Figueroa, R. (2008). Structure, empowerment and the liberalization of cross-national abortion rights. *Politics and Gender*, 4, 265–284.

Asal, V., Murdie A., & Sommer, U. (2017). Rainbows for rights: The role of LGBT activism in gay rights promotion. *Societies Without Borders*, 12(1) 1–19.

Asal, V., Sommer, U., & Harwood, P. (2013). Original sin: A cross national study of the legality of homosexual acts. *Comparative Political Studies*, 46(3), 320–351.

Asuagbor, L. (2016, March 18). *Status of Implementation of the Protocol to the African Charter on Human and People's Rights on the Rights of Women in Africa.*

Avdeev A., Blum A., & Troitskaya, I. (1995). The history of abortion statistics in Russia and the USSR from 1900 to 1991. *Population: An English Selection*, 7, 39–66

Avdeyeva, O. (2007). When do states comply with international treaties? Policies on violence against women in post-Communist countries. *International Studies Quarterly*, 51, pp. 877–900.

Bader, V. (2007). *Secularism or democracy? Associational governance of religious diversity.* Amsterdam: Amsterdam University Press.

Bahrain Mirror. (2018, April 7). *Chamber of Commerce rejects motion to grant female employees abortion leaves.* Retrieved from bahrainmirror.com/en/news/46272.

Bahraini Census. (2010). Retrieved from www.census2010.gov.bh/_index_en.php

Bahry, L. (1997). The opposition in Bahrain: A Bellwether for the Gulf? *Middle East Policy*, 5(2), 42–57.

Bakht, N. (2007). Religious arbitration in Canada: Protecting women by protecting them from religion. *Canadian Journal of Women and Law*, 19, 119–144.

Banda, F. (2006). Blazing a trail: The African Protocol on Women's Rights comes into force. *Journal of African Law*, 50(1), 72–84.

Barnea, M. F., & Schwartz, S. H. (1998). Values and voting. *Political Psychology*, 19(1), 17–40.

Barnett, M. N., & Finnemore, M. (1999). The politics, power, and pathologies of international organizations. *International Organization*, 53(4), 699–732.

Barnhart, M. G. (2009). Buddhist family values: Fertility and technological intervention in the quest for enlightenment. In *Faith and fertility: Attitudes towards reproductive practices in different religions from ancient to modern time*, edited by E. Blyth and R. Landau (pp. 158–178). London: Jessica Kingsley Publishers.

Barton, J. R., & Murray, W. E. (2002). The end of transition? Chile 1990–2000. *Bulletin of Latin American Research*, 21(3), 329–338.

Basinga, P., Moore, A. M., Singh, S. D., Carlin, E. E., Birungi, F., & Ngabo, F. (2012). Abortion incidence and postabortion care in Rwanda. *Studies in Family Planning*, 43 (1), 11–20.

Bauer, G., & Burnet, J. E. (2013). Gender quotas, democracy, and women's representation in Africa: Some insights from democratic Botswana and autocratic Rwanda. *Women's Studies International Forum 41*, 103–112.

BBC Country Profiles. (2012). Chile timeline. Retrieved July 30, 2018, www .bbc.co.ukhttp://news.bbc.co.uk/2/hi/americas/country_profiles/1222905.stm

BBC News. (2017). *Chile abortion: Court approves easing total ban*. Retrieved August 1, 2018, www.bbc.comhttps://www.bbc.com/news/world-latin-america-41005517

BBC News. (2004, November 18). *Chile introduces right to divorce*. Retrieved from http://news.bbc.co.uk/2/hi/americas/4021427.stm

BBC Rwanda Profile. (2018). *Rwanda profile – Timeline*. Retrieved July 18, 2018, from www.bbc.com/news/world-africa-14093322

Behuria, A. K. (2004). Sunni-Shia relations in Pakistan: The widening divide. *Strategic Analysis, 28*(1), 157–176.

Bélanger, D., & Flynn, A. (2009). The persistence of induced abortion in Cuba. Exploring the notion of an "abortion culture." *Studies in Family Planning, 40*(1), 13–26.

Bellamak, T. (2018). *Terry Bellamak: Law commission has its work cut out on abortion*. Retrieved July 26, 2018, from www.nzherald.co.nz/nz/news/article.cfm? c_id=1&objectid=12026649

Benne, R. (2010). *Good and bad ways to think about religion and politics*. Grand Rapids, MI: Wm. B. Eerdmans Publishing.

Berkman, M. B., & O'Connor, R. E. (1993). Do women legislators matter? Female legislators and state abortion policy. *American Politics Quarterly, 21*(1), 102–124.

Berkovitch, N. (1999a). *From motherhood to citizenship: Women's rights and international organizations*. Baltimore: JHU Press.

Berkovitch, N. (1999b). The emergence and transformation of the international women's movement. In *Constructing world culture: International nongovernmental organizations since 1875*, edited by J. Boli & G. M. Thomas (pp. 100–126). Stanford: Stanford University Press.

Bhalotra, S., & Clots-Figueras, I. (2014). Health and the political agency of women. *American Economic Journal: Economic Policy, 6*(2), 164–97.

Bird, K. (2014). Ethnic quotas and ethnic representation worldwide. *International Political Science Review, 35*(1), 12–26.

Blackman, A. D. (2018). Religion and foreign aid. *Politics and Religion, 11*(3), 1–31.

Blofield, M. (2001). *The politics of "moral sin": A study of abortion and divorce in Catholic Chile since 1990*. Santiago: FLACSO-Chile.

Bogaards, M. (2009). How to classify hybrid regimes? Defective democracy and electoral authoritarianism. *Democratization, 16*(2), 399–423.

Boli, J., & Thomas, G. M. (1999). *Constructing world culture: International nongovernmental organizations since 1875*. Stanford: Stanford University Press.

Booth, C., & Bennett, C. (2002). Gender mainstreaming in the European Union: Towards a new conception and practice of equal opportunities? *European Journal of Women's Studies, 9*(4), 430–446.

Boulay, M., Tweedie, I., & Fiagbey, E. (2008). The effectiveness of a national communication campaign using religious leaders to reduce HIV-related stigma in Ghana. *African Journal of AIDS Research, 7*(1), 133–141.

Boyle, E., Kim, M., & Longhofer, W. (2015). Abortion liberalization in world society, 1960–2009. *American Journal of Sociology, 121*(3), 882–913.

Bratton, K. A. (2005). Critical mass theory revisited: The behavior and success of token women in state legislatures. *Politics & Gender, 1*(1), 97–125.

Braun, D., & Gilardi, F. (2006). Taking "Galton's problem" seriously: Towards a theory of policy diffusion. *Journal of Theoretical Politics, 18*(3), 298–322.

Brookes, B. (2016). *A history of New Zealand women*. Wellington, NZ: Bridget Williams Books.

Brookman-Amissah, E., & Bando Mayo, J. (2004). Abortion law reform in sub-Saharan Africa: No turning back. *Reproductive Health Matters, 12*(24), 227–234.

Brossard, D., Scheufele, D., Kim, E., & Lewenstein, B. (2009). Religiosity as a perceptual filter: Examining processes of opinion formation about nanotechnology. *Public Understanding of Science, 18*(5), 546–558.

Bulliet, R. W. (2002). The crisis within Islam. *The Wilson Quarterly, 26*(1), 11–19.

Burnet, J. (2008). Gender balance and the meanings of women in governance in post-genocide Rwanda. *African Affairs, 107*(428), 361–386.

Burnet, J. E. (2011). Women have found respect: Gender quotas, symbolic representation, and female empowerment in Rwanda. *Politics & Gender, 7*(3), 303–334.

Bush, S. S. (2011). International politics and the spread of quotas for women in legislatures. *International Organization, 65*(1), 103–137.

Buvinic, M., Gupta, M. D., Casabonne, U., & Verwimp, P. (2013). *Violent conflict and gender inequality: An overview*. Washington, DC: The World Bank.

Campbell, R. (2004). Gender, ideology and issue preference: Is there such a thing as a political women's interest in Britain? *The British Journal of Politics & International Relations, 6*(1), 20–44.

Carey, J. M., & Shugart, M. S. (1995). Incentives to cultivate a personal vote: A rank ordering of electoral formulas. *Electoral Studies, 14*(4), 417–439.

Carlsnaes, W., Risse-Kappen, T., Risse, T., & Simmons, B. A. (2002). *Handbook of international relations*. London: Sage.

Carothers, T. (2002). The end of the transition paradigm. *Journal of Democracy, 13*(1), 5–21.

Casas, L., & Vivaldi, L. (2014). Abortion in Chile: The practice under a restrictive regime. *Reproductive Health Matters, 22*(44), 70–81.

Castles, F. G. (2003). The world turned upside down: Below replacement fertility, changing preferences and family-friendly public policy in 21 OECD countries. *Journal of European Social Policy, 13*(3), 209–227.

Caul, M. (2001). Political parties and the adoption of candidate gender quotas: A cross-national analysis. *The Journal of Politics, 63*(4), 1214–1229.

Celis Brunet, A., Castro, R., & Scroggie, M. (2009). *Religion and law in the non-confessional Chilean state*. Provo, Utah: International Center for Law and Religion Studies, Brigham Young University.

Celis, K., & Childs, S. (2008). Introduction: The descriptive and substantive representation of women: New directions. *Parliamentary Affairs, 61*(3), 419–425.

Chen, L. J. (2010). Do gender quotas influence women's representation and policies? *The European Journal of Comparative Economics, 7*(1), 13–60.

Childs, S. (2001). In their own words: New Labour women and the substantive representation of women. *The British Journal of Politics & International Relations, 3*(2), 173–190.

Childs, S., & Krook, M. L. (2008). Critical mass theory and women's political representation. *Political Studies*, 56(3), 725–736.

Childs, S., & Krook, M. L. (2006). Should feminists give up on critical mass? A contingent yes. *Politics & Gender*, 2(4), 522–530.

Childs, S., & Lovenduski, J. (2012). Political representation. In *The Oxford handbook of gender and politics*, edited by G. Waylen, K. Celis, J. Kantola, & L. Weldon. Oxford: Oxford University Press.

Childs, S., & Withey, J. (2004). Women representatives acting for women: Sex and the signing of Early Day Motions in the 1997 British Parliament. *Political Studies*, 52, 552–564.

Chile's Constitution of 1980. (1980). Retrieved from www.constituteproject.org/consti tution/Chile_2012.pdf

Chirwa, D. M. (2006). Reclaiming (wo)manity: The merits and demerits of the African Protocol on Women's Rights. *Netherlands International Law Review*, 53 (1), 63–96.

Cingranelli, D. L., Richards, D. L., & Clay, C. K. (2014). *The CIRI human rights dataset*. Retrieved from www.humanrightsdata.com.

Clausen, J. A. (1968). *Socialization and society*. Boston: Little Brown & Company.

Clayton, A., & Zetterberg, P. (2018). Quota shocks: Electoral gender quotas and government spending priorities worldwide. *The Journal of Politics*, 80(3), 916–932.

Clayton, R., & Gladden, J. (1974, June). The five dimensions of religiosity: Toward demythologizing a sacred artifact. *Journal for the Scientific Study of Religion*, 13(2), 135–143.

Cohen, J. L., & Arato, A. (1994). *Civil Society and Political Theory*. Cambridge: MIT Press.

Combs, M. W., & Welch, S. (1982). Blacks, whites and attitudes toward abortion. *Public Opinion Quarterly*, 46, 510–520.

Cook, E. A., Jelen, T. G., & Wilcox, C. (1993). State political cultures and public opinion about abortion. *Political Research Quarterly*, 46, 771–781.

Cortell, A. P., & Davis Jr, J. W. (1996). How do international institutions matter? The domestic impact of international rules and norms. *International Studies Quarterly*, 40(4), 451–478.

Council of Europe. (2011). *Council of Europe Convention on Preventing and Combating Violence against Women and Domestic Violence*. Istanbul: Author.

Cudworth, E. (2007). *The modern state: Theories and ideologies*. Edinburgh: Edinburgh University Press.

Curtin, J. (1997). *Gender and political leadership in New Zealand*. Parliamentary Library: Research Note 14, 1997–1998.

Dahlerup, D. (2006). The story of the theory of critical mass. *Politics & Gender*, 2(4), 511–522.

Dahlerup, D. (1988). From a small to a large minority: Women in Scandinavian Politics. *Scandinavian Political Studies*, 11(4), 275–298.

Dahlerup, D., & Freidenvall, L. (2005). Quotas as a "fast track" to equal representation for women: Why Scandinavia is no longer the model. *International Feminist Journal of Politics*, 7(1), 26–48.

Damian, C. I. (2010). Abortion from the perspective of Eastern religions: Hinduism and Buddhism. *Romanian Journal of Bioethics*, 8(1), 124–136.

Davis, K. (2009). The emperor is still naked: Why the Protocol on the Rights of Women in Africa leaves women exposed to more discrimination. *Vanderbilt Journal of Transnational Law, 42*, 949–992.

Davison, I. (2018, June 19). *New Zealand's abortion rate rises slightly, though teen abortions fall*. Retrieved from www.nzherald.co.nz/nz/news/article.cfm?c_id=1&objectid=12073574

DeJong, J. (2001). The role and limitations of the Cairo International Conference on Population and Development. *Social Science and Medicine, 51*, 941–953.

De Paola, M., Lombardo, R., & Scoppa, V. (2009). *Can gender quotas break down negative stereotypes? Evidence from changes in electoral rules. Working Paper*. Calabria, Italy: University of Calabria, Department of Economics and Statistics.

De Walque, D., & Verwimp, P. (2009). *The demographic and socio-economic distribution of excess mortality during the 1994 genocide in Rwanda*. Brussels: The World Bank, Development Research Group.

Devlin, C., & Elgie, R. (2008). The effect of increased women's representation in Parliament: The case of Rwanda. *Parliamentary Affairs, 61*(2), 237–254.

Diamond, L. (1999). *Developing democracy: Toward consolidation*. Baltimore: Johns Hopkins University Press.

Diamond, L. (2002). Thinking about hybrid regimes. *Journal of Democracy, 13*(2), 21–35.

Diaz, M. M. (2005). *Representing women? Female legislators in West European Parliaments*. Colchester, UK: ECPR Press.

Dietrich, S., & Murdie, A. (2017). Human rights shaming through INGOs and foreign aid delivery. *The Review of International Organizations, 12*(1), 95–120.

Djupe, P. A., & Gilbert, C. P. (2008). *The political influence of churches*. New York: Cambridge University Press.

Doan, L. (2010). *Rwandan women and the 1994 genocide: The effect on their social and political roles*. Washington, DC: Georgetown University.

Doh, J. P., & Guay, T. R. (2004). Globalization and corporate social responsibility: How non-governmental organizations influence labor and environmental codes of conduct. *Management and International Review, 44*(2), 7–29.

Dominguez, J. (1994). *Parties, elections, and political participation in Latin America*. New York: Routledge.

Dovi, S. (2002). Preferable descriptive representatives: Will just any woman, black, or Latino Do? *American Political Science Review, 96*(4), 729–743.

Dreher, A. (2006). Does globalization affect growth? Evidence from a new Index of Globalization. *Applied Economics, 38*(10), 1091–1110.

Driessen, M. D. (2010). Religion, state and democracy: Analyzing two dimensions of church-state relations. *Politics and Religion, 3*, 55–80.

Dryzek, J. S., & Niemeyer, S. (2008). Discursive representation. *The American Political Science Review, 102*(4), 481–493.

Dunn, E., & Hann,C. (1996). *Civil society: Challenging Western models*. New York: Psychology Press.

Ebeku, K. S. (2004). A new hope for African women: Overview of Africa's protocol on women's rights. *Nordic Journal of African Studies, 13*(3), 264–274.

Echavarri, R. & Husillos, J. (2016). The missing link between parents' preferences and daughters' survival: The moderator effect of societal discrimination. *World Development, 78,* 372–85.

Edmond, J. (2016). *1960s abortion law unacceptable for 21st century women of New Zealand.* Retrieved July 25, 2018, from www.stuff.co.nzwww.stuff.co.nz/dominion-post/comment/81738291/1960s-abortion-law-unacceptable-for-21st-century-women-of-new-zealand

Edwards, B., & Foley, M. W. (1998). Civil society and social capital beyond Putnam. *American Behavioral Scientist, 42*(1), 124–139.

Edwards, J. (2013). *Painful birth: How Chile became a free and prosperous society.* Landham, MD: University Press of America.

El Desconcierto. (2018, February 10). Retrieved from www.eldesconcierto.cl/2018/02/10/la-historia-del-primer-aborto-legal-realizado-en-el-hospital-san-jose/

Elkins, Z., & Simmons, B. (2005). On waves, clusters, and diffusion: A conceptual framework. *The Annals of the American Academy, 598,* 33–51.

Ellina, C. (2003). *Promoting women's rights: Politics of gender in the European Union.* New York: Routledge.

Encuesta Nacional Bicentenario. (2017). Encuesta Nacional Bicentenario 2017: Religión. Retrieved from https://encuestabicentenario.uc.cl (in Spanish)

Engeli, I. (2009). The challenges of abortion and assisted reproductive technologies policies in Europe. *Comparative European Politics, 7,* 56–74.

Engeli, I., Green-Pedersen, C., & Larsen, L. (2013). The puzzle of permissiveness: Understanding policy processes concerning morality issues. *Journal of European Public Policy, 20*(3), 335–352.

European Parliament. (2003, December 4). *Oral Question (H-0794/03) for Question Time at the part-session in December 2003 pursuant to Rule 43 of the Rules of Procedure by Dana Scallon to the Council.*

Fallon, K. M., Swiss, L., & Viterna, J. (2012). Resolving the democracy paradox: Democratization and women's legislative representation in developing nations, 1975 to 2009. *American Sociological Review, 77*(3), 380–408.

Family First Lobby Press Release. (2008, June 10). *Abortion Supervisory Committee Deserves Criticism. Retrieved from* www.scoop.co.nz/stories/PO0806/S00090.htm

Fastnow, C., Grant, J. T., & Rudolph, T. J. (1999). Holy roll calls: Religious tradition and voting behavior in the US House. *Social Science Quarterly, 80*(4), 687–701.

Fincher, R. A. (1994). International Conference on Population and Development. *Environmental Policy and Law, 24*(6), 309–312.

Finnemore, M. (1996). *National interests in international society.* Ithaca, NY: Cornell University Press.

Finnemore, M. (1993). International organizations as teachers of norms: The United Nations educational, scientific, and cultural organization and science policy. *International Organization, 47*(4), 565–597.

Finnoff, K. (2012). Intimate partner violence, female employment, and male backlash in Rwanda. *The Economics of Peace and Security Journal, 7*(2), 14–24.

Fleet, M., & Smith, B. H. (1997). *The Catholic Church and democracy in Chile and Peru.* Notre Dame, IN: University of Notre Dame Press.

Foley, M. W., & Edwards, B. (1996). The paradox of civil society. *Journal of Democracy, 7*(3), 38–52.

Forman-Rabinovici, A., & Sommer, U. (2018a). An impediment to gender equality? Religion's influence on development and reproductive policy. *World Development,* 105, 48–58. Retrieved from https://doi.org/10.1016/j.worlddev.2017.12.024

Forman-Rabinovici, A., & Sommer, U. (2018b). Reproductive health policy-makers: Comparing the influences of international and domestic institutions on abortion policy. *Public Administration,* 96(1), 185–199. Retrieved from https://doi.org/10.1111/padm.12383

Fortin-Rittberger, J., & Rittberger, B. (2014). Do electoral rules matter? Explaining national differences in women's representation in the European Parliament. *European Union Politics,* 15(4), 496–520.

Fox, J. (2018). *An introduction to religion and politics: Theory and practice.* New York: Routledge.

Fox, J. (2001). Religion as an overlooked element of international relations. *International Studies Review,* 3(3), 53–73.

Franceschet, S., & Piscopo, J. (2008). Gender quotas and women's substantive representation: Lessons from Argentina. *Politics and Gender,* 4, 393–425.

Franceschet, S., Krook, M., & Piscopo, J. M. (2012). *The impact of gender quotas.* New York: Oxford University Press.

Fukuyama, F. (2001). Social capital, civil society and development. *Third World Quarterly,* 22(1), 7–20.

Ganatra, B., Tunçalp, Ö., Bart Johnston, H., Johnson, B. R., Gülmezoglu, A. M., & Temmerman, M. (2014). From concept to measurement: Operationalizing the WHO's definition of unsafe abortion. *Bulletin of the World Health Organization,* 92, 155.

Garnett, R. W. (2009). A hands-off approach to religious doctrine: What are we talking about? *Notre Dame Law Review,* 84(2), 837–864.

Gelb, J. (1996). Abortion and reproductive choice: Policy and politics in Japan. In *Abortion politics: Public policy in cross-cultural perspective,* edited by M. Githens & D. M. Stetson(pp. 119–137). Abington on Thames, United Kingdom: Routledge.

Gelman, A. (2006). Multilevel (hierarchical) modeling: What it can and cannot do. *Technometrics,* 48(3), 432–435.

Germain, A., & Kidwell, J. (2005). The unfinished agenda for reproductive health: Priorities for the next 10 Years. *International Family Planning Perspectives,* 31(2), 90–93.

Gerntholtz, L., Gibbs, A., & Willan, S. (2011). The African Women's Protocol: Bringing attention to reproductive rights and the MDGs. *PLOS Medicine,* 8(4), 1–4.

Gerson, C. M. (2005). Toward an international standard of abortion rights: Two obstacles. *Chicago Journal of International Law,* 5(2),753–61.

Gidron, B., Bar, M., & Katz, H. (2004). *The Israeli third sector: Between welfare state and civil society.* New York: Kluwer Academic/Plenum Publishers.

Gilardi, F. (2012). Transnational diffusion: Norms, ideas, and policies. In *Handbook of International Relations* edited by W. Carlsnaes, T. Risse, & B. Simmons (pp. 453–477). Thousand Oaks, CA: Sage Publications.

Gill, A. (1998). *Rendering unto Caesar: The Catholic Church and the state in Latin America.* Chicago: The University of Chicago Press.

Githens, M., & Stetson, D. M. (1996). *Abortion politics: Public policy in cross-cultural perspective.* Abingdon on Thames, United Kingdom: Routledge.

Glasier, A., & Gülmezoglu, M. (2006). Putting sexual and reproductive health on the agenda. *The Lancet, 368*(9547), 1550–1551.

Glock, C. Y. (1972). On the study of religious commitment. In *Religion's influence in contemporary society: Readings in the sociology of religion*, edited by J. E. Faulkner (pp. 38–56). Marietta, OH: Charles E. Merrill.

Gonzalez, N. (2009). *The Sunni-Shia conflict: Understanding sectarian violence in the Middle East.* Orange County, CA: Nortia Press.

Goodman, R., & Jinks, D. (2004). How to influence states: Socialization and international human rights law. *Duke Law Journal, 54*(3), 621–703.

Goodman, R., & Jinks, D. (2003). Measuring the effects of human rights treaties. *European Journal of International Law, 14*(1), 171–183.

Gourevitch, P. (1998). *We wish to inform you that tomorrow we will be killed with our families: Stories from Rwanda.* Gordonsville, VA: Picador.

Government Offices of Sweden. (2018, August). *Handbook of Sweden's feminist foreign policy.* Retrieved from https://www.government.se/reports/2018/08/handbook-swedens-feminist-foreign-policy/

Grant, R., & Keohane, R. O. (2005). Accountability and abuses of power in world politics. *American Political Science Review, 99*, 29–44.

Green, E. (2018, January 16). *As Pope Francis visits, Chileans question their allegiance to the Catholic Church.* Retrieved from www.usatoday.com/story/new s/world/2018/01/16/pope-francis-visits-chileans-question-their-allegiance-catholic-church/1035515001

Greenhill, B. (2010). The company you keep: International socialization and the diffusion of human rights norms. *International Studies Quarterly, 54*(1), 127–145.

Grey, S. (2006). Numbers and beyond: The relevance of critical mass in gender research. *Politics and Gender, 2*(4), 492–502.

Grey, S. (2002). Does size matter? Critical mass and New Zealand's female MPs. *Parliamentary Affairs, 55*, 19–29.

Grim, B., & Finke, R. (2006). International religion indexes: Government regulation, government favoritism, and social regulation of religion. *Interdisciplinary Journal of Research on Religion, 2*(1), 2–40.

Grimshaw, P. (2000). Settler anxieties, indigenous peoples, and women's suffrage in the colonies of Australia, New Zealand, and Hawai'i, 1888 to 1902. *Pacific Historical Review, 69*(4), 553–572.

Grimshaw, P. (1972). *Women's suffrage in New Zealand.* Oxford: Oxford University Press.

Grossman, D., Grindlay, K., & Burns, B. (2016). Public funding for abortion where broadly legal. *Contraception, 94*(5), 453–460.

Grzymala-Busse, A. (2012). Why comparative politics should take religion (more) seriously. *The Annual Review of Political Science, 15*, 421–442.

Guiraudon, V. (2000). European courts and foreigners' rights: A comparative study of norms diffusion. *International Migration Review, 34*(4), 1088–1125.

Guttmacher Institute. (2013, April). *Fact sheet: Abortion in Rwanda.* Retrieved from www.guttmacher.org/fact-sheet/abortion-rwanda

Gygli, S., Florian H., Potfrake, N., & Sturm, J. E. (2019). *The KOF Globalisation Index – revisited. Review of International Organizations.* New York: Springer. Retrieved from https://doi.org/10.1007/s11558-019-09344-2

Haas, P. M. (1992). Introduction: Epistemic communities and international policy coordination. *International Organization*, 46(1), 1–35.

Haddad, L. B., & Nour, N. M. (2009). Unsafe abortion: Unnecessary maternal mortality. *Reviews in Obstetrics and Gynecology*, 2(2), 122–126.

Hafner-Burton, E. M. (2005). Trading human rights: How preferential trade agreements influence government repression. *International Organization*, 59(3), 593–629.

Hage, J. (2005). *Studies in legal logics*. The Netherlands: Springer.

Hamilton, H. (2000). *Rwanda's women: The key to reconstruction*. Retrieved July 18, 2018, from www.reliefweb.int: https://reliefweb.int/report/rwanda/rwandas-women-key-reconstruction

Hanson, E. O. (1987). *The Catholic Church in world politics*. Princeton: Princeton University Press.

Hathaway, O. A. (2002). Do human rights treaties make a difference? *Yale Law Journal*, 112, 1935–2042.

He, Q. (1996). The crucial role of the United Nations in maintaining international peace and security. *Legal Aspects of International Organizations*, 6(1), 77–90.

Hempel, M. (1996). Reproductive health and rights: Origins of and challenges to the ICPD agenda. *Health Transition Review*, 6(1), 73–85.

Herring, E. (2002). Between Iraq and a hard place: A critique of the British government's case for UN economic sanctions. *Review of International Studies*, 28, 39–56.

Hessini, L. (2005). Global progress in abortion advocacy and policy: An assessment of the decade since ICPD. *Reproductive Health Matters*, 13(25), 88–100.

Hessini, L., Brookman-Amissah, E., & Crane, B. (2006). Global policy change and women's access to safe abortion: The Impact of the World Health Organization's guidance in Africa. *African Journal of Reproductive Health*, 10(2), 14–27.

Hildebrandt, A. (2015). What shapes abortion Law? – A global perspective. *Global Policy*, 6(4), 418–428.

Hofmann, D. A. (1997). An overview of the logic and rationale of hierarchical linear models, *Journal of Management*, 23(6), 723–744.

Htun, M. (2004). Is gender like ethnicity? The political representation of identity groups. *Perspectives on Politics*, 2(3), 439–458.

Htun, M. (2003). *Sex and the state: Abortion, divorce, and the family under Latin American dictatorships and democracies*. Cambridge: Cambridge University Press.

Htun, M., & Power, T. (2006). Gender, parties, and support for equal rights in the Brazilian Congress. *Latin American Politics and Society*, 48(4), 83–104.

Htun, M., & Weldon, S. L. (2018). *The logics of gender justice: State action on women's rights around the world*. Cambridge: Cambridge University Press.

Htun, M., & Weldon, S. L. (2012). The civic origins of progressive policy change: Combating the violence against women in global perspective, 1975–2005. *American Political Science Review*, 106(3), 548–569.

Htun, M., & Weldon, S. L. (2010). When do governments promote women's rights? A framework for the comparative analysis of sex equality policy. *Perspectives on Politics*, 8(1), 207–216.

Hurley, E. (2017, November 7). *Record level of women in New Zealand Parliament*. Retrieved from www.newshub.co.nz/home/politics/2017/11/record-levels-of-women-in-new-zealand-parliament.html

Hyde, S. D. (2017). *The pseudo-democrat's dilemma: Why election observation became an international norm*. Ithaca, NY: Cornell University Press.

Instituto Nacional de Estadisticas. (2006, October). *Compendio estadistico 2006*. Madrid: Author.

Inter-Parliamentary Union. (2018, April). *Women in Parliaments*. Geneva: Author. Retrieved from http://archive.ipu.org/wmn-e/arc/classif010418.htm

Iversen, T., & Rosenbluth, F. (2008). Work and power: The connection between female labor force participation and female political representation. *Annual Review of Political Science, 11*, 479–495.

Jackson, R., & Sørensen, G. (2016). *Introduction to international relations: Theories and approaches* (6th ed.). Oxford: Oxford University Press.

Jacobson, J. L. (2000). Transforming family planning programmes: Towards a framework for advancing the reproductive rights agenda. *Reproductive Health Matters, 8*(15), 21–32.

Jain, S. (2003). The right to family planning, contraception and abortion: The Hindu view. In *Sacred rights: The case for contraception and abortion in world religion*, edited by D. C. Maguire (pp. 129–143). New York: Oxford University Press.

Jan, T., Dahlberg, S., Holmberg, S., Rothstein, B., Hartmann, F., & Svensson, R. (2015). *The Quality of Government Standard Dataset, version Jan 15*. Retrieved October 19, 2015, from www.qog.pol.gu.se.

Jelen, T. G. (2014). The subjective bases of abortion attitudes: A cross national comparison of religious traditions. *Politics and Religion, 7*, 550–567.

Jelen, T. G., & Wilcox, C. (2003). Causes and consequences of public attitudes toward abortion: A review and research agenda. *Political Research Quarterly, 56*(4), 489–500.

Joecks, J., Pull, K., & Vetter, K. (2013). Gender diversity in the boardroom and firm performance: What exactly constitutes a "critical mass?". *Journal of Business Ethics, 118*(1), 61–72.

Johnson, J., & Saarinen, A. (2013). Twenty-first-century feminisms under repression: Gender regime change and the Women's Crisis Center Movement in Russia. *Signs 38*(3), 543–567.

Jonas, O. (2012). The practice of polygamy under the scheme of the Protocol to the African Charter on Human and Peoples Rights on the Rights of Women in Africa: A critical appraisal. *Journal of African Studies and Development, 4*(5), 142–149.

Jones, M. P. (2008). Gender quotas, electoral laws, and the election of women: Evidence from the Latin American vanguard. *Comparative Political Studies, 42*(1), 56–81.

Joshi, D. K. (2013). The representation of younger age cohorts in Asian Parliaments: Do electoral systems make a difference? *Representation, 49*(1), 1–16.

Joshi, S., & Sivaram, A. (2014). Does it pay to deliver? An evaluation of India's safe motherhood program. *World Development, 64*, 434–47.

Karolak, M. (2010). Religion in a political context: The case of the Kingdom of Bahrain. *Asia Journal of Global Studies, 4*(1), 4–20.

Katzenstein, P. J. (1996). *The culture of national security*. New York: Columbia University Press.

Keck, M. E., & Sikkink, K. (1999). Transnational advocacy networks in international and regional politics. *International Social Science Journal, 51*(159), 89–101.

Kelly, S. (2009). Recent gains and new opportunities for women's rights in the Gulf Arab states. *Women's Rights in the Middle East and North Africa: Gulf Edition*, 1–8. New York: Freedom House.

Kelly, S., & Breslin, J. (2010). *Women's rights in the Middle East and North Africa: Progress amid resistance*. Lanham, MD: Rowman & Littlefield Publishers.

Kenworthy, L., & Malami, M. (1999). Gender inequality in political representation: A worldwide comparative analysis. *Social Forces*, 78(1), 235–268.

Khagram, S. (2004). *Dams and development: Transnational struggles for water and power*. Ithaca, NY: Cornell University Press.

Khagram, S., Riker, J. V., & Sikkink, K. (2002). *Restructuring world politics: Transnational social movements, networks, and norms*. Minneapolis: University of Minnesota Press.

Kimenyi, B. (2011). *What the law says about abortion*. Retrieved July 17, 2018, from www.newtimes.co.rw: www.newtimes.co.rw/section/read/97435.

King, J. S. (2012). Genetic tests: Politics and fetal diagnostics collide. *Nature, 491*, 33–34.

Kingsbury, B., Krisch, N., & Stewart, R. B. (2005). The emergence of global administrative law. *Law and Contemporary Problems*, 68(3/4), 15–61.

Kittilson, M. C. (2005). In support of gender quotas: Setting new standards, bringing visible gains. *Politics and Gender*, 1(4), 638–644.

Knill, C., Preidel, C., & Nebel, K. (2014). Brake rather than barrier: The impact of the Catholic Church on morality policies in Western Europe. *West European Politics*, 37(5), 845–866.

Koh, H. H. (1999). How is international human rights law enforced? *Indiana Law Journal*, 74, 1397–1417.

Kortmann, M. (2018). When are churches allowed to discriminate? How churches' role in public service delivery affects employment equality regulations. *Acta Politica*, 1–22.

Kozak, P. (2018). *Chile president-elect reveals hardline cabinet with ties to Pinochet*. Retrieved August 1, 2018, from www.theguardian.com/world/2018/jan/23/chile-president-elect-sebastian-pinera-andres-chadwick

Kozak, P. (2017). *'A triumph of reason': Chile approves landmark bill to ease abortion ban*. Retrieved August 1, 2018, from www.theguardian.com/global-development/2017/aug/22/chile-abortion-bill-michelle-bachelet-a-triumph-of-reason-ease-abortion-ban

Krook, M. L. (2006). Reforming representation: The diffusion of candidate gender quotas worldwide. *Politics and Gender, 2*, 303–327.

Krook, M. L., Franceschet, S., & Piscopo, J. M., eds. (2009). *The impact of gender quotas: A research agenda*. First European Conference on Politics and Gender. Oxford: Oxford University Press.

Krook, M., & O'Brien, D. Z. (2010). The politics of group representation: Quotas for women and minorities worldwide. *Comparative Politics*, 42(3), 253–272.

Krook, M., & Zetterberg, P. (2014). Electoral quotas and political representation: comparative perspectives. *International Political Science Review*, 35(1), 3–11.

Kwibuka, E. (2017, October 6). *Government moves to relax anti-abortion law*. New York: The New Times.

La Mattina, G. (2017). Civil conflict, domestic violence and intra-household bargaining in post-genocide Rwanda. *Journal of Development Economics, 124*, 168–198.

Levitsky, S., & Way, L. A. (2002). Elections without democracy: The rise of competitive authoritarianism. *Journal of Democracy, 13*(2), 51–65.

Lieberson, S. (1969). Measuring population diversity. *American Sociological Review, 34* (6), 850–862.

Lindsley, L. (1987). The Beagle Channel settlement: Vatican mediation resolves a century-old dispute. *Journal of Church and State, 29*, 435–456.

Lipson, C. (1991).Why are some international agreements informal? *International Organizations, 45*(4), 495–538.

Louër, L. (2013). Sectarianism and coup-proofing strategies in Bahrain. *Journal of Strategic Studies, 36*(2), 245–260.

Lovenduski, J. (2001). Women and politics: Minority representation or critical mass? *Parliamentary Affairs, 54*(4), 743–758.

Lovenduski, J., & Outshoorn, J. (1986). *The new politics of abortion.* London: Sage Publications.

Luna, J. (2013). Religious parties in Chile: The Christian Democratic Party and the Independent Democratic Union. *Democratization, 20*(5), 917–938.

MacFarquhar, N. (September 7, 2010) *U.N. officials say 500 were victims of Congo Rapes.* New York: The New York Times.

Macionis, J. J., & Gerber, L. M. (2011). *Sociology.* Toronto: Pearson Canada.

Magaloni, B. (2006). *Voting for autocracy: Hegemonic party survival and its demise in Mexico.* Cambridge: Cambridge University Press.

Malesky, E., & Schuler, P. (2010). Nodding or needling: Analyzing delegate responsiveness in an authoritarian parliament. *American Political Science Review, 104*(3), 482–502.

Mallat, C. (1988). Religious militancy in contemporary Iraq: Muhammad Baqer as-Sadr and the Sunni-Shia paradigm. *Third World Quarterly, 10*(2), 699–729.

Mamudu, H., Cairney, P., & Studlar, D. (2015). Global public policy: Does the new venue for transnational tobacco control challenge the old way of doing things? *Public Administration, 93*(4), 856–873.

Mansbridge, J. (1999). Should blacks represent blacks and women represent women? A contingent "yes." *The Journal of Politics, 61*(3), 628–657.

Maoz, Z., & Henderson, E. A. (2013). The World Religion Dataset, 1945–2010: Logic, estimates, and trends. *International Interactions, 3*, 265–291.

March, J. G., & Olsen, J. P. (1998).The institutional dynamics of international political orders. *International Organization, 52*(4), 943–969.

Marima, T. (2017, August 16). *Rwanda: World Leader for Women in Politics (Unless They Oppose Kagame).* Retrieved from www.newsdeeply.com/womenandgirls/articles/2017/08/16/rwanda-world-leader-for-women-in-politics-unless-they-oppose-kagame

Marshall, M., Gurr, T., & Jaggers, K. (2017, July 13). *Polity IV Project: Political regime characteristics and transitions, 1800–2015.* Retrieved from Center for Systemic Peace www.systemicpeace.org/inscrdata.html

Martin, J. E. (2015, February 1). *Parliament.* Retrieved from *Te Ara: The Encyclopedia of New Zealand* https://teara.govt.nz/en/parliament

Martin, L. L. (2000). *Democratic commitments: Legislatures and international cooperation.* Princeton: Princeton University Press.

Martinsson, J. (2011). *Global norms: Creation, diffusion, and limits.* Washington DC: International Bank for Reconstruction and Development/ World Bank.

Masci, D. (2016, June 21). *Where major religious groups stand on abortion*. Retrieved from www.pewresearch.org/fact-tank/2016/06/21/

Matland, R. E. (1998). Women's representation in national legislatures: Developed and developing countries. *Legislative Studies Quarterly*, 23(1), 109–125.

Mavisakalyan, A. (2014). Women in cabinet and public health spending: Evidence across countries. *Economics of Governance*, 15(3), 281–304.

McBride Stetson, D. (2001). *Abortion politics, women's movements, and the democratic state: A comparative study of state feminism*. New York: Oxford University Press.

McConnell, M. W. (2013). Why protect religious freedom? *The Yale Law Journal*, 123 (3), 770–810.

McCoy, J., & Hartlyn, J. (2009). The relative powerlessness of elections in Latin America. In *Democratization by elections: A new mode of transition*, edited by S. Lindberg. Baltimore: Johns Hopkins University Press.

McMurry, M. (1978). Religion and women's sex role traditionalism. *Sociological Focus*, 11(2), 81–95.

Meacham, C. E. (1994). *The role of the Chilean Catholic Church in the New Chilean democracy*. Journal of Church and State, 36, 277–299.

Merriman, S. A. (2009). *Religion and the state: An international analysis of roles and relationships*. Santa Barbara, CA: ABC-CLIO, LLC.

Meyer, J., Boli, J., Thomas, G., & Ramirez, F. (1997). World society and the nation-state. *American Journal of Sociology*, 103(1), 144–181.

Miller, A. F. (2013). The non-religious patriarchy: Why losing religion HAS NOT meant losing white male dominance. *CrossCurrents*, 63(2), 211–226.

Mimiko, N. O. (2012). *Globalization: The politics of global economic relations and international business*. Durham, NC: Carolina Academic Press.

Ministry of Information Affairs, The Kingdom of Bahrain. (2014, September 2). *Population and Demographics*. Retrieved from www.mia.gov.bh/en/Kingdom-of-Bahrain/Pages/Population-and-Demographic-Growth.aspx

Minkenberg, M. (2003). The policy impact of church-state relations: Family policy and abortion in Britain, France, and Germany. *West European Politics*, 26(1), 195–214.

Minkenberg, M. (2002). Religion and public policy: Institutional, cultural and political impact on the shaping of abortion policies in Western democracies. *Comparative Political Studies*, 35(2), 221–247.

Mirow, M. C. (2004). International law and religion in Latin America: The Beagle Channel Dispute. *Suffolk Transnational Law Review*, 28(1), 1–29.

Moir, J. (2018, May 27). *Vote on abortion law reform could happen in NZ Parliament next year*. Retrieved from www.stuff.co.nz/national/politics/104246447/vote-on-abortion-law-reform-could-happen-in-nz-parliament-next-year

Morse, Y. L. (2012). The era of electoral authoritarianism. *World Politics*, 64(1), 161–198.

Mujuzi, J. D. (2008). The Protocol to the African Charter on Human and Peoples' Rights on the Rights of Women in Africa: South Africa's reservations and interpretative declarations. *Law, Democracy & Development*, 12(2), 41–61.

Mulligan, C. B., Ricard, G., & Sala-i-Martin, X. (2004). Do democracies have different public policies than nondemocracies? *Journal of Economic Perspectives*, 18(1), 51–74.

Murdie, A. M., & Davis, D. R. (2012). Shaming and blaming: Using events data to assess the impact of human rights INGOs. *International Studies Quarterly*, 56, 1–16.

Murdie, A., & Peksen, D. (2015). Women's rights INGO shaming and the government respect for women's rights. *The Review of International Organizations*, 10(1), 1–22.

Muriaas, R. L., Tønnessen, L., & Wang, V. (2013). Exploring the relationship between democratization and quota policies in Africa. *Women's Studies International Forum*, 41, 89–93.

Mutisi, M. (2012). Local conflict resolution in Rwanda: The case of Abunzi mediators. In *Integrating traditional and modern conflict resolution experiences from selected cases in Eastern and the Horn of Africa*, edited by M. Mutisi & K. Sansculotte-Greenidge (pp. 41–74). Durban, South Africa: Accord.

Mylonas, H., & Roussias, N. (2008). When do votes count? Regime type, electoral conduct, and political competition in Africa. *Comparative Political Studies*, 41(11), 1466–1491.

n.a. (2014). *A brief history of abortion laws in New Zealand*. Retrieved July 24, 2018, from www.abortionservices.org.nz

Nabaneh, S. (2012). *A purposive interpretation of Article 14 (2) (c) of the African Women's Protocol to Include Abortion on Request and for Socio-Economic Reasons*. Maputo, Mozambique: Eduardo Mondlane University, Faculty of Law.

National Commission for Truth and Reconciliation. (1990). *Report of the Chilean National Commission on Truth and Reconciliation*. Retrieved from the U.S. Institute of Peace www.usip.org/sites/default/files/resources/collections/truth_commissions/Chile90-Report/Chile90-Report.pdf

National Statistics Institute. (2018, January 1). *Resultados Censo 2017*. Madrid: Author.

Naughton, C. (2017). *Abort mission: A recommendation for reform of New Zealand's abortion law*. Otago: University of Otago.

Neumayer, E. (2005). Do international human rights treaties improve respect for human rights? *Journal of Conflict Resolution*, 49(6), 925–953.

New Zealand Ministry of Culture and Heritage. (2016). *Political and constitutional timeline*. Retrieved July 24, 2018, from www.nzhistory.govt.nz: https://nzhistory.govt.nz/politics/milestones

Newbury, C. (1998). Ethnicity and the politics of history in Rwanda. *Africa Today*, 45 (1), 7–24.

Ngwena, C. G. (2010). Inscribing abortion as human rights: Significance of the Protocol to the Rights of Women in Africa. *Human Rights Quarterly*, 32(4), 783–864.

Nickel, J. W. (2005). Who needs freedom of religion? *University of Colorado Law Review*, 76, 941–964.

Norrander, B., & Wilcox, C. (1999). Public opinion and policymaking in the States: The case of post-Roe abortion policy, *Policy Studies Journal*, 27(4), 707–722.

Norris, P., & Inglehart, R. (2002). Islamic culture and democracy: Testing the "Clash of Civilizations" thesis. *Comparative Sociology*, 1(3–4), 235–263.

Norwood, C. (2016, December 30). The year in religion and politics. *The Atlantic* Retrieved from www.theatlantic.com/politics/archive/2016/12/2016-religion-and-politics/511736/

Nteta, T. M., & Wallsten, K. J. (2012). Preaching to the choir? Religious leaders and American opinion on immigration reform. *Social Science Quarterly*, 93(4), 891–910.

Obelkevich, J., Roper, L., & Samuel, R. (2013). *Disciplines of faith: Studies in religion, politics and patriarchy*. New York: Routledge.

O'Brien, D. Z. (2012). Gender and Select Committee Elections in the British House of Commons. *Politics & Gender*, 8(2), 178–204.

O'Connor, R. E., & Berkman, M. B. (1995). Religious determinants of state abortion policy. *Social Science Quarterly*, 76(2), 447–459.

OECD. (2018a). Chile. Paris: OECD, Development Centre. Retrieved from www .genderindex.org/country/chile/#_ftn10

OECD. (2018b). OECD data. Paris: OECD Development Centre. Retrieved from Gender Wage Gap https://data.oecd.org/earnwage/gender-wage-gap.htm

OECD. (2016, April 2). *Share of births outside of marriage*. Paris: OECD, Social Policy Division. Retrieved from www.oecd.org/els/family/SF_2_4_Share_births_outside_ marriage.pdf

Office of the Historian of the U.S. Department of State. (2018). Retrieved July 30, 2018, from www.history.state.gov: https://history.state.gov/milestones/1969–1976/allende

Office of the Special Adviser on Gender Issues and Advancement of Women. (2000). *United Nations Security Council Resolution 1325 (2000) on Women, Peace and Security*. New York: U.N. Department of Economic and Social Affairs.

Olson, L., Cadge, W., & Harrison, J. (2006). Religion and public opinion about same-sex marriage. *Social Science Quarterly*, 87(2), 340–360.

O'Regan, V. R. (2000). *Gender matters: Female policymakers' influence in industrialized nations*. Westport, CT: Praeger Publishers.

Organization of American States (OAS). (1994). *Inter-American Convention on the Prevention, Punishment and Eradication of Violence against Women ("Convention of Belem do Para")*. Washington, DC: Author.

Ottaway, M. (2003). *Democracy challenged: The rise of semi-authoritarianism*. Washington DC: Carnegie Endowment for International Peace.

Outshoorn, J. (1996). The stability of compromise: Abortion politics in Western Europe. In *Abortion politics: Public policy in cross-cultural perspective*, edited by M. Githens & D. McBride Stetson (pp. 145–164). London: Routledge.

Oyarce, G. (2015, October 12). *Madres de menores violadas defienden el aborto*. www .theclinic.cl/2015/10/12/madres-de-menores-violadas-defienden-el-aborto/

Pande, R., & Ford, D. (2011). *Gender quotas and female leadership: A review. World Development Report 2012*. Washington, DC: World Bank Group.

Parish, M. (2010). An essay on the accountability of international organizations. *International Organizations Law Review*, 7(2), 277–342.

Park, S. (2005). Norm diffusion within international organizations: A case study of the World Bank. *Journal of International Relations and Development*, 8(2), 111–141.

Paxton, P. (1997). Women in national legislatures: A cross-national analysis. *Social Science Research*, 26(4), 442–464.

Paxton, P., & Kunovich, S. (2003). Women's political representation: The importance of ideology. *Social Forces*, 82(1), 87–113.

Paxton, P., Kunovich, S., & Hughes, M. M. (2007). Gender in politics. *Annual Review of Sociology*, 33, 263–284.

Perrett, R.W. (2000). Buddhism, abortion and the middle way. *Asian Philosophy*, 10(2), 101–114.

Petchesky, R. P. (2003). *Global prescriptions: Gendering health and human rights*. London: Zed Books.

Peter, C. M., & Kibalama, E. (2006). *Searching for sense and humanity: Civil society and the struggle for a better Rwanda.* Kampala, Uganda: Fountain Publishers.

Peterson, J. (2009). Bahrain: Reform – promise and reality. In *Political Liberalization in the Persian Gulf*, edited by J. Teitelbaum (pp. 157–185). London: Hurst Publishers.

Pew Research Center. (2015). *Pew Research Center Spring 2015 survey: Importance of Religion.* Washington, DC: Pew-Templeton.

Pew Research Center. (2012). *The global religious landscape.* Washington DC: Pew-Templeton.

Pew Research Center. (2010). *Pew Research Center's Religion & Public Life Project: Bahrain.* Retrieved from www.globalreligiousfutures.org/countries/bahrain/reli gious_demography#/?affiliations_religion_id=0&affiliations_year=2010

Pew Research Center. (2009). *Mapping the global Muslim population.* Pew Forum on Religion & Public Life. Washington, DC: Author.

Picken, D. (2018, June). *Big Read: Abortion law reform – what's at stake?* New Zealand Herald. Retrieved Oct. 18, 2018, from www.nzherald.co.nz/nz/news/article.cfm? c_id=1&objectid=12070558

Pietilä, H., & Vickers, J. (1990). *Making women matter: The role of the United Nations.* London: Zed Books.

Pillai, V., & Wang, G.-Z. (1999). *Women's reproductive rights in developing countries.* Farnham, UK: Ashgate.

Pitkin, H. (1967). *The concept of representation.* Berkeley: University of California Press.

Pitkin, H. F. (2004). Representation and democracy: Uneasy alliance. *Scandinavian Political Studies*, 27(3), 335–342.

Plantenga, J., Remery, C., Figueiredo, H., & Smith, M. (2009). Towards a European Union gender equality index. *Journal of European Social Policy*, 19(1), 19–33.

Plotke, D. (1997). Representation is democracy. *Constellations*, 4(1), 19–34.

Pollack, M. (1999). *New right in Chile.* New York: Springer

Pollack, M. A., & Hafner-Burton, E. (2000). Mainstreaming gender in the European Union. *Journal of European Public Policy*, 7(3), 432–456.

Pollack Petchesky, R. (1995). From population control to reproductive rights: Feminist fault lines. *Reproductive Health Matters*, 3(6), 152–161.

Potts, M., & Campbell, M. (2002). History of contraception. *Gynecology and Obstetrics*, 6(8), 18–22.

Power, M. (2004). Gender and Chile's split culture. *ReVista: Harvard Review of Latin America*, 32–34. Retrieved July 30, 2018, from https://revista.drclas.harvard.edu/book/ gender-and-chiles-split-culture

Powley, E. (2006). *Rwanda: The impact of women legislators on policy outcomes affecting children and families.* New York: UNICEF.

Prada, E. (2016). *Induced Abortion in Chile.* Retrieved August 1, 2018, from www .guttmacher.org/report/induced-abortion-chile

Protocol to the African Charter on Human and Peoples' Rights on the Rights of Women in Africa. Retrieved May 18, 2016, from www.achpr.org/instruments/women-protocol/ratification/

Quene,' H., & Van den Bergh, H. (2004). On multi-level modeling of data from repeated measures designs: A tutorial, *Speech Communication*, 43, 103–121.

Quota Project: Global Database of Quotas for Women (2017). Retrieved June 8, 2015, from www.quotaproject.org/index.cfm

Rainey, V. (2018, January 2). *'Help me before my relatives kill me': Aiding abortion in the Middle East*. Retrieved from www.middleeasteye.net/news/help-me-my-relatives-kill-me-aiding-abortion-middle-east

Raustiala, K. (2005). Form and substance in international agreements. *American Journal of International Law*, 99(3), 581–614.

Reanda, L. (1981). Human rights and women's rights: The United Nations approach. *Human Rights Quarterly*, 3(11), 11–31.

Rehfeld, A. (2006). Towards a general theory of political representation. *Journal of Politics*, 68(1), 1–21.

Reinisch, A. (2001). Developing human rights and humanitarian law accountability of the Security Council for the Imposition of Economic Sanctions. *American Journal of International Law*, 95(4), 851–872.

Reuters. (2017, August 21). *Chile court ruling ends abortion ban; new law allows in limited cases*. Retrieved from https://uk.reuters.com/article/uk-chile-abortion/chile-court-ruling-ends-abortion-ban-new-law-allows-in-limited-cases-idUKKCN1B122I?il=0

Reynolds, A. (1999). Women in the legislatures and executives of the world: Knocking at the highest glass ceiling. *World Politics*, 51(4), 547–572.

Reynolds, J., & May, M. (2014). Religion, motherhood, and the spirit of capitalism. *Social Currents*, 1(2), 173–188.

Reyntjens, Filip (2011). Constructing the truth, dealing with dissent, domesticating the world: Governance in post-genocide Rwanda. *African Affairs*, 110(438), 1–34.

Risse, T. (2007). Transnational actors and world politics. In *Corporate ethics and corporate governance*, edited by C. Z. Walther, K. Richter, & M. Holzinger (pp. 251–286). Berlin: Springer.

Risse, T. (2000). "Let's argue!": Communicative action in world politics. *International Organization*, 54(1), 1–39.

Robbers, G. (2001). Religious freedom in Germany. *Brigham Young University Law Review*, 2, 643–668.

Roe v. Wade, 410 U.S. 113 (1973).

Rohter, L. (2005, January 30). *Divorce ties Chile in knots*. Retrieved from www.nytimes.com/2005/01/30/weekinreview/divorce-ties-chile-in-knots.html

Rosenbluth, F., Salmond, R., & Thies, M. F. (2006). Welfare works: Explaining female legislative representation. *Politics & Gender*, 2(2), 165–192.

Ross, M. L. (2008). Oil, Islam and women. *The American Political Science Review*, 102(1), 107–123.

Roy, E. (2017, Sept 5). New Zealand election: Jacinda Ardern pledges to decriminalise abortion. Retrieved Oct 2018, from www.theguardian.com/world/2017/sep/05/jacinda-ardern-decriminalise-abortion-new-zealand-election

Rwirahira, R. (2018, January 22). *Rwanda's Proposed Abortion Amendment Takes Procedure Out of the Courts*. Retrieved July 2018, from www.newsdeeply.com/womenandgirls/articles/2018/01/22/rwandas-proposed-abortion-amendment-takes-procedure-out-of-the-courts

Ryall, D. (2001). The Catholic Church as a transnational actor. In *Non-state actors in world politics*, edited by D. Josselin & W. Wallace (pp. 41–58). Hampshire, United Kingdom: Palgrave Publishers.

Salamon, L. M., Anheier, H. K., List, R., Toepler, S., & Sokolowski, S. W. (1999). *Civil society in comparative perspective*. Baltimore: The Johns Hopkins Center for Civil Society Studies.

Salmon, T. C., & Imber, M. F. (2008). *Issues in international relations* (2nd ed). New York: Routledge.

Sapiro, V. (1998). When are interests interesting? The problem of political representation of women. In *Feminism and Politics*, edited by A. Phillips (pp. 161–192). New York: Oxford University Press.

Saward, M. (2006). The representative claim. *Comparative Political Theory*, 5, 297–318.

Say, L., Chou, D., & Gemmell, A. et al. (2014). Global causes of maternal death: A WHO systemic analysis. *The Lancet Global Health*, 2(6), e323–e333.

Schabas, W. A. (1996). Justice, democracy, and impunity in post-genocide Rwanda: Searching for solutions to impossible problems. *Criminal Law Forum*, 7(3), 523–560.

Scheufele, D., Corley, E., Shih, T.-J., Dalrymple, K., & Ho, S. (2009). Religious beliefs and public attitudes toward nanotechnology in Europe and the United States. *Nature Nanotechnology*, 4, 91–94.

Schindler, K. (2010). *Who does what in a household after genocide: Evidence from Rwanda. Discussion Paper, 1072*. Berlin: DIW Berlin.

Schwartz, F. J., & Pharr, S. J. (2003). *The state of civil society in Japan*. Cambridge: Cambridge University Press.

Schwarz, R. (2004). The paradox of sovereignty, regime type and human rights compliance. *The International Journal of Human Rights*, 8(2), 199–215.

Schwindt-Bayer, L. (2015). *Chile's gender quota: Will it work?* Houston: Institute for Public Policy, Rice University.

Schwindt-Bayer, L. A., & Mishler, W. (2005). An integrated model of women's representation. *The Journal of Politics*, 67(2), 407–428.

Scrutton, A. (16 March 2015). Margot Wallström: Can Sweden's feminist foreign minister be both radical and influential – and make the country a 'moral great power'?. *The Independent*.

Sedge, G., Singh, S., Henshaw, S. K., & Bankole, A. (2011). Legal abortion worldwide in 2008: Levels and recent trends. *Perspectives on Sexual and Reproductive Health*, 37 (2), 84–94.

Seikaly, M. (1994). "Women and social change in Bahrain." *International Journal of Middle East Studies*, 26(3), 415–426.

Semashko, N. A. 1924. *Health Protection in the USSR*. London: Gollancz

Shachar, A. (2005). Religion, state and the problem of gender: New modes of citizenship and governance in diverse societies. *McGill Law Journal*, 50, 49–88.

Shain, R. N. (1986). A cross-cultural history of abortion. *Clinics in Obstetrics and Gynaecology*, 13(1), 1–17.

Shannon, V. P. (2000). Norms are what states make of them: The political psychology of norm violation. *International Studies Quarterly*, 44(2), 293–316.

Sherkat, D. E. (2000). "That they be keepers of the home": The effect of conservative religion on early and late transitions into housewifery. *Review of Religious Research*, 41(3), 344–358.

Shipan, C. R., & Volden, C. (2008). The mechanisms of policy diffusion. *American Journal of Political Science*, 52(4), 840–857.

Sigmund, P. E. (1986). Revolution, counterrevolution, and the Catholic Church in Chile. *The ANNALS of the American Academy of Political and Social Science, 483*(1), 25–35.

Simmons, B. A. (1998). Compliance with international agreements. *Annual Review of Political Science, 1*(1), 75–93.

Simmons, B., & Elkins, Z. (2004). The globalization of liberalization: Policy diffusion in the international political economy. *American Political Science Review, 98*(1), 171–89.

Simmons, B. A., & Martin, L. (2012). International organisations and institutions. In *Handbook of International Relations*, edited by W. Carlsnaes, T. Risse, & B. A. (pp. 326–351). London: Sage Publications.

Singh, S., Remez, L., Sedgh, G., Kwokand, L., & Onda, T. (2018). Abortion worldwide 2017: Uneven progress and unequal access. New York: Guttmacher Institute.

Smidt, C. E. (2005). Religion and American attitudes toward Islam and an invasion of Iraq. *Sociology of Religion, 66*(3), 243–261.

Smith, J., Chatfield, C., & Pagnucco, R. (1997). *Transnational social movements and global politics: Solidarity beyond the state*. New York: Syracuse University Press.

Solodoch, O., & Sommer, U. (2018). Explaining the birthright citizenship lottery: Longitudinal and cross-national evidence for key determinants. *Regulation & Governance* https://doi.org/10.1111/rego.12197

Sommer, U. (2018). Women, demography and politics: How lower fertility rates lead to democracy." *Demography, 55*(2), 559–586. https://doi.org/10.1007/s13524-018-0655-x

Sommer, U. (2017). International effects on the security wall rulings of the Israeli High Court. *Israel Studies Review, 33*, 43–65.

Sommer, U., & Asal, V. (2018). Political and legal antecedents of affirmative action: A comparative framework. *Journal of Public Policy*. Retrieved from https://doi.org/10.1017/S0143814X18000089

Sommer, U., & Frishman, O. (2016). Translating justice: The International Organization of Constitutional Courts" *Law & Policy, 38*(2), 124–142

Ssenyonjo, M. (2007). Culture and the human rights of women in Africa: Between light and shadow. *Journal of African Law, 51*(1), 39–67.

Staffan, L. (ed.). (2009). *Democratization by elections: A new mode of transitions*. Baltimore: Johns Hopkins University Press.

Stats NZ Tatauranga Aotearoa. (2018, June 19). *Abortion statistics: Year ended December 2017*. Retrieved from www.stats.govt.nz/information-releases/abortion-statistics-year-ended-december-2017

Stepan, A. (2000). Religion, democracy, and the "twin tolerations." *Journal of Democracy, 11*(4), 37–57.

Stockemer, D. (2011). Women's parliamentary representation in Africa: The impact of democracy and corruption on the number of female deputies in national parliaments. *Political Studies, 59*, 693–712.

Stockemer, D. (2009). Women's parliamentary representation: Are women more highly represented in (consolidated) democracies than in non-democracies? *Contemporary Politics, 15*(4), 429–443.

Stone, D., & Ladi, S. (2015). Global public policy and transnational administration. *Public Administration, 93*(4), 839–855.

Strassner, V. (2018, January 15). Chile: La iglesia y su rol en la transición pactada a la democracia. Retrieved from www.laizquierdadiario.com/Chile-la-Iglesia-y-su-rol-en-la-transicion-pactada-a-la-democracia

Sultana, A. (2011). Patriarchy and women's subordination: A theoretical analysis. Arts Faculty Journal, 4, 1–18.

Swiss, L., Fallon, K. M., & Burgos, G. (2012). Does critical mass matter? Women's political representation and child health in developing countries. Social Forces, 91(2), 531–558.

T13 Radio. (2017, September 18). Te Deum: Iglesia Católica reafirma postura contra el aborto y matrimonio igualitario. Retrieved from Tele13 Radio 103.3FM www.t13.cl /noticia/nacional/te-deum-iglesia-catolica-reafirma-postura-aborto-y-matrimonio-igualitario

Tadjo, V. (2010) Genocide: The changing landscape of memory in Kigali. African Identities, 8(4), 379–388.

Tatalovitch, R., & Schier, D. (1993). The persistence of ideological cleavage in voting on abortion legislation in the House of Representatives, 1973–1988. American Politics Quarterly, 21(1), 125–139.

Tatauranga Aotearoa. (2018, June 19). Abortion statistics: Year ended December 2017. Retrieved from www.stats.govt.nz/information-releases/abortion-statistics-year-ended-december-2017

Taylor, R. (1990). Modes of civil society. Public Culture, 3(1), 95–118.

Taylor, V., & Whittier, N. (1995). Analytical approaches to social movement culture: The culture of the women's movement. In H. Johnston & B. Klandermans, Social movements and culture, edited by H. Johnston & B. Klandermans (pp. 163–187). Minneapolis: University of Minnesota Press.

Te Aka Matua o te Ture. (2018, Feb). Abortion law reform. Retrieved Oct 18, 2018, from www.lawcom.govt.nz: https://www.lawcom.govt.nz/abortion

Toumi, H. (2016, June 12). Bahrain officially bans mixing politics with religion. Retrieved from Gulf News https://wwrn.org/articles/46011/

Towns, A. E. (2012). Norms and social hierarchies: Understanding international policy diffusion "from below." International Organization, 66(2), 179–209.

TradeArabia News Service. (2010, February 21). Bahrain women in high-risk abortions. Retrieved from www.tradearabia.com/news/HEAL_175194.html

Tribble, S. (2018a). Causes for the debate: Pros and cons of female voting rights. Retrieved July 23, 2018, from www.sthistorysuffrage.weebly.com

Tribble, S. (2018b). Consequences of the campaign. Retrieved July 24, 2018, from https:// sthistorysuffrage.weebly.com/consequences-of-the-campaign.html

True, J., & Mintrom, M. (2001). Transnational networks and policy diffusion: The case of gender mainstreaming. International Studies Quarterly, 45, 27–57.

Tzannatos, Z. (1999). Women and labor market changes in the global economy: Growth helps, inequalities hurt and public policy matters. World Development, 27(3), 551–569.

United Nations. (n.d.). About UN membership. Retrieved from www.un.org/en/sec tions/member-states/about-un-membership/index.html

United Nations. (2015a). Sustainable development goals. New York: United Nations Publications.

United Nations. (2015b). 14.16. New York: United Nations Publications.

United Nations. (1999). *United Nations treaty collection: Treaty reference guide.* New York: United Nations Publications.

United Nations Department of Economic and Social Affairs Population Division. (2007). *World abortion policies 2007.* New York: United Nations Publications. Retrieved from www.un.org/esa/population/publications/2007_Abortion_Policies_Chart/2007_WallChart.pdf.

United Nations Department of Economic and Social Affairs Population Division. (2002). *Abortion policies: A global review.* New York: United Nations Publications.

U.N. Economic and Social Affairs. (2002a). *Abortion policies – A global review, Volume III Oman to Zimbabwe.* New York: United Nations Publications.

U.N. Economic and Social Affairs. (2002b). *Abortion policies – A global review, Volume II Gabon to Norway.* New York: United Nations Publications.

UNFPA. (1995). *Programme of Action of the International Conference on Population Development.* New York: United Nations Publications.

Union, A. O. *Protocol to the African Charter on Human and Peoples' Rights on the Rights of Women in Africa.* African Union, Maputo.

U.N. Outreach Programme on the Rwanda Genocide. (2007). *Rwanda: A brief history of the country. Retrieved July 18, 2018, from* www.un.org/en/preventgenocide/rwanda/education/rwandagenocide.shtml

U.N. Women. (2018a). *Chile endorses women's leadership in politics and aims for women to direct 40 per cent of public enterprises by 2018.* Retrieved July 30, 2018, from www.unwomen.org: www.unwomen.org/en/get-involved/step-it-up/commitments/chile

U.N. Women. (2018b). HeForShe. Retrieved from www.heforshe.org/en

United Nations Department of Economic and Social Affairs Population Division. (2007). *World abortion policies 2007.* New York: United Nations Publications. www.un.org/esa/population/publications/2007_Abortion_Policies_Chart/2007_WallChart.pdf.

United Nations Development Programme. (2016). Human development data (1990–2015). Retrieved from http://hdr.undp.org/en/data

United Nations Development Programme. (2010). *Human development report: 2010.* New York: U.N. Publications Department

United Nations Development Programme. (2005). *Human development report: 2005.* New York: United Nations Publications Department.

United Nations General Assembly. (1979). *Convention on the elimination of all forms of discrimination against women (CEDAW).* New York: United Nations Publications.

United Nations Population Fund. (n.d.). *International Conference on Population and Development.* Retrieved March 14, 2018, from www.unfpa.org/icpd

United Nations Rwanda. (2013, 6 Oct). *Women secure 64 per cent of seats in Rwandan parliamentary elections.* Retrieved 6 July, 2018, from www.rw.one.un.org/press-center/news/women-secure-64-cent-seats-rwandan-parliamentary-elections

U.S. Department of State. (2008). *International Religious Freedom Report 2008.* Retrieved from www.state.gov/j/drl/rls/irf/2008/108518.htm

Uvin, P. (2001). Difficult choices in the new post-conflict agenda: The international community in Rwanda after the genocide. *Third World Quarterly, 22*(2), 177–189.

Valdivia Ortiz De Zárate, V. (2003). Terrorism and political violence during the Pinochet years: Chile, 1973–1989. *Radical History Review, 85*(1), 182–190.

Vallier, I. (1971). The Roman Catholic Church: A transnational actor. *International Organization*, 25(3), 479–502.

Verbit, M. F. (1970). The components and dimensions of religious behavior: Toward a reconceptualization of religiosity. In *American Mosaic, Social Patterns of Religion in the United States*, edited by P. Hammond, & B. Johnson (pp. 24–39). New York: Random House.

Viljeon, F. (2009). An introduction to the Protocol to the African Charter on Human and Peoples' Rights on the Rights of Women in Africa. *Washington and Lee Journal of Civil Rights and Social Justice*, 16(11), 11–46.

Vincent, A. (2001 [1992]). Conceptions of the state. In *Encyclopedia of government and politics*, edited by M. E. Hawkesworth & M. Kogan (pp. 43–55). New York: Routledge.

Vivanco, J., & Undurraga, V. (2017). *How Chile ended its draconian ban on abortion*. Retrieved August 1, 2018, from www.nytimes.com/2017/09/01/opinion/chile-abortion-ban.html

Vlassoff, M., Shearer, J., Walker, D., & Lucas, H. (2008). *Economic impact of unsafe abortion-related morbidity and mortality: Evidence and estimation challenges (Vol. 59)*. Brighton, United Kingdom: Institute of Development Studies.

Vreeland, J. R. (2006). *The International Monetary Fund (IMF): Politics of conditional lending*. Oxfordshire, United Kingdom: Routledge.

Vogelstein, R., & Bro, A. (2019, January 30). *Sweden's feminist foreign policy, long may it reign*. Retrieved from https://foreignpolicy.com/2019/01/30/sweden-feminist-foreignpolicy/

Wald, K. D., & Wilcox, C. (2006). Getting religion: Has political science rediscovered the faith factor? *American Political Science Review*, 100(4), 523–529.

Walker, J. A. (2012). Early marriage in Africa – Trends, harmful effects and interventions. *African Journal of Reproductive Health*, 16(2), 231–240.

Wallace, C., Haerpfer, C., & Abbott, P. (2009). Women in Rwandan politics and society. *International Journal of Sociology*, 38(4), 111–125.

Walzer, M. (1990, October). *The civil society argument: Gunnar Myrdal Lecture*. Stockholm, Sweden: University of Stockholm.

Wandia, M. (2004). *Not yet a force for freedom: The Protocol on the Rights of Women in Africa*. Oxon, United Kingdom: Pambazuka News.

Wang, Q., & Sun X. (2016). The role of socio-political and economic factors in fertility decline: A cross-country analysis. *World Development*, 87, 360–70.

Wangnerud, L. (2009). Women in parliaments: Descriptive and substantive representation. *Annual Review of Political Science*, 12, 51–69.

Wangnerud, L. (2000). Testing the politics of presence: Women's representation in the Swedish Riksdag. *Scandinavian Political Studies*, 23(1), 67–91.

Warhurst, J. (2008). The Catholic Lobby: Structures, policy styles and religious networks. *The Australian Journal of Public Administration*, 67(2), 213–230.

Warner, C. M. (2000). *Confessions of an interest group: The Catholic Church and political parties in Europe*. Princeton: Princeton University Press.

Warner, G. (2018) *Rwanda ranks in the top 5 for gender equity. Do its teen girls agree?* National Public Radio, 17 April 2018.

Warwick. (2014). *The Chilean dictatorship*. Retrieved July 30, 2018, from https://warwick.ac.uk/fac/arts/english/currentstudents/undergraduate/modules/fulllist/first/e

n123/contemporary2014/deathandthemaiden/historicalcontext/
thechileandictatorship/

Waylen, G. (2008). Enhancing the substantive representation of women: Lessons from transitions to democracy. *Parliamentary Affairs, 61*(3), 518–534.

Welch, S., & Studlar, D. T. (1996). The opportunity structure for women's candidacies and electability in Britain and the United States. *Political Research Quarterly, 49*(4), 861–874.

Westfall, A., & Chantiles, C. (2016). The political cure: Gender quotas and women's health. *Politics & Gender, 12*(3), 469–490.

Wilcox, C. (1990). Race differences in abortion attitudes: Some additional evidence. *Public Opinion Quarterly, 54,* 248–255.

Williams, M. (1998). *Voice, trust, and memory: Marginalized groups and the failings of liberal representation.* Princeton, NJ: Princeton University Press.

Wing, S. D. (2012). Human rights-based approaches to development: Justice and legal fiction in Africa. *Polity, 44*(4), 504–522.

Women in National Parliaments. (2015, December 1). Retrieved from Inter-Parliamentary Union www.ipu.org/english/home.htm

Wood Jr, J. E. (1986). Church lobbying and public policy. *Journal of Church and State, 28,* 183–192.

Woodhead, L. ([2001]2003). Feminism and the sociology of religion: From gender-blindness to gendered difference. In *The Blackwell Companion to Sociology of Religion,* edited by R. K. Fenn (pp. 67–84). Hoboken, NJ: Blackwell Publishing:

World Bank. (2018). *GDP per capita (current US$).* Retrieved from The World Bank: https://data.worldbank.org/indicator/NY.GDP.PCAP.CD

World Bank. (2017, July 1.) *GDP ranking.* Retrieved from http://data.worldbank.org/data-catalog/GDP-ranking-table

World Bank Group. (2015a). *Current health expenditure (% of GDP).* Washington, DC: World Bank. Retrieved from https://data.worldbank.org/indicator/SH.XPD.CHEX.GD.ZS.

World Bank Group. (2015b). *Government expenditure on education, total (% of GDP).* Washington, DC: World Bank. Retrieved from https://data.worldbank.org/indicator/SE.XPD.TOTL.GD.ZS.

World Economic Forum. (2017). *The global gender gap report.* Geneva: Author.

World Health Organization. (2003). *Safe abortion: Technical and policy guidance for health systems.* Geneva: Author.

World Values Survey Association. (1981–2014). Longitudinal Aggregate v. 20150418. World Values Survey Association. Aggregate File Producer: JD Systems. Retrieved from www.worldvaluessurvey.org).

Wright, S. (2010). *Fixing the kingdom: Political evolution and socio-economic challenges in Bahrain. Occasional Paper No. 3.* Washington, DC: Georgetown University, Center for International and Regional Studies.

Yamane, D. A. (2005). *The Catholic Church in state politics: Negotiating prophetic demands and political realities.* Oxford: Sheed & Ward.

Yanda, K., Smith, S., & Rosenfield, A. (2003). Reproductive health and human rights. *International Journal of Gynecology and Obstetrics, 82,* 275–283.

Vogelstein, R., & Bro, A. (2019, January 30). *Sweden's Feminist Foreign Policy, Long May It Reign.* Retrieved from https://foreignpolicy.com/2019/01/30/sweden-feminist-foreignpolicy/

Yom, S. L., & Gause III, F. G. (2012). Resilient royals: How Arab monarchies hang on. *Journal of Democracy*, 23(4), 74–88

Yuval-Davis, N. ([1992]2005). Fundamentalism, multiculturalism and women in Britain. In *'Race,' culture and difference*, edited by J. Donald, & A. Rattansi (pp. 278–292). London: Sage Publications.

Zetterberg, P. (2008). The downside of gender quotas? Institutional constraints on women in Mexican State Legislatures. *Parliamentary Affairs*, 61(3), 442–460.

Zwingel, S. (2012). How do norms travel? Theorizing international women's rights in transnational perspective. *International Studies Quarterly*, 56(1), 115–129.

Index